Strategies & Tactics for the MPRE

Strategies & Tactics
for the MPRE

Multistate Professional Responsibility Exam

Sixth Edition

This edition revised by
Alex Ruskell
Director of Academic Success and Bar Preparation
University of South Carolina School of Law

Prior editions by
Lazar Emanuel, J.D.
Kimm Alayne Walton, J.D.

Wolters Kluwer

Published by Wolters Kluwer in New York.

Wolters Kluwer Legal & Regulatory U.S. serves customers worldwide with CCH, Aspen Publishers, and Kluwer Law International products. (www.WKLegaledu.com)

To contact Customer Service, e-mail customer.service@wolterskluwer.com, call 1-800-234-1660, fax 1-800-901-9075, or mail correspondence to:

> Wolters Kluwer
> Attn: Order Department
> PO Box 990
> Frederick, MD 21705

Printed in the United States of America.

2 3 4 5 6 7 8 9 0

ISBN 978-1-4548-9189-5

About Wolters Kluwer Legal & Regulatory U.S.

Wolters Kluwer Legal & Regulatory U.S. delivers expert content and solutions in the areas of law, corporate compliance, health compliance, reimbursement, and legal education. Its practical solutions help customers successfully navigate the demands of a changing environment to drive their daily activities, enhance decision quality and inspire confident outcomes.

Serving customers worldwide, its legal and regulatory portfolio includes products under the Aspen Publishers, CCH Incorporated, Kluwer Law International, ftwilliam.com and MediRegs names. They are regarded as exceptional and trusted resources for general legal and practice-specific knowledge, compliance and risk management, dynamic workflow solutions, and expert commentary.

This book is dedicated to Jimmy and Mary Frances.

Table of Contents

Strategies & Tactics for the MPRE

Part One
Plan of Attack for the MPRE

A. Introduction

Along with graduating from law school and passing a state bar exam, you must pass the Multistate Professional Responsibility Examination (MPRE) if you want to practice law in most jurisdictions in the United States (all but three). The MPRE is designed to test your knowledge of two relatively short documents, the American Bar Association (ABA) Model Rules of Professional Conduct and the ABA Model Code of Judicial Conduct, as well as your "understanding of the generally accepted rules, principles, and common law regulating the legal profession in the United States." Any amendments to the ABA Model Rules or Model Code will not appear on the MPRE until one year after the ABA's approval of those amendments.

The exam consists of 60 multiple-choice questions, 10 of which are not included in your final score (these are questions being tested by the examiners — you won't be able to tell the difference between a scored question and a test question). Each question has only one correct answer out of the four options.

The standard score scale ranges from 50 (low) to 150 (high). The conversion of your raw score (the number of questions you get right) to a scaled score (the score reported by the MPRE) involves a statistical process that adjusts for variations in the difficulty of different MPRE exams so that any particular scaled score will represent the same level of knowledge from test to test. For example, if a particular MPRE exam is considered easier than previous exams, the raw scores will be adjusted downward to account for this difference. The passing grade is different from state to state, but it is generally a scaled score between 75 and 86. To find the passing grade for your state, contact the state board of bar examiners.

By the time you finish your law school course in ethics or professional responsibility, you will have developed a general sense of the range of ethical problems lawyers face every working day. However, to get past the MPRE, you need to know how to apply this general sense to specific fact patterns created by the MPRE examiners.

Importantly, PEOPLE FAIL THE MPRE ALL OF THE TIME! Consequently, you can't simply wander into the exam room on test day and hope for the best. There are two things that you need to do: one is to get familiar with the ethics rules, and the other is to get a sense of the kinds of questions that appear on the MPRE.

As you may know by now, the ABA Code and Rules are incredibly tedious to read. So, you'd be well advised to expand your preparation into a few more tools than simply trying to read the Code and Rules themselves. Along with this book, you should use the Law in a Flash card set on Professional Responsibility, which you will find at just about any law school bookstore. The flashcards offer more than 900 cards testing every aspect of the ABA Rules and Code. They define the basic rules and then give you hundreds of hypothetical fact patterns just like the ones tested on the MPRE. They have been revised and updated to reflect the most recent changes in the Model Rules of Professional Conduct and the Model Code of Judicial Conduct. The cards take only about 8–10 hours to review. They incorporate modern learning techniques that not only teach you the rules, but also how to apply those rules to facts quickly and effectively.

Of course, you can use any source to review the ethics rules, such as outlines or hornbooks. The point is that you have to *know* the rules, and, more importantly, *how those rules are applied*. Other than that, you have to learn the structure and technique of MPRE questions, and that's what this book will show you. Part One shows you how to attack MPRE questions, and in Part Two, you'll get a chance to put this plan of attack into practice on some model MPRE Questions and Answers. Part Three contains an additional three practice exams (180 questions) and corresponding answers to help you hone your skills.

If you were expecting to review thousands of questions for the MPRE — relax. This book is designed to teach you the law and analysis you will need to pass the MPRE through the use of the practice questions contained herein.

Incidentally, many of the questions in this book are real MPRE questions, although some have been modified to reflect recent changes in test format. They're in this book courtesy of the National Conference of Bar Examiners (NCBE). So you don't have to worry that the questions in this book may not resemble the ones you'll see on your MPRE — many were written by the very same people! Questions 11–60 in Practice Exam 3 are not actual MPRE questions, but they closely resemble the NCBE questions in content and style.

B. Basic Information About the MPRE

Background — The MPRE is created and administered by the NCBE, which is also responsible for the Multistate Bar Examination and the Uniform Bar Examination. The MPRE is currently administered in virtually every state, as well as the District of Columbia. All but three jurisdictions require the MPRE for admission (only Maryland, Wisconsin, and Puerto Rico do not require the test).

When Offered — The MPRE is administered three times a year — in Spring, Summer, and Fall (usually March, August, and November, although it has been known to vary). In many states, you can take the MPRE before you finish law school. Generally, you should take the MPRE as soon as you complete your course on Professional Responsibility (since you will have just studied the subject). However, check with your local bar or your school's Academic Support or Bar Preparation Program to get advice on the best time to take the exam. Some jurisdictions allow you to take the MPRE long after you have taken the bar exam. Some jurisdictions require a minimum amount of law credits before accepting an MPRE score. Some jurisdictions will not allow you to take the MPRE until after you have taken the bar exam. Importantly, some jurisdictions have time limitations for how long a test score remains valid (sometimes less than two years), so if you are not sure where you are planning to practice, you might want to wait until your third year in the event you have to take more than one bar exam to find a job. However, if you are planning to sit for the bar in a state where you have to have a passing score on the MPRE before you can sit for the bar exam, it's a good idea to take it early enough so that, if you do fail, you'll have another chance to take it before the time you were planning to sit for the bar.

Format and Length — The MPRE is made up of 60 multiple-choice questions. It lasts two hours. It is similar to the Multistate Bar Examination in the sense that each question includes a fact pattern followed by four answer choices, from which you are supposed to choose the "best" response. Later in Part One, you'll see lots of examples of this question format, and you'll learn to analyze it down to its most essential elements.

Coverage — The MPRE covers the ABA Model Rules of Professional Conduct, as well as the ABA Model Code of Judicial Conduct. It doesn't attempt to cover the code of any individual state. (In actual practice you may find that the codes governing professional responsibility in your state differ in substantial respects from the ABA Rules and Code.)

The MPRE also tests the applicant's "understanding of the generally accepted rules, principles and common law regulating the legal profession"; in these items, the correct answer will be governed by the view reflected in the majority of cases, statutes, or regulations on the subject. In testing issues such as litigation sanctions or the attorney-client evidentiary privilege, the Federal Rules of Civil Procedure and the Federal Rules of Evidence apply.

The entire subject of legal malpractice, which is of vital concern to lawyers and which is tested on the MPRE, is not mentioned as such in the Model Rules.

Scoring — Your MPRE score is determined by how many questions you answer correctly; there's no penalty for incorrect answers. The lesson to be learned from this is that it pays to answer every question, even if you're not exactly sure what the correct answer is.

How to Register for the MPRE — To register for the MPRE, visit the website online: http://www.ncbex.org/exams/mpre/registration/

C. What the MPRE Tests

1. Scope of Questions

Questions on the ABA Model Rules and related sources dealing with the conduct of lawyers and law firms make up 90–94 percent of all the questions on the MPRE. The remaining questions test the applicant's knowledge of the Model Code of Judicial Conduct.

The outline of subjects published by the NCBE lists the items tested. Occasionally, other items are added, but the NCBE's outline is a good guide to the weight you should give each subject as you study. Not all of the items are tested each time, but if you've covered them all in your studies, you can't miss.

The NCBE's outline of MPRE subjects, and the approximate weight given to each, follows:

I. Regulation of the Legal Profession (6–12 percent)

  A. Powers of Courts and Other Bodies to Regulate Lawyers

  B. Admission to the Profession

  C. Regulation After Admission — Lawyer Discipline

D. Mandatory and Permissive Reporting of Professional Misconduct

E. Unauthorized Practice of Law — by Lawyers and Nonlawyers

F. Multijurisdictional Practice

G. Fee Division with a Nonlawyer

H. Law Firm and Other Forms of Practice

I. Responsibilities of Partners, Managers, Supervisory, and Subordinate Lawyers

J. Restrictions on Right to Practice

II. The Client-Lawyer Relationship (10–16 percent)

A. Formation of Client-Lawyer Relationship

B. Scope, Objective, and Means of the Representation

C. Decision-Making Authority — Actual and Apparent

D. Counsel and Assistance Within the Bounds of the Law

E. Termination of the Client-Lawyer Relationship

F. Client-Lawyer Contracts

G. Communications with the Client

H. Fees

III. Client-Confidentiality (6–12 percent)

A. Attorney-Client Privilege

B. Work-Product Doctrine

C. Professional Obligation of Confidentiality — General Rule

D. Disclosures Expressly or Impliedly Authorized by Client

E. Other Exceptions to the Confidentiality Rule

IV. Conflicts of Interest (12–18 percent)

A. Current Client Conflicts — Multiple Clients and Joint Representation

B. Current Client Conflicts — Lawyer's Personal Interest or Duties

C. Former Client Conflicts

D. Prospective Client Conflicts

E. Imputed Conflicts

F. Acquiring an Interest in Litigation

G. Business Transactions with Clients

H. Third-Party Compensation and Influence

I. Lawyers Currently or Formerly in Government Service

J. Former Judge, Arbitrator, Mediator, or Other Third-Party Neutral

V. Competence, Legal Malpractice, and Other Civil Liability
   (6–12 percent)

A. Maintaining Competence

B. Competence Necessary to Undertake Representation

C. Exercising Diligence and Care

D. Civil Liability to Client, Including Malpractice

E. Civil Liability to Nonclients

F. Limiting Liability for Malpractice

G. Malpractice Insurance and Risk Prevention

VI. Litigation and Other Forms of Advocacy (10–16 percent)

A. Meritorious Claims and Contentions

B. Expediting Litigation

C. Candor to the Tribunal

D. Fairness to Opposing Party and Counsel

E. Impartiality and Decorum of the Tribunal

F. Trial Publicity

G. Lawyer as Witness

VII. Transactions and Communications with Persons Other than Clients
   (2–8 percent)

A. Truthfulness in Statements to Others

B. Communications with Represented Persons

C. Communications with Unrepresented Persons

D. Respect for Rights of Third Persons

VIII. Different Roles of the Lawyer (4–10 percent)

A. Lawyer as Advisor

B. Lawyer as Evaluator

C. Lawyer as Negotiator

D. Lawyer as Arbitrator, Mediator, or Other Third-Party Neutral

E. Prosecutors and Other Governmental Lawyers

F. Lawyer Appearing in Nonadjudicative Proceeding

G. Lawyer Representing an Entity or Other Organization

IX. Safekeeping Funds and Other Property (2–8 percent)

A. Establishing and Maintaining Client Trust Accounts

B. Safekeeping Funds and Other Property of Clients

C. Safekeeping Funds and Other Property of Third Persons

D. Disputed Claims

X. Communication About Legal Services (4–10 percent)

A. Advertising and Other Public Communications About Legal Services

B. Solicitation — Direct Contact with Prospective Clients

C. Group Legal Services

D. Referrals

E. Communications Regarding Fields of Practice and Specialization

XI. Lawyers' Duties to the Public and the Legal System (2–4 percent)

A. Voluntary Pro Bono Service

B. Accepting Appointments

C. Serving in Legal Services Organizations

D. Law Reform Activities Affecting Client Interests

E. Criticism of Judges and Adjudicating Officials

F. Political Contributions to Obtain Engagements or Appointments

G. Improper Influence on Government Officials

H. Assisting Judicial Misconduct

XII. Judicial Ethics (2–8 percent)

A. Maintaining the Independence and Impartiality of the Judiciary

B. Performing the Duties of Judicial Office Impartially, Competently, and Diligently

C. Ex Parte Communications

D. Disqualification

E. Extrajudicial Activities

2. Important Terminology

Model Rule 1.0 defines the important terminology you will need to understand in order to answer a question:

(a) "Belief" or "believes" denotes that the person involved actually supposed the fact in question to be true. A person's belief may be inferred from circumstances.

(b) "Confirmed in writing," when used in reference to the informed consent of a person, denotes informed consent that is given in writing by the person or a writing that a lawyer promptly transmits to the person confirming an oral informed consent. See paragraph (e) for the definition of "informed consent." If it is not feasible to obtain or transmit the writing at the time the person gives informed consent, then the lawyer must obtain or transmit it within a reasonable time thereafter.

(c) "Firm" or "law firm" denotes a lawyer or lawyers in a law partnership, professional corporation, sole proprietorship, or other association authorized to practice law; or lawyers employed in a legal services organization or the legal department of a corporation or other organization.

(d) "Fraud" or "fraudulent" denotes conduct that is fraudulent under the substantive or procedural law of the applicable jurisdiction and has a purpose to deceive.

(e) "Informed consent" denotes the agreement by a person to a proposed course of conduct after the lawyer has communicated adequate information and explanation about the material risks of and reasonably available alternatives to the proposed course of conduct.

(f) "Knowingly," "known," or "knows" denotes actual knowledge of the fact in question. A person's knowledge may be inferred from circumstances.

(g) "Partner" denotes a member of a partnership, a shareholder in a law firm organized as a professional corporation, or a member of an association authorized to practice law.

(h) "Reasonable" or "reasonably" when used in relation to conduct by a lawyer denotes the conduct of a reasonably prudent and competent lawyer.

(i) "Reasonable belief" or "reasonably believes" when used in reference to a lawyer denotes that the lawyer believes the matter in question and that the circumstances are such that the belief is reasonable.

(j) "Reasonably should know" when used in reference to a lawyer denotes that a lawyer of reasonable prudence and competence would ascertain the matter in question.

(k) "Screened" denotes the isolation of a lawyer from any participation in a matter through the timely imposition of procedures within a firm that are reasonably adequate under the circumstances to protect information that the isolated lawyer is obligated to protect under these rules or other law.

(l) "Substantial" when used in reference to degree or extent denotes a material matter of clear and weighty importance.

(m) "Tribunal" denotes a court, an arbitrator in a binding arbitration proceeding or a legislative body, administrative agency or other body acting in an adjudicative capacity. A legislative body, administrative agency or other body acts in an adjudicative capacity when a neutral official, after the presentation of evidence or legal argument by a party or parties, will render a binding legal judgment directly affecting a party's interests in a particular matter.

(n) "Writing" or "written" denotes a tangible or electronic record of a communication or representation, including handwriting, typewriting, printing, photostating, photography, audio or video recording, and electronic communications. A "signed" writing includes an electronic sound, symbol or process attached to or logically associated with a writing and executed or adopted by a person with the intent to sign the writing.

The MPRE also lists several key words and phrases you should know:

(1) "Subject to discipline" asks whether the conduct described in the question would subject the lawyer to discipline under the provisions of the ABA Model Rules of Professional Conduct. In the case of a judge, the test question asks whether the judge would be subject to discipline under the ABA Model Code of Judicial Conduct.

(2) "May" or "proper" asks whether the conduct referred to or described in the question is professionally appropriate in that it (a) would not subject the lawyer or judge to discipline; (b) is not inconsistent with the preamble, comments, or text of the ABA Model Rules of Professional Conduct or the ABA Model Code of Judicial Conduct; and (c) is not inconsistent with generally accepted principles of the law of lawyering.

(3) "Subject to litigation sanction" asks whether the conduct described in the question would subject the lawyer or the lawyer's law firm to sanction by a tribunal such as fine, fee forfeiture, disqualification, punishment for contempt, or other sanction.

(4) "Subject to disqualification" asks whether the conduct described in the question would subject the lawyer or the lawyer's law firm to disqualification as counsel in a civil or criminal matter.

(5) "Subject to civil liability" asks whether the conduct described in the question would subject the lawyer or the lawyer's law firm to civil liability, such as claims arising from malpractice, misrepresentation, or breach of fiduciary duty.

(6) "Subject to criminal liability" asks whether the conduct described in the question would subject the lawyer to criminal liability for participation in or for aiding and abetting criminal acts, such as prosecution for insurance or tax fraud, destruction of evidence, or obstruction of justice.

(7) When a question refers to discipline by the "bar," "state bar," or "state disciplinary authority," it refers to the appropriate agency in the jurisdiction with authority to administer the standards for

admission to practice and for maintenance of professional competence and integrity. Whenever a lawyer is identified as a "certified specialist," that lawyer has been so certified by the appropriate agency in the jurisdiction in which the lawyer practices. The phrases "informed consent" and "consent after consultation" have the same meaning

You should make sure you have a clear understanding of how the MPRE defines its terms. Otherwise, answering questions correctly will be extremely difficult.

D. Attacking the MPRE

1. Getting Familiar with the Question Format

MPRE questions are arranged in this way: They start with a fact pattern set around a common problem in legal ethics. This is followed by the "call" of the question, which directs you to what point of ethics the examiners are trying to test you on. Finally, there are four answer options. You are expected to choose the one that best answers the call. Here's a typical example:

An attorney represented a buyer in a real estate transaction. Due to the attorney's negligence in drafting the purchase agreement, the buyer was required to pay for a survey that should have been paid by the seller. The attorney fully disclosed this negligence to the buyer, and the buyer suggested that he would be satisfied if the attorney simply reimbursed the buyer for the entire cost of the survey.

Although the buyer might have recovered additional damages if a malpractice action were filed, the attorney reasonably believed that the proposed settlement was fair to the buyer. He sent the buyer a letter stating that the buyer should consider seeking independent representation before making a decision. Then, in order to forestall a malpractice action, the attorney agreed to make the reimbursement. The attorney drafted a settlement agreement, and it was executed by both the attorney and the buyer.

Was the attorney's conduct proper?

(A) Yes, because the attorney advised the buyer in writing that the buyer should seek independent representation before deciding to enter into the settlement agreement.

(B) Yes, because the attorney reasonably believed that the proposed settlement was fair to the buyer.

(C) No, because the attorney settled a case involving liability for malpractice while the matter was still ongoing.

(D) No, because the buyer was not separately represented in negotiating and finalizing the settlement agreement.

In this question, the first and second paragraphs make up the fact pattern. The final sentence, "Was the attorney's conduct proper?" is the "call" of the question — it tells you specifically what to look for in the answer options. Items A through D are the "answer options." One of these is the best response, and the other three are "distracters" — basically, answer options that are trying to "distract" you away from the right one. (Incidentally, the best response is A.)

2. Reading the Fact Patterns

On the MPRE, you have two minutes to read each question, answer it, and move on. This means you have to grasp the ethics rules and understand how to apply them, and you need to read and respond quickly. Most of all, you need to know what to look for. The most important thing to keep in mind about the MPRE is that it's very limited in the range of questions that it can raise. As with all standardized multiple-choice tests, the MPRE simply cannot test gray areas; the facts must clearly point toward one and only one correct answer for the question to be "psychometrically" sound — that is, for the question to be a valid measure of competence. In other words, there can't be a reasonable argument about which answer is the right answer.

Ultimately, although the examiners may be knowledgeable and crafty, there are only so many fact patterns they can concoct. They are testing you and every other law student in the country on your knowledge of the ethical rules, and they need to make sure that you understand the most important ones and follow them in your later practice. Consequently, in making the exam, they don't try to find the most obscure point or comment in the rules simply to trick you. In many ways, the MPRE is more similar to a driving test than a typical law school exam. In a driving test, the test-maker's goal is to make sure you know what a stop sign means, not what the paint on the sign is made from. What this means in practical terms is best shown by example.

Let's say that you and your best friend study for the MPRE together, and you both have an equally detailed knowledge of the rules of ethics;

in fact, your knowledge of the rules is identical. For any given question on the MPRE to be valid as a testing device, you would both have to choose the same answer when confronted by any particular question. If you *didn't,* the question cannot be said to have tested your knowledge. Because you both had the same knowledge of the rules, the facts and the questions should have led you to the same result. If you each answered differently, and if this one question were the difference between passing and failing the MPRE, one of you would pass and the other would fail, *even though your knowledge of the rules was identical.* From the examiners' point of view, this would make the test invalid, because the test would fail its own purpose of distinguishing among students on the basis of their knowledge.

For instance, say a question involves a lawyer's representation of multiple parties who may have a conflict of interest. The issue is: Can the lawyer represent all of them in light of this potential conflict? Clearly, before a lawyer can properly ask the consent of the parties to a multiple representation, he or she must *reasonably believe* he or she can represent all the parties adequately. "Reasonableness" is a standard that is totally fact-dependent. Therefore, if the examiners wanted to test you on whether the lawyer *could* properly represent all the parties in this basic circumstance, they would have to write the question to make it unmistakably clear in the facts that the lawyer's belief was reasonable.

If the examiner didn't do this, the question would not be a valid test of the rule requiring consent in advance of all parties to a multiple-party representation. In fact, if a question that is offered on the MPRE doesn't "perform as intended" — a term describing an ambiguous question that sneaks by the drafting committee — it is dropped from the exam.

If this theory for testing the validity of a test question isn't all that clear to you now, don't worry. The only thing that really matters is that you appreciate its impact on what you should look for in MPRE fact patterns. Looking at some of these points individually may clarify matters.

a. Pay special attention to statements about the lawyer's or the client's state of mind

In many ethics rules, the propriety of a lawyer's conduct depends on whether he or she *knows* or *believes* something. His or her knowledge or belief will determine whether some act on his or her part is mandated or prohibited. Pay special attention to words or phrases like "knows," "knowingly," "concludes," "becomes convinced," "believes," and "reasonably believes." In fact, on many ethical issues, the attorney's belief about a fact or an event is more important than the fact or event itself.

Take a typical question about a lawyer's role in recommending a candidate for admission to the bar. According to the Rules, a lawyer cannot *"knowingly* make a false statement of material fact" in connection with an applicant's admission to the bar. Model Rule 8.1.

Looking at the Rule carefully, you should notice that it doesn't matter whether the person the lawyer recommends later turns out to be a drug dealer; as long as *the lawyer didn't know the true facts* at the time he or she made the recommendation, he or she will not be subject to discipline.

Take another example — the problem of conflicts of interest. In most conflict cases, the conflict can be remedied by obtaining the informed consent of the affected clients whether they are prospective, current, or former clients. However, before the lawyer can even *seek* a client's consent, he or she must *reasonably believe* he or she can carry on the representation of that client without adverse affect on his or her representation of another client. Model Rule 1.7. Here again, it doesn't really matter whether his or her belief ultimately proves to be sound; as long as the lawyer *reasonably believed* at the time that he or she undertook the representation that he or she could do so without adversely affecting either party, the lawyer will not be subject to discipline.

The lesson here is that it's important to pay attention to the MPRE's description of the attorney's state of mind — i.e., his or her beliefs and knowledge — in determining whether he or she has acted ethically.

b. Pay attention to the lawyer's motivation when he or she acts or fails to act

Just as the extent of an attorney's knowledge can determine the propriety or impropriety of his or her behavior, so too can his or her reasons for undertaking, or failing to undertake, the behavior. You should always make special note of the reason for an attorney's actions. Often, that will help you in assessing the propriety of his or her conduct.

For example, on a question dealing with permissive or mandatory withdrawal from representation, the attorney's reasons for withdrawing will be crucial in determining whether the withdrawal is ethical. Some questions will raise obvious issues of motivation, but others will insert more insidious circumstances in which motivation may play a less obvious but equally critical role.

Take, for instance, the question of whether to call a particular witness at trial. Ordinarily, whether to call a particular witness is the exclusive decision of the attorney, not the client. Model Rule 1.2. Under ordinary circumstances, the attorney has acted perfectly properly if he or she decides *not* to call a particular witness after careful deliberation.

But suppose he or she decides not to call a particular witness because it would take too much time and energy on his or her part to find and prepare the witness. Then his or her motives would raise issues both of incompetent representation under Model Rule 1.1, and of a lack of reasonable diligence under Model Rule 1.3. When the lawyer's behavior raises questions about his or her *motivation,* you have to analyze that motivation carefully to determine whether the behavior itself was proper.

c. Ignore "window dressing" — pay attention to the lawyer's core behavior

In some MPRE questions, the examiners test your knowledge of the ethical rules by surrounding unethical behavior with the "trappings" of propriety. This is to test whether you can tell the trees from the forest — that is, to see if you can find evidence of unethical conduct when it's surrounded by misleading "goodies."

For example, lawyers have a duty to provide competent service to their clients. Model Rule 1.1. A question that asked only, "Is a lawyer subject to discipline for providing incompetent service," free of other facts, wouldn't lead anyone into answering "No," however little the test-taker actually knew about the rules of ethics.

So this simple question, without more, wouldn't make a very good MPRE question. But suppose the lawyer *tells* the client that he is not competent to handle the matter, and the client insists that he handle it anyway, because the lawyer is the only lawyer she really trusts. Say also that the client is the lawyer's biggest client, and that the client says she will take her business elsewhere if the lawyer doesn't accept the matter. Now suppose that the client signs an affidavit acknowledging that the lawyer has advised her that he doesn't believe that he is skilled enough to handle the matter competently, and promising that she will not sue him for malpractice regardless of the outcome of the case. Even though the facts have been embellished, the "nub" of the matter is still the same — the lawyer is incompetent to handle the matter. Simply by adding seemingly relevant new facts — namely, the client's insistence on the lawyer's handling the work, her waiver of the right to competent representation, and her agreement not to sue — a question that was too easy to use has been transformed into a more appropriate one.

Ultimately, the way to insulate yourself against the trap that's been set for you by these kinds of embellishments is to strip them all away and ask yourself what's really going on. Start with the undisputed fact that, underneath it all, the lawyer will provide incompetent service. Then work your way up from there to see if any of the additional facts — here, those additional facts are client consent and waiver — change the nature of that core issue. The answer here is "No." A lawyer who provides incompetent service cannot take comfort in client consent. The requirement of competent representation is unqualified and inflexible.

If you maintain your focus in this way, you will make it extremely difficult for the examiners to confuse you by layering on facts that don't really change the underlying issue. In fact, the most common way that the examiners try to distract you from the right answer is to "fix" the Rule violation with a good outcome, client consent, or the fact that the attorney or judge would have done things the same way even if there was not a potential breach of ethics. Thus, always be wary of such "no-harm, no-foul" fact scenarios and answer options.

3. Reading the "Call" of the Question

The "call" of the question contains the instructions that you are expected to follow in choosing among the answers. The call flows logically from the facts, but it can take many forms. It can be very general — for instance, it can ask simply if the attorney's conduct was proper, improper, or subject to discipline — or it can be specific, inquiring into a particular aspect of the attorney's conduct. The call of the question is critical, because your answer cannot be correct unless it is responsive to what the question is asking. In writing a question, an examiner is trying to get you to choose a response that shows you understand a specific point of law. As previously stated, if the question cannot lead a prepared student to respond correctly, the question (and ultimately the test) is invalid. Importantly, the call tells you specifically what that examiner is looking for by limiting issues or highlighting specific facts or relationships. If you do not pay close attention to the call, you cannot possibly get a question correct. Just to make this point absolutely clear, here is a somewhat silly example of a question without a call:

A student wants to start a successful law firm.

(A) Pass the bar.

(B) Recommendations.

(C) Name it "SUE THEM ALL, WIN BIG BUCKS!"

(D) Dogs.

As you can see, a question without a call is impossible to answer. Does this question want you to pick the first thing the student has to do? Does this question want you to pick the thing the student can't do ethically? Does this question want you to pick the way the student should market the firm? Does this question want you to pick the least likely thing the student will need? Without the call, this question is worthless.

a. "General" call

When a general call is used, the prevailing issue should spring to mind as you read the fact pattern. Here's an example:

> An attorney is a member of the bar and a salaried employee of the trust department of a bank. As part of his duties, he prepares a monthly newsletter concerning wills, trusts, estates, and taxes that the bank sends to all of its customers. The newsletter contains a recommendation to the customer to review his or her will in light of the information contained and, if the customer has any questions, to take the will to the bank's trust department where the trust officer will answer any questions without charge. The trust officer is not a lawyer. If the trust officer is unable to answer the customer's questions, the trust officer refers the customer to the attorney.

> Is the attorney subject to discipline for the foregoing?

> **(A)** Yes, because the attorney is giving legal advice to persons who are not his clients.

(**B**) Yes, because the attorney is aiding the bank in the unauthorized practice of law.

(**C**) No, because no charge is made for the attorney's advice.

(**D**) No, because it is the attorney's duty to carry out the bank's instructions.

As you read this fact pattern, the one fact that should have popped out at you is that the attorney is helping a nonlawyer (the bank) to practice law. Consequently, the prime issue is the unauthorized practice of law.

If, for whatever reason, you have a problem spotting the issue in a "general call" question, try the following tactic: Rephrase the questions by turning it around. Here, you might ask yourself: "Why *shouldn't* the attorney be subject to discipline on these facts?" Or, "Why *would* he be?"

Take note: If a question asks you whether a particular act is unethical, you can be *pretty* sure that the attorney's done something that fits a particular clause of one of the ethics rules, or one of the exceptions to the rule, or that the conduct itself is unethical — otherwise, the question wouldn't be a very good testing item.

b. "Specific call"

Most MPRE questions call for more specific answers. For example: "Is it proper for the attorney to represent both parties in the contempt proceedings?" "Is the attorney subject to discipline if he asserts such a defense?" "Is it proper for the attorney to supply the judge with the requested list of writings on the subject of custody?" "Is it proper for the attorney to grant the extension of time without consulting the client?" Unlike a general call, the specific call will usually define the issue you're looking for. Looking at these particular calls more closely should help to clarify this point.

"Is it proper for the attorney to represent both parties in the contempt proceedings?"

The issue here is almost certainly *conflict of interest,* because you're being asked whether it would be proper to represent two people in the same proceeding at the same time.

"Is the attorney subject to discipline if he asserts such a defense?"

Here, the issue probably relates to frivolous claims or fraud. The Rules specify that an attorney shall not knowingly make a false statement of material fact or law to a tribunal. Model Rule 3.3. They also prohibit a lawyer from bringing or defending a proceeding unless there is a nonfrivolous basis for doing so. Model Rule 3.1.

> "Is it proper for the attorney to supply the judge with the requested list of writings on the subject of custody?"

The issue here is obviously ex parte contact with judges.

> "Is it proper for the attorney to grant the extension of time without consulting the client?"

The issue is undoubtedly the relative control of the attorney and the client over the process of decision making during the representation or trial. The issue is given away by the words *"without consulting the client."*

If you found this exercise difficult, it's probably because you aren't — not yet, anyway — sufficiently familiar with the Model Rules. Once you've learned them and how they relate to MPRE fact patterns, it will be easier for you to find the issues raised by the MPRE, especially when the call of the question is specific.

c. Spotting the issue when it's not obvious from the fact pattern

In either general or specific call questions, if you can't find the issue in the facts, study the answer options. They will usually give the issue away. Obviously, the right answer will suggest the issue, but at least one or two of the other answers may suggest it as well.

That's because the examiners go to great lengths to craft some of the wrong answers as distracters. While these also point to or suggest the main issue, they manage to avoid it, however narrowly. Here's an example:

> A plaintiff and defendant are next-door neighbors and bitter personal enemies. The plaintiff is suing the defendant over an alleged trespass. Each party believes, in good faith, in the correctness of his position. After the plaintiff had retained an attorney, he told the attorney, "I do not want you to grant any delays or courtesies to the defendant or his lawyer. I want you to insist on every technicality."

The attorney has served the defendant's attorney with a demand to answer written interrogatories. The defendant's attorney, because of the illness of his secretary, has asked the attorney for a five-day extension of time within which to answer them.

Granting the extension would not hurt the plaintiff in any way.

Is the attorney subject to discipline if she grants the defendant's attorney's request for a five-day extension?

(A) Yes, because the attorney is acting contrary to her client's instructions.

(B) Yes, because the attorney did not first inform the plaintiff of the request and obtain the plaintiff's consent to grant it.

(C) No, because granting the extension would not prejudice the plaintiff's rights.

(D) No, because the defendant's attorney was not at fault in causing the delay.

Look carefully at the language in the various answer options here: "granting the extension"; " . . . the plaintiff's consent"; " . . . client's instructions." All of them suggest that this is an inquiry into the relative decision-making roles of the lawyer and the client. The best response is C. Why? Because it recognizes that the underlying reason for assigning different levels of control over decision making to the lawyer and the client *is to avoid prejudice to the client's basic rights.* At the same time, it recognizes that lawyers may take such action as is impliedly authorized to carry out representation and that clients normally defer to the special knowledge and skill of their lawyer regarding technical and tactical issues during litigation. Model Rule 1.2, Comments [1] and [2].

The other options are skillful distracters. Answer A suggests that a lawyer always has to get his or her client's consent on issues of litigation tactics. This is not the case. Answer B is wrong for the same reason as A. Answer D is easy to eliminate. The issue is whether a delay would prejudice the plaintiff's rights, regardless of what caused the delay. Whether the defendant's attorney was at fault in causing the delay is immaterial to the attorney's decision to grant the request for an extension.

4. Reading the Answers and Choosing the Best Response

As with any standardized test, the best — and sometimes the only — way to arrive at the best response is to eliminate all the options that are *definitely wrong.*

This means that the most important skill you can apply to the MPRE is the ability to perceive when an answer is definitely wrong. There are several ways to hone this skill:

- Learn the general principles for determining when an answer is wrong,

- Review the substantive rules that are most likely to trip you up, and

- Learn the traps the examiners expect you to fall into.

You'll learn all three of these skills in the next few pages. But one point you simply can't ignore is this — the most important element in your success is early and constant review of the Rules themselves. Unlike the LSAT and most other standardized exams, the MPRE is not a test of general intelligence or knowledge. It's based on your intimate knowledge of a specific set of rules, which, stripped to their bare bones, cover less than 100 pages of text. That is, it's designed to test your knowledge of a limited subject, and you can't expect to pass it without having at least a reasonable familiarity with the Model Rules and the Model Code of Judicial Conduct. The advice on the next few pages assumes that you've already done your substantive review.

The instructions below will do two things for you. First, they'll ensure that you aren't tripped up by the MPRE's format, and that you'll always get the right answer if you know the rule. Also, these instructions will help you find your way to the right answer when you're not really sure what that answer ought to be. The bottom line is, if you are reasonably familiar with the ethics rules, understand how to apply the rules, and you apply the principles in this chapter, *the* MPRE *cannot beat you!*

a. General principles of elimination

The most important skill you can take to the MPRE is the ability to identify when an answer is clearly wrong. What makes this more difficult than you may think is the extraordinary skill applied by the examiners in creating the wrong answers. Perhaps you've heard it said that you can tell the quality of a superhero movie by watching the bad guy — the better the villain, the better the movie. Well, on standardized exams, the better the wrong answers, the more difficult the exam. The MPRE is difficult exactly because the examiners are exceptionally successful in masking the wrong answers to make them seem right. In this section, you'll learn how to "unmask" the wrong answers and make them easier to spot. Once you know how to eliminate the wrong answers with skill and confidence, you'll be able to pick out the *right* answer every time. Here, then, are the rules you need to know.

(1) If you know the right answer for sure, ignore these instructions.

If there is no question in your mind that one answer is correct, choose it and move on. If you've studied the substance of the Rules and read and practiced with this book, you should find the right answer on a first or second reading. If you do spot the right answer right away, mark your answer sheet and go on to the next question.

(2) Eliminate any answers you know are wrong, and then concentrate on the remaining answer choices.

In many cases you will immediately recognize that at least one and perhaps two of the answer choices are wrong. If you can spot three, great — you're left with the one option that has to be right. Don't bother to look a second time at answer options that are clearly wrong; cross them off in your test booklet if necessary to take your mind off them, and concentrate on the other possibilities.

(3) Remember that many of the answers will seem to draw on the same issue.

This rule isn't set in stone, but the nature of the exam makes it likely that several answers will focus on the same issue. Remember, what makes a standardized test difficult is the seeming resemblance between the *wrong* answers and the *right* one. This leads to one simple rule: *in general,* if there is a single answer option that seems very different from the other options, it's probably not the best answer. For example, if a multiple-choice exam was trying to test whether you knew that the sun was a star, and the answer options were "star," "nebula," "constellation," and "duck," you can generally get rid of "duck" immediately.

(4) Analyze the ways in which a particular answer can be wrong.

There are several clues to concluding that an answer is wrong. An answer is wrong if:

(a) It misapplies a rule of ethics to the facts. This is far and away the most common type of distracter; this will be discussed this in detail under "Traps Set by the Examiners."

(b) It misstates the ethics rules. This is also relatively common.

(c) It misstates or deliberately confuses the facts. An answer of this kind is so clearly wrong that it fools only the least prepared applicants; for this reason, it's not used very often.

b. A few general rules to remember

Here are a few general rules you should keep in mind. They will save you a lot of time in choosing the right answer.

(1) Don't be confused by a question that suggests that the lawyer's conduct, though questionable, has not prejudiced the client.

This is a very common MPRE trap — the facts describe conduct by a lawyer that is wrong, but then tell you that the misconduct has not affected the client adversely. When this happens in an MPRE fact pattern, you can bet your bottom dollar that at least one of the distracters will suggest that the lawyer's conduct was proper because his client wasn't "prejudiced," or "adversely affected," or the like. For this reason, it's important to keep the following basic rule in mind — even if things work out all right for the client, the lawyer may still be subject to discipline for violating the Rules in the first place. To avoid picking the wrong answer in this kind of question, you need to know the Model Rules in all their subtleties. (Note: *To recover in a malpractice case, the client has to show not only that the lawyer's conduct was negligent or improper, but that the conduct was the direct cause of the client's loss or injury.*)

For example, say a lawyer allows a paralegal in his office to conduct a deposition or perform some other act that constitutes the practice of law. The lawyer will be subject to discipline for assisting a person who is not a member of the bar in the unauthorized practice of law (Model Rule 5.5(a)) *even if* that person renders competent service. As another example, suppose a lawyer neglects the client's work over an extended period; he or she may be subject to discipline *even if* he or she finally manages to file the client's claim before the statute of limitations runs out.

The way to think of this behavior is that it is similar to the crime of burglary: Once a person's broken into a dwelling of another at night with the intent to commit a felony therein, it doesn't matter what he or she does after that — he or she can change his or her mind and exit without touching anything — he or she is still guilty of burglary. It's the same with some lawyer infractions. Once a lawyer has engaged in unethical conduct, it doesn't really matter what the consequence of that conduct is to the client; the lawyer has violated the ethics rules and he or she is subject to discipline.

(2) When it comes to fees, less is better.

Occasionally the MPRE will ask about the propriety of a fee that is in dispute. Remember that the Model Rules specify that a lawyer's fee shall be reasonable (Model Rule 1.5(a)); it's a safe bet, therefore, that a lower fee will be perceived as more reasonable than a higher one. Thus, when a question asks what part of a fee a lawyer may properly keep, you're generally safe if you opt for the choice that best protects the client's interests in the money under dispute. Here's an example:

A client retained an attorney to appeal the client's criminal conviction and to seek bail pending appeal. The agreed fee for the appearance on the bail hearing was $50 per hour. The attorney received $800 from the client, of which $300 was a deposit to secure the attorney's fee and $500 was for bail costs in the event that bail was obtained. The attorney maintained two office bank accounts: a "Fee Account," in which all fees were deposited and from which all office expenses were paid, and a "Client Fund Account." The attorney deposited the $800 in the "Client Fund Account" and expended six hours of time on the bail hearing. The effort to obtain bail was unsuccessful. Dissatisfied, the client immediately demanded return of the $800.

It is now proper for the attorney to:

(A) transfer the $800 to the "Fee Account."

(B) transfer $300 to the "Fee Account" and leave $500 in the "Client Fund Account" until the attorney's fee for the final appeal is determined.

(C) transfer $300 to the "Fee Account" and send the client a $500 check on the "Client Fund Account."

(D) send the client a $500 check and leave $300 in the "Client Fund Account" until the matter is resolved with the client.

With no other thought in mind than the general rule that "less for the lawyer, more for the client" is better than the alternative, you can see that the best response would have to be D, because it's the one in which the attorney gets to keep less than he does in any other response.

(3) If a Rule forbids communication between two persons, it doesn't matter who initiates the communication.

The Model Rules contain many provisions that forbid communication between a lawyer and someone else. Examples:

A lawyer shall not communicate with a person he or she knows to be represented by another attorney without that attorney's consent; a lawyer shall not communicate *ex parte* with a judge, juror, or prospective juror; or a lawyer shall not contact or solicit professional employment either in person or by live telephone from any person who is not a lawyer, family member, or former client. Model Rules 4.2, 3.5, & 7.3.

The rule to remember is that when communication by a lawyer is banned, it's banned in almost every instance regardless of who contacts whom first. (Except, of course, that the lawyer may discuss a matter with a prospective client who initiates the contact.) Thus, for instance, if a juror tries to strike up a conversation with one of the lawyers in a case, the lawyer has to terminate the conversation immediately. It's quite common on the MPRE for a distracter to suggest that a communication is proper because someone other than the lawyer in the fact pattern initiated the contact. Don't be fooled by this device!

(4) An attorney may not engage in conduct that would cause a judge to violate the Model Code of Judicial Conduct.

Sometimes an MPRE fact pattern will point to a judge who has violated the Model Code of Judicial Conduct with the help of a lawyer. A common example concerns a judge who contacts a lawyer because he or she happens to be an expert on a particular issue in a case, instead of relying solely on the briefs submitted by counsel.

Although there's nothing in the Model Rules that discourages a lawyer from advising a judge on the law, the Model Code of Judicial Conduct itself requires that a judge refrain from relying on the advice unless the judge first tells the lawyers in the case the name of the expert consulted and the substance of his or her advice, and gives the lawyers a chance to respond. Model Code of Judicial Conduct, Rule 2.9(A)(2). Remember, therefore, that it's not enough to know the Model Rules. When a judge is involved, you have to include the Model Code of Judicial Conduct in your analysis of a lawyer's conduct. Under Model Rule 8.4(f), a lawyer can't knowingly aid a judge in violating the law *or the Model Code of Judicial Conduct.* Thus, if a judge's conduct violates the Model Code of Judicial Conduct and a lawyer has helped the judge in that conduct, the lawyer has violated the ethics rules.

(5) A client's insistence on a course of conduct doesn't relieve the lawyer of the responsibility to observe the Rules.

Sometimes an MPRE fact pattern will feature an attorney who has violated the Rules at the insistence of the client — for example, asserting an unmeritorious or baseless claim for the sake of harassing the adversary, or taking on work when the lawyer isn't competent to handle it. Rule to remember: The client's insistence on improper conduct by the lawyer doesn't relieve the lawyer of the obligation not to engage in the conduct.

c. Traps set by the examiners

Knowing the tricks the examiners use to lure you into choosing the wrong answer can save you from the temptation to pick them instead of the right answer. When the examiners create an MPRE, their central concern is to preserve the integrity of the exam. They want people who know the Rules to pass the exam, and people who don't know the Rules to fail. (In fact, this is the only way they can convince the states to include the exam as part of their licensing requirements.) So, what they do is to set "traps" for the unwary.

It's almost as though they deliberately calculate and anticipate the mistakes students are likely to make and build around them. They design and construct "distracters" — wrong answers — precisely to lure everyone into making these very mistakes.

(1) The "Hmmm, that sounds familiar" trap

This is the most common — and most insidious — trap on the MPRE. Many law students have a tendency to review for exams only until they can respond by rote. They don't bother to analyze the material to the point of real understanding, and they especially don't bother to apply the material to real facts. The MPRE examiners know this about law students, so they construct answers that seem right because they correctly state a Rule or a part of a Rule — *EXCEPT THAT* the Rule they state is not the Rule that applies to the facts. Here's an example:

> An attorney represented a landlord in a variety of matters over several years. The attorney's engagement letter did not specifically state that he would provide anything other than legal advice. An elderly widow living on public assistance filed suit against the landlord alleging that the landlord withheld without justification the security deposit on a rental unit that she had vacated three years ago. She brought the action for herself, without counsel, in small claims court. The attorney investigated the claim and learned that it was legally barred by the applicable statute of limitations, although the widow's underlying claim was meritorious. The attorney told the landlord of the legal defense, but emphasized that the widow's claim was just and that, in all fairness, the security deposit should be returned to the widow. The attorney told the landlord:

"I strongly recommend that you pay her the full amount with interest. It is against your long-term business interests to be known in the community as a landlord who routinely withholds security deposits even though the tenant leaves the apartment in good condition. Paying the claim now will prevent future headaches for you."

Ultimately, the landlord paid the widow's claim. Was the attorney's conduct proper?

(A) Yes, because the landlord did not object to the attorney's advice and paid the widow's claim.

(B) Yes, because the attorney may refer to both legal and nonlegal considerations in advising a client.

(C) No, because the attorney's engagement letter did not inform the landlord that the attorney's advice on the matter would include both legal and nonlegal considerations.

(D) No, because in advising the landlord to pay the full claim, the attorney failed to represent zealously the landlord's legal interests.

Look at option D. This is a tempting choice because it sounds familiar; you may even say to yourself, "I've seen something like this in one of the Rules, so it must be right." In fact, that language is contained in Model Rule 1.3, Comment [1]. The problem is that the language used — the responsibility of a lawyer to act with zeal — is not what the facts are getting at. Ultimately, option D is wrong because it's not directed at whether the attorney's advice, which went beyond purely technical legal advice, was proper, and that's the issue here.

Option C does the same thing, but this time it suggests a different but equally inapplicable Rule. The idea of an engagement letter will ring a bell, but such a letter to the client is concerned with fees. Its purpose is to make clear what services the lawyer will provide and what he or she will charge for them, not in what form he or she will render advice. Model Rule 1.5.

Ultimately, these answer options are tempting because they reference the Rules in a way that is familiar, and unless you realize that the pivotal issue here concerns the appropriate scope of a lawyer's advice to a client, you might choose C or D. Don't think examiners don't realize this when they create answer options like this! (Incidentally, the best response is B. A lawyer should exercise professional judgment and give candid advice, which may rely on considerations other than purely technical legal advice.)

The only way to insulate yourself against this kind of trap is to study and know the Rules. If you are sufficiently familiar with the Rules, you'll be able to distinguish one Rule from another.

(2) Stating part of a Rule, and omitting a part that would change the result

A frequent trick in distracters is the partial statement of a Rule, or the statement of a Rule without including a relevant or controlling exception. For example:

An attorney filed an action on behalf of a client for breach of contract. In fact, the client had no legal basis for the suit, but wanted to harass the defendant. To induce the attorney to file the action, the client made certain false statements of material fact to the attorney, which the attorney included in the complaint filed against the defendant.

At the trial of the case, the client took the stand and testified as set forth in the complaint. The trial court ordered judgment for the client. After entry of judgment, the client wrote the attorney a letter marked "Confidential," in which the client admitted that she had lied to the attorney and had testified falsely in the case.

Upon complaint of the defendant, who claimed the attorney had knowingly used false testimony in the case, disciplinary proceedings were instituted against the attorney.

Is it proper for the attorney to use the client's letter in the attorney's defense in the disciplinary proceedings?

(A) Yes, because it is necessary to do so in order to protect the attorney's rights.

(B) Yes, because the client had committed a fraud on the court in which the case was tried.

(C) No, because the attorney learned the facts from the client in confidence.

(D) No, because disclosure by the attorney could result in the client's prosecution for perjury.

Look at option C. It suggests the *general* Rule prohibiting a lawyer from revealing any information relating to the representation of a client without the client's consent, but it ignores the *exception* to this Rule, which is core to these facts. The exception is that a lawyer *may reveal* a client confidence to defend him- or herself in a controversy with the client or against a criminal charge or civil claim for conduct involving the client, or to respond to allegations in any proceeding concerning the representation. Model Rule 1.6(b). Because the exception is the important point here, the correct answer is A. Thus, *whenever* an answer option seems to state a prevailing Rule, be on your guard — don't accept the statement at face value — scan your memory to verify that the Rule has been stated either completely or in *pertinent* part, and pay special attention to all the exceptions you know.

(3) Focusing on an issue that wasn't addressed in the "call" of the question

Sometimes when you read a fact pattern on the MPRE, an issue you've learned well will jump off the page at you. You'll immediately assume that's the issue on which the question is focusing, but don't let yourself be distracted. Focus *only* on what's asked in the *call* of the question. If it's a specific call, and it doesn't elicit the issue that first jumped out at you, you can be sure that one of the distracters will rely on that very issue — and, of course, it's one of the three wrong answers. (Remember, this rule applies only to questions following a *specific* call. If the call of the question is general — for example, "Is the attorney subject to discipline for his conduct?" — then the issue you first spotted may well be the basis for the correct answer.)

d. "Because" is your friend

Most answer choices will say "yes" or "no," followed by "because." The word "because" is a *definite,* as opposed to a *conditional,* modifier. Simply put, when "because" is the modifier, it must *necessarily* be true that the reasoning leads to the result. For an answer beginning with "because" to be correct, the following three elements must exist.

(1) Resolve central issue

The reasoning must address and resolve an issue central to the call of the question — or, at least, an issue more central than any other response.

(2) Unequivocally reflect facts

The facts in the reasoning must *completely* and *unequivocally* confirm the facts in the basic fact pattern. For instance, if an option states, "because there was a conflict between two of his clients," the facts must *clearly* show a conflict between the two clients.

(3) Agreement between result and reasoning

The result must be consistent with the reasoning. For instance, if the reasoning tells you, "because the representation was competent," the result must be that the representation is proper. Keep in mind, however, that if the lawyer's competence isn't the central issue, this element *alone* will not necessarily make the option the best response.

Although this is fairly technical, the example below should illustrate this further.

> Four years ago, an attorney was a judge in a state court of general jurisdiction and heard a plaintiff's civil case against a defendant. The plaintiff prevailed and secured a judgment for $50,000, which was sustained on appeal. Since then, the attorney has resigned from the bench and returned to private practice. The defendant has filed suit to enjoin enforcement of the judgment on the grounds of extrinsic fraud in its procurement. The plaintiff has now asked the attorney to represent the plaintiff in defending the suit to enjoin enforcement. The attorney's conduct of the first trial will not be in issue, and he did not believe the present suit was brought in bad faith.
>
> Is it proper for the attorney to accept the representation of the plaintiff in this matter?

(A) Yes, because the attorney would be upholding the decision of the court.

(B) Yes, because the attorney's conduct of the first trial will not be in issue.

(C) No, because the attorney does not believe the present suit is brought in bad faith.

(D) No, because the attorney had acted in a judicial capacity on the merits of the original case.

You should have determined that the *problem* here is the conflict of interest that can arise when a lawyer moves from the judiciary to private practice. The Rule is that a lawyer can't represent anyone in connection with a matter in which the lawyer participated personally and substantially as a judge, unless all parties to the proceeding give informed, written consent. Model Rule 1.12(a).

Let's look at option D. Now, go through the three elements for the "because" modifier to see if D is correct. Remember, the shorthand for those three elements is: (1) resolves a central issue; (2) unequivocally reflects the facts; and (3) shows agreement between result and reasoning.

First, does option D address and resolve a central issue? Yes, it does; the issue is whether the attorney can properly represent the plaintiff, and this turns on whether his conflict of interest prevents him from doing so. D cites the Rule on conflicts of interest for former judges, the central issue, so D passes the first hurdle.

The second hurdle is determining whether the reasoning unequivocally reflects the facts. It does. You're told that the attorney was the judge in the original suit, and the new suit deals with the enforceability of that judgment. Thus, as option D indicates, the attorney did in fact participate "personally and substantially" as a judge in the original case.

Finally, the result and the reasoning must agree. Because the reasoning in D is true, then a conflict of interest must exist that would prevent the attorney from representing the plaintiff. Option D tells you that it would not be proper for the attorney to represent the plaintiff under these facts. Thus, the result and the reasoning agree. (Note, incidentally, that representing the plaintiff would not only be improper — it would subject the attorney to discipline; but, then, every disciplinable act or omission is necessarily improper.)

Now that you've seen how you can determine if a "because" option is correct, you can see how you can conclude thatsome "because" answers are *incorrect*. Look at option A, which also begins with the modifier "because." Look directly at the three "hurdles," the first one first. Does the reasoning of the option address and resolve a central issue? *No.* The central issue is conflict, so it doesn't matter whether the attorney is upholding his decision or not; what matters is that he was acting as judge in the first trial and that this creates an irreconcilable conflict in the second trial.

Because option A fails to clear the first hurdle, you can move on to the next option; you've eliminated A as an acceptable response.

If you have difficulty determining whether a "because" option is correct, there is a way that may help you. Combine the reasoning of the answer with the call of the question to create an "if-then" statement. If the "if-then" statement is true, the answer is correct. If you do this with answer A, you wind up with the following statement: "If the attorney is upholding the decision of the court, then it would be proper for the attorney to represent the plaintiff." As you can see, the "if" clause is the reasoning in the original answer, and the "then" statement restates the call of the question. For the statement to be true, the "if" clause must provide a valid reason for the resulting "then" element. In answer A, it doesn't — the fact that the attorney isn't challenging the judgment doesn't resolve the conflict of interest in favor of his representing the plaintiff.

Incidentally, did you notice what kind of a "distracter" option A is? It's one in which the reasoning evokes a Rule that seems correct but *doesn't apply* to the facts. Option A evokes the lawyer's duty of loyalty to former clients — i.e., the Rule that states a lawyer can't represent a new client with interests adverse to a former client in a substantially related matter. Model Rule 1.9(a). (For instance, a lawyer can't seek to rescind on behalf of a new client a contract he or she drafted for an old client, or challenge the validity of a will for a descendant that he or she prepared and witnessed for the decedent.) Option A suggests that because the attorney isn't challenging his own judgment, his representation of the plaintiff is proper. Of course, this is wrong, because the conflict exists *independently* of whether the attorney is challenging his own decision. Nonetheless, you can see why bringing up another Rule makes A a good distracter.

E. Finding the Right Answer

Learning how to analyze answers correctly can do more for you than simply help you avoid pitfalls. If you put to work all of the principles discussed here, you'll frequently be able to pick the right answer to an MPRE question on first reading! Of course, you shouldn't rush to judgment, because the MPRE is an important exam; the point is that you can learn to increase your confidence and trust your instincts. Your ability to do this is built on something mentioned earlier — namely the tension between the flexibility inherent in the ethics rules and the need for concrete answers to standardized multiple-choice questions. As a result of this tension, the answer options often contain so many qualifying facts that they lead you directly to the one best choice. For example, here are the four answer options to a past MPRE question:

(A) Yes, because the attorney's time was not completely occupied with work for other clients.

(B) Yes, because the attorney neglected the representation of the passenger.

(C) No, because the passenger's suit was filed before the statute of limitations ran.

(D) No, because the attorney returned the $1,000 retainer to the passenger.

Without first having read the corresponding fact pattern, you should be able to guess the best response. A quick glance at each of the options should tell you that the facts probably revolve around a lawyer who didn't act promptly enough in representing his or her client. Remember, good distracters often focus on the same issue as the best response does. This should suggest to you that the issue raised by the fact pattern requires an analysis of the standard set by Mode Rule 1.3 to determine whether a lawyer has acted diligently and promptly in representing the client. You know that the Rule requires a lawyer to act with "reasonable diligence and promptness." You also know that a lawyer should control his or her workload to avoid neglecting one client in favor of others and that unreasonable delay is unacceptable even if the client's interests are not affected in substance. That makes it easy to eliminate options A and C. Option D cannot be the right answer because the issue is neglect of the passenger's interests, not the retainer. With all of that in mind, the best answer is almost certainly option B.

To prove the validity of this approach, here are the facts to this same question:

> An attorney was retained by a passenger on a bus who had been injured in a collision between the bus and a truck. Although he was busy, his time was not completely occupied with work for other clients. The passenger paid the attorney a retainer of $1,000 and agreed further that the attorney should have a fee of 25 percent of any recovery before filing suit, 30 percent of any recovery after suit was filed but before judgment, and 35 percent of any recovery after trial and judgment. The attorney promptly called the lawyer for the bus company and told him she was representing the passenger and would like to talk about a settlement. The attorney made an appointment to talk to the lawyer for the bus company, but did not keep the appointment. The attorney continued to put off talking to the lawyer for the bus company.

> Meanwhile, the passenger became concerned because she had heard nothing from the attorney. The passenger called the attorney's office but was told the attorney was not in and would not call back. The passenger was told not to worry because the attorney would look after her interests. After 10 months had passed, the passenger went to another attorney for advice. The other attorney advised the passenger that the statute of limitations would run in one week and, with the passenger's consent, immediately filed suit for the passenger. The attorney, upon the passenger's demand, refunded the $1,000 the passenger had paid.

> Is the attorney subject to discipline?

As you can see, the facts confirm that B is the best response. This should give you the confidence to trust your instincts as you measure the answer options under facts such as these. Here is another example of four answer options.

(A) Yes, because the attorney has no interest in the case.

(B) Yes, because the judge believes that the attorney's advice is needed to serve the interests of justice.

(C) No, because all parties in the case did not first give their written consent to the judge's consultation with the attorney.

(D) No, because the judge did not inform the parties of the attorney's identity and the substance of the attorney's advice and ask for responses.

Try to deduce what facts are behind these options. You can logically assume that the judge has consulted the attorney (who is probably not an attorney for one of the parties — option A tells us that he has no interest in the case). That's implied by all of the answer options, and, as you know by now, distracters are only effective if they contain elements common to the correct answer. Consequently, it seems Model Code of Judicial Conduct Rule 2.9(A)(2) is at issue here. It permits a judge to consult a disinterested party on applicable law providing he or she follows certain guidelines. The answer options should tell you that the fact pattern probably concerns a judge who asked an uninterested party for advice concerning a proceeding before him or her and that option D is probably the best answer. Here are the facts from that question:

> A judge is presiding in a case that has, as its main issue, a complicated point of commercial law. The lawyers have not presented the case to the judge's satisfaction, and the judge believes she needs additional legal advice. The judge's former partner in law practice is an attorney and expert in the field of law that is at issue. The attorney has no interest in the case. The judge believes the advice is necessary, so she contacts the attorney without telling any of the parties involved.

> Was it proper for the judge to consult the attorney?

As you can see, reading the facts, as in the last example, only reinforces your judgment that the best answer is option D. Here is one more set of options:

(A) Yes, because the client instructed the attorney not to tell anyone about the jewelry box.

(B) Yes, because the disclosure would be detrimental to the client's interests.

(C) No, because the jewelry box was not involved in the dispute between the client and his partner.

(D) No, because the disclosure is necessary to enable the attorney to defend against a criminal charge.

Looking at these options, you can reasonably assume that the facts revolve around confidentiality. A lawyer has a duty not to reveal information relating to the representation of a client without the client's consent. Model Rule 1.6(a). An exception to the Rule, however, is the lawyer's right to defend himself or herself against a criminal charge based on conduct in which the client was involved. Model Rule 1.6(b)(5). Because option D clearly outlines this exception to the client-confidentiality rule, it is very likely the best answer.

The facts to this question bear this out:

> An attorney had been representing the client for several months in a matter involving the ownership of some antique jewelry. The client claimed he purchased the jewelry for his wife with his own funds. The client's business partner claimed the jewelry was a partnership purchase in which he had a one-half interest. While the matter was pending, the client brought a valuable antique jewelry box to the attorney's office and said:
>
>> "Keep this in your vault for me. I bought it before I went into business with my partner. Do not tell him or anyone else about it until my matter with my partner is settled."
>
> Later that same day, a police officer, who was in the attorney's office on another matter, saw the jewelry box when a clerk opened the vault to put in some papers. The police officer recognized it as one that had recently been stolen from a collector. The attorney was arrested and later charged with receiving stolen property.
>
> Is the attorney subject to discipline if the attorney reveals that the client brought the box to her office?

If you are sufficiently well versed in analyzing answer options to MPRE questions and relating them to the facts, you'll be so well prepared for the MPRE that you could well pass the exam just by reasoning your way through the options without reading the questions! But don't get the wrong idea. In no way should you skip the facts.

On the contrary, you should read and reread every fact pattern before you consider the options. And then trust the skills and the instinct you've developed by reviewing and understanding the Rules, studying this book, and reasoning your way to the right answers.

Good luck!

Part Two
Model Questions and Answers

Part Two contains 60 questions reproduced from MPRE Sample Questions VI and MPRE Online Practice Exam 1, published by the National Conference of Bar Examiners. However, some of the questions have been modified to reflect recent changes to the test format. With these model questions, you should be able to put into practice the plan of attack you learned in Part One. The 60 model questions are followed by an explanation and analysis of the answer options. The answers begin on page 89 and reflect the Model Rules of Professional Conduct and the Model Code of Judicial Conduct.

A couple of brief words of advice before you get started. First of all, don't pay attention to timing as you read. On the real MPRE, you'll have two minutes for each question. But for now, put that out of your mind. When you practice here, it's much more important to pay attention to applying the principles from Part One than to beat the clock. Speed will come naturally as you become more proficient at reading the questions and choosing among the answers. Save working on speed until you do the questions in Part Three.

Also, if you pick the wrong answer option, don't stop after you read the correct response; read why the option you chose is wrong. (It's a good idea to make a study sheet of these "near misses" as you answer the questions — see more on what to do with this sheet in Part Three.) Each response is designed to show you not only the correct Rule, but, far more importantly, the mistake you made when you chose the wrong response. You may actually learn more from analyzing the wrong answer than from reviewing the right answer!

Importantly, also go over the answer choices for questions you get right. You might have gotten the right answer for the wrong reason, which means you don't clearly understand the applicable law.

In terms of breaking up the questions, you'd be wise to do ten or so model questions, check your results, and then proceed. Breaking your review down into small chunks like this, and reviewing answers as you go, gives you a chance to identify and correct any mistakes you make before they become habits. If you feel very confident from the start, though, there's no reason why you can't just do all 60 questions at once and then review the answers.

A. Model Questions

Question 1. *you can maintain education other than CLE*

An attorney practices in a state that <u>does not require lawyers to participate</u> in continuing legal education courses. After the attorney forms a partnership with several other lawyers, the majority decides that the firm will not pay for continuing legal education courses since they are not required by the state. Consequently, the attorney tells the firm he will not attend any continuing legal education courses because they all cost money. However, he decides to study legal issues on his own to keep up to date, since he has no malpractice insurance.

Is it proper for the attorney to refuse to attend any continuing legal education courses?

(A) Yes, because the state does not offer free continuing legal education courses.

(B) Yes, because the attorney will independently undertake continuing study and education in the law.

(C) No, because the attorney cannot maintain competence without attending continuing legal education courses.

(D) No, because the attorney does not have malpractice insurance.

Question 2.

An attorney is a newly admitted member of the bar. A partner in his firm was recognized as an expert in securities regulation law. A corporation retained the firm to qualify the corporation's stock for public sale. After accepting the matter, the partner preferred to spend his time on cases with larger fee potential, so he assigned the corporation matter to the attorney. The attorney told the partner he knew nothing about securities regulation law and that he had too little time to prepare himself for the corporation's sale without substantial help from the partner. The partner refused to help and directed the attorney to proceed.

Was the partner's conduct proper in this matter?

(A) Yes, because as a member of the bar, the attorney is licensed to handle any legal matter.

(B) Yes, because the partner may withdraw from a case if work on it would cause him unreasonable financial hardship.

(C) No, because the partner knew the attorney was not competent to handle the matter, and the partner failed to provide supervision adequate to protect the client's interest.

(D) No, because the corporation had not given the partner permission to assign the attorney to work on the matter.

Question 3.

An attorney is a member of the bar in one state and is also licensed as a stockbroker in another. In his application for renewal of his stockbroker's license the attorney knowingly filed a false financial statement. Soon thereafter, the attorney is convicted in the second state for knowingly filing a false financial statement.

Is the attorney subject to discipline as a member of the bar of the first state?

(A) Yes, because his actions involve dishonesty or misrepresentation.

(B) Yes, because he was first convicted of a criminal offense in the second state.

(C) No, because his action was not done in his capacity as an attorney.

(D) No, because his action was not in the first state.

Question 4.

An attorney is a sole practitioner whose practice is largely in the areas of tax, wills, estates, and trusts. The attorney learned of a new Internal Revenue Service (IRS) regulation that probably affects the trust provisions in a will she prepared for a client two years ago. The attorney has not represented the client since she drew up the will, and believes another lawyer now represents her. She also has no interest in drawing up a new one for the client.

Is the attorney subject to discipline if she calls the former client and advises her of the new IRS ruling and the need to revise the will?

(A) Yes, because the attorney has reason to believe that the former client has another lawyer.

(B) Yes, because the attorney would be soliciting legal business from a person who is not a current client.

(C) No, because the attorney does not plan on preparing a new will for the former client.

(D) No, because the client is a former client of the attorney.

Question 5.

An attorney was retained to appeal the client's criminal conviction and to seek bail pending appeal. The agreed fee for the appearance on the bail hearing was $50 per hour. The attorney received $800 from the client, of which $300 was a deposit to secure the attorney's fee, and $500 was for bail costs in the event that bail was obtained. The attorney maintained two office bank accounts: a "Fee Account," in which all fees were deposited and from which all office expenses were paid, and a "Clients' Fund Account." The attorney deposited the $800 in the "Clients' Fund Account" the week before the bail hearing. The attorney expended six hours of time on the bail hearing. The effort to obtain bail was unsuccessful. Dissatisfied, the client immediately demanded return of the $800.

It is now proper for the attorney to:

(A) transfer the $800 to the "Fee Account."

(B) transfer $300 to the "Fee Account" and leave $500 in the "Clients' Fund Account" until the attorney's fee for the final appeal is determined.

(C) transfer $300 to the "Fee Account" and send the client a $500 check on the "Clients' Fund Account."

(D) send the client a $500 check and leave $300 in the "Clients' Fund Account" until the matter is resolved.

Question 6.

A judge has been assigned to try a criminal prosecution by the state against a defendant. Ten years previously, the judge, while serving as a deputy attorney general in the state, led an investigation of the defendant for suspected criminal conduct. The investigation did not establish any basis for prosecution. None of the matters previously investigated is involved in or affects the present prosecution. The judge had completely forgotten the earlier investigation, and had no prejudice toward the defendant.

Is it proper for the judge to try the case?

(A) Yes, because none of the matters previously investigated is involved in or affects the present case.

(B) Yes, because there is no indication the judge might be prejudiced against the defendant because of the prior investigation.

(C) No, because the judge had substantial responsibility in initiating the previous investigation of defendant.

(D) No, because the judge had substantial responsibility in determining that the previous investigation did not establish any basis for prosecution.

Question 7.

An attorney represented a landlord in a variety of matters over several years. The attorney's engagement letter did not specifically state that he would provide anything other than legal advice. An elderly widow living on public assistance filed suit against the landlord alleging that the landlord withheld without justification the security deposit on a rental unit that the widow vacated three years ago. She brought the action for herself, without counsel, in small claims court. The attorney investigated the claim and learned that it was legally barred by the applicable statute of limitations, although the widow's underlying claim was meritorious. The attorney told the landlord of the legal defense, but emphasized that the widow's claim was just and that, in all fairness, the security deposit should be returned to her. The attorney told the landlord:

> "I strongly recommend that you pay the widow the full amount with interest. It is against your long-term business interests to be known in the community as a landlord who routinely withholds security deposits even though the tenant leaves the apartment in good condition. Paying the claim now will prevent future headaches for you."

Ultimately, the landlord paid the widow's claim. Was the attorney's conduct proper?

(A) Yes, because the landlord did not object to the attorney's advice and paid the widow's claim.

(B) Yes, because the attorney may refer to both legal and nonlegal considerations in advising a client.

(C) No, because the attorney's engagement letter did not inform the landlord that the attorney's advice on the matter would include both legal and nonlegal considerations.

(D) No, because in advising the landlord to pay the full claim, the attorney failed to represent zealously the landlord's legal interests.

Question 8.

An attorney is a member of the bar and a salaried employee of a bank's trust department. As part of his duties, he prepares a monthly newsletter concerning wills, trusts, estates, and taxes, which the bank sends to all of its customers. The newsletter contains a recommendation to the customer to review his or her will in light of the information contained and, if the customer has any questions, to bring the will to the bank, where the attorney will review the customer's will and answer the customer's legal questions. The bank provides the attorney's services to its customers for no charge.

Is the attorney subject to discipline for the foregoing?

(A) Yes, because by sending out the newsletter the attorney is giving legal advice to persons who are not his clients.

(B) Yes, because the attorney is assisting the bank in the unauthorized practice of law.

(C) No, because no charge is made for the attorney's advice.

(D) No, because the attorney is a member of the bar.

Question 9.

An attorney was recently admitted to practice and was hired as a new associate at a large firm employing over 100 lawyers. The attorney was working late one night when he received a telephone call from his cousin. His cousin said that he was calling from the police station where he had just been arrested for possession of cocaine with intent to distribute. He was permitted to make only one phone call, and the attorney was the only lawyer he knew. The attorney responded that he had no criminal law experience and that his firm did not handle criminal cases. Nevertheless, his cousin pleaded with the attorney to come to the police station and see what he could do to get him out on bail. The attorney replied that he would do what he could.

The attorney went to the police station and using what information he recalled from his criminal law and procedure courses attempted to get his cousin released on bail. However, as a result of his inexperience, the attorney was unable to secure his cousin's release that night. The next morning, the attorney found an experienced criminal lawyer for his cousin, who obtained his cousin's release within one hour.

Was the attorney's conduct proper?

(A) Yes, because neither referral nor consultation was practical under the circumstances.

(B) Yes, because the attorney was a close relative.

(C) No, because the attorney had no special training or experience in criminal cases.

(D) No, because the attorney did not have the requisite level of competence to accept representation in the case.

Question 10.

A business attorney entered into a partnership with a certified public accountant. The partnership provided legal and other assistance to clients in connection with business and tax planning, tax filings, and other personal and corporate business matters. The accountant performed only work that she was authorized to perform as a certified public accountant. The attorney made reasonable efforts to ensure that the accountant did not interfere with the attorney's compliance with his professional obligations as a lawyer.

Is the attorney subject to discipline?

(A) Yes, because some of the activities of the partnership consisted of the practice of law.

(B) Yes, because lawyers may not form partnerships with nonlawyers.

(C) No, because the accountant performed only work that she was authorized to perform as a certified public accountant.

(D) No, because the attorney made reasonable efforts to ensure that the accountant did not interfere with the attorney's compliance with his professional obligations as a lawyer.

Question 11.

An attorney is widely regarded as an exceptionally competent practitioner in the field of criminal law. A client of the attorney became the subject of a grand jury investigation in a matter that could result in a felony indictment. The client lacked sufficient funds to pay for the attorney's services beyond the grand jury stage. He asked the attorney to provide limited representation for a flat fee. Under the arrangement he proposed, the attorney would advise the client concerning the grand jury investigation, but the representation would end when an indictment was returned or the grand jury decided not to indict. The attorney fully advised the client of the practical and legal aspects of the client's proposal.

Is it proper for the attorney to accept this limited representation?

(A) Yes, because the client and not the attorney suggested the arrangement.

(B) Yes, because the attorney and the client may agree to limit the scope of the representation so long as the limitation is reasonable under the circumstances.

(C) No, because the attorney should not limit the scope of the representation based on the client's ability to pay.

(D) No, because the scope of the representation may not be limited in a criminal case.

Question 12.

An attorney represents a client who is under indictment for homicide. In the course of the representation, the client told the attorney that she had previously killed two other people. These murders are completely unrelated to the murder indictment for which the attorney is providing representation. With the client's consent, the attorney made a tape recording of the client's confession regarding the unrelated homicides. At the attorney's request, the client also drew a map of the remote locations of the victims' graves from the unrelated killings. Those bodies have not been found by the police, and the client is not a suspect in either crime, both of which remain unsolved.

Is the attorney subject to discipline if he fails to voluntarily disclose to the authorities his knowledge of the two prior murders and the locations of the victim's bodies?

(A) Yes, because as an officer of the court, the attorney must disclose any knowledge that he has, whether privileged or not, concerning the commission of the prior crimes by his client.

(B) Yes, because the attorney is impeding the state's access to significant evidence.

(C) No, because the attorney did not represent or advise his client with respect to the prior crimes.

(D) No, because the information was obtained by the attorney in the course of the representation.

Question 13.

A client has asked an attorney to represent her in obtaining compensation for a tract of land that is being condemned by the state department of transportation to build a new highway. Two years ago, the attorney had been employed by the department and had been assigned to search title on several tracts of land, including the one owned by the client. The attorney remembers a department engineer had drafted a confidential memorandum advising against running a new highway across the client's land because of a potential adverse environmental impact. Because of this information, the attorney believes it is possible to prevent the condemnation of the client's land or to increase the settlement amount.

What is the proper action for the attorney to take?

(A) Represent the client on the issue of damages only and not disclose the information that might prevent the condemnation.

(B) Represent the client and attempt to prevent the condemnation by using the information about the adverse environmental impact.

(C) Refuse to represent the client but disclose to her the information about the adverse environmental impact.

(D) Refuse to represent the client and not disclose the information about the adverse environmental impact.

Question 14.

An assistant district attorney was in charge of the presentation before a grand jury of evidence that led to an indictment charging 32 defendants with conspiracy to sell controlled drugs. Shortly after the grand jury returned the indictments, the attorney resigned as assistant district attorney and became an associate in the law office of an attorney for one of the indicted codefendants. The former district attorney did not reveal any confidence or secret learned while he was an assistant district attorney, but he also did not expressly state he would not participate in the case.

Is it proper for that attorney to continue to represent the codefendant?

(A) Yes, because the former assistant district attorney did not reveal to the attorney any confidence or secret learned while an assistant district attorney.

(B) Yes, because a public prosecutor must make timely disclosure to the defense attorney of any exculpatory evidence.

(C) No, because the former assistant district attorney did not agree to not participate in the representation of the codefendant.

(D) No, because the former assistant district attorney had substantial responsibility for the indictment of the codefendant.

Question 15.

An attorney filed an action on behalf of his client for breach of contract. In fact, the client had no legal basis for suit, but wanted to harass the defendant. In order to induce the attorney to file the action, the client made certain false statements of material fact to the attorney, which the attorney included in the complaint filed against the defendant.

At the trial of the case, the client took the stand and testified as set forth in the complaint. The trial court ordered judgment for the client. After entry of judgment, the client wrote the attorney a letter marked "Confidential," in which the client admitted that she had lied to the attorney and had testified falsely in the case.

Upon complaint of the defendant, who claimed the attorney had knowingly used false testimony in the case, disciplinary proceedings were instituted against the attorney.

Is it proper for the attorney to use the client's letter in the attorney's defense in the disciplinary proceedings?

(A) Yes, because it is necessary to do so in order to protect the attorney's rights.

(B) Yes, because the client had committed a fraud on the court in which the case was tried.

(C) No, because the attorney learned the facts from the client in confidence.

(D) No, because disclosure by the attorney could result in the client's prosecution for perjury.

Question 16.

An attorney who is a sole practitioner limits his practice to personal injury cases. He regularly places advertisements in local newspapers that state that his practice is limited to personal injury cases, including medical malpractice. After seeing one of the attorney's ads, a man approached the attorney for representation in a medical malpractice case. After a 30-minute interview, the attorney told the man that he was too busy to take his case because it appeared quite complicated. He further offered to refer the man to another lawyer who regularly practiced in the field. He reminded the man that he should see another lawyer promptly before the statute of limitations expired and he lost his right to sue.

Although the attorney did not charge the man for the interview, the man was upset at wasting 30 minutes of his time. The man did not contact another lawyer until eight months later, when he learned that the statute of limitations on his claim had expired six months after his interview with the attorney. In fact, the man had a meritorious medical malpractice claim.

Is the attorney subject to civil liability?

(A) Yes, because the attorney falsely advertised his availability for medical malpractice cases.

(B) Yes, because the attorney did not advise the man as to the date the statute of limitations would expire.

(C) No, because the attorney did not violate any duty owed to the man.

(D) No, because the attorney offered to refer the man to another medical malpractice lawyer.

Question 17.

An attorney is employed by a client who is a fugitive from justice under indictment for armed robbery. The attorney, after thorough legal research and investigation of the facts furnished by the client, reasonably believes the indictment is fatally defective and should be dismissed as a matter of law. The attorney advised the client of his opinion and urged the client to surrender. The client told the attorney that she would not surrender.

The attorney informed the district attorney that he represented the client and that he had counseled her to surrender but that she refused to follow his advice. The attorney has not advised his client on how to avoid arrest and prosecution and does not know where she is hiding.

Is the attorney subject to discipline if he continues to represent the client?

(A) Yes, because the client is engaging in continuing illegal conduct.

(B) Yes, because the client refused to accept the attorney's advice and surrender.

(C) No, because the attorney is not counseling the client to avoid arrest and prosecution.

(D) No, because the attorney reasonably believes the indictment is defective.

Question 18.

An attorney represented a real estate developer who was trying to buy several properties. The attorney arranged a meeting with an owner of two large parcels of land, hoping to arrange a sale to the developer.

When the attorney scheduled this meeting, he neither knew nor asked whether the owner was represented by counsel in the matter. Shortly after the meeting began, the owner disclosed that he had retained counsel to assist in the sale of the two parcels of land, but that his lawyer could not be present that day. He further stated that he would be meeting with his lawyer the next day. The attorney asked the owner if they could talk anyway, and stated that he wouldn't ask the owner to sign anything until his lawyer had a chance to look over anything they discussed.

The owner, an experienced businessman and negotiator, agreed to continue as suggested, and a tentative agreement was soon worked out.

Was the attorney's conduct proper?

(A) Yes, because the owner knowingly agreed to continue the discussions without his own lawyer being present.

(B) Yes, because the attorney did not present the owner with any documents to sign during the meeting.

(C) No, because the attorney negotiated with the owner after learning that the owner was represented by a lawyer in the matter.

(D) No, because the attorney failed to ascertain whether the owner was represented by a lawyer before beginning the negotiation session.

Question 19.

An attorney prepared a will for a client and acted as one of the subscribing witnesses to the client's execution of the will. The will left all of the client's estate to his son. Later, at the client's request, the attorney prepared a second will for the client and acted as one of the subscribing witnesses to the client's execution of the second will. The second will left one-half of the client's estate to his son and the other one-half to his housekeeper. The client died and the housekeeper has offered the second will for probate.

If the son requests that the attorney represent him in opposing probate of the second will on the grounds of fraud and undue influence, is it proper for the attorney to do so?

(A) Yes, because after the client's death the attorney may represent his son.

(B) Yes, because the client's son is a beneficiary under both wills.

(C) No, because an attorney guarantees the validity of a will that he or she prepares.

(D) No, because the attorney would be taking a position adverse to a will she prepared and witnessed.

Question 20.

A judge was trying a case without a jury. After both parties had completed the presentation of evidence and arguments, the judge took the case under advisement.

After the case was under advisement for several weeks, the attorney heard rumors that the judge was having difficulty determining the issue of factual causation and was uncertain about the applicable law. Immediately after hearing these rumors, the attorney telephoned the judge, told the judge of the rumors the attorney had heard, and asked if the judge would like to reopen the case for additional evidence and briefing from both parties.

Thereafter, the judge reopened the case for further testimony and requested supplementary briefs from both parties.

Was it proper for the attorney to communicate with the judge?

(A) Yes, because both parties were given full opportunity to present their views on the issues in the case.

(B) Yes, because the attorney did not make any suggestion as to how the judge should decide the matter.

(C) No, because the attorney communicated with the judge on a pending matter without advising opposing counsel.

(D) No, because the attorney caused the judge to reopen a case that had been taken under advisement.

Question 21.

An attorney represented a seller in negotiating the sale of his ice cream parlor. The seller told the attorney in confidence that, although the business had once been very profitable, recent profits had been stable but modest. As the negotiations proceeded, the buyer appeared to be losing interest in the deal. Hoping to restore the buyer's interest, the attorney stated, "The ice cream business is every American's dream: happy kids, steady profits, and a clear conscience." The buyer bought the ice cream parlor but was disappointed when his own profits proved to be modest.

Is the attorney subject to discipline?

(A) Yes, because the attorney made a false statement of fact to the buyer.

(B) Yes, because the attorney exaggerated the profitability of the business.

(C) No, because the attorney represented the seller, not the buyer.

(D) No, because the attorney's statement constitutes acceptable puffing in negotiations.

Question 22.

An attorney has a radio commercial that states:

"Do you have a legal problem? Are you being sued? Call me, a licensed attorney at law. Initial conference charge is $25 for one hour. Act now and protect your interests. Call at 1234 Main Street; telephone area code (101)

123-4567." All of the statements were true, and the broadcast could not be heard outside of the state in which the attorney was licensed.

Is the attorney subject to discipline for the commercial?

(A) Yes, because the attorney's qualifications are not stated.

(B) Yes, because the radio broadcast may encourage litigation.

(C) No, because all the statements in the radio broadcast are true.

(D) No, because the radio broadcast is not heard outside the state in which the attorney is licensed.

Question 23.

An attorney, recently admitted to practice, opened an office near a residential neighborhood and published the following advertisement in the local newspaper.

COUPON

Get Acquainted With

Your Neighborhood Lawyer

A. Attorney

Suite 2 — 1100 Magnolia Avenue

Sunshine City, State 01000

Telephone: (555) 555-5555

In order to acquaint you with our services, we are offering a one-hour consultation to review your estate plans, including your wills, trusts, and similar documents, all at the nominal cost of $25 to anyone presenting this coupon. Call now for an appointment.

Everything in the advertisement was true. Is the attorney subject to discipline?

(A) Yes, because the attorney is soliciting business from persons with whom the attorney had no prior relationship.

(B) Yes, because the attorney requires the use of a coupon.

(C) No, because the attorney provides the services described for the fee stated.

(D) No, because the attorney is not seeking business from persons who are already represented by a lawyer.

Question 24.

An attorney was retained by a client to incorporate client's business, which previously had been operated as a sole proprietorship. The attorney noticed in the client's file copies of some correspondence from the client to another attorney concerning the possibility of that attorney incorporating the client's business. The attorney questioned the client to make certain that any attorney-client relationship between the other attorney and the client had been terminated. The client told the attorney,

"It certainly has been terminated. When I discussed the matter with that guy six months ago, he asked for a retainer of $1,000, which I paid him. He did absolutely nothing after he got the money, even though I called him weekly, and finally, last week when I again complained, he returned the retainer. But don't say anything about it because he is an old friend of my family, and I was just happy I got the money back."

The attorney believed the other attorney was guilty of professional misconduct, although the attorney did not think the other attorney usually acted in this manner. The client just wanted to drop the matter.

Is the attorney subject to discipline if she does not report her knowledge of the other attorney's conduct to the appropriate authority?

(A) Yes, because the attorney believes the other attorney was clearly guilty of professional misconduct.

(B) Yes, because the attorney did not believe the other attorney usually neglected matters entrusted to him.

(C) No, because the client was satisfied by the other attorney's return of the retainer.

(D) No, because the client has not agreed that the attorney may report the information.

Question 25.

An attorney represented a client as a plaintiff in a personal injury matter under a standard contingent fee contract. The client agreed to settle the case for $1,000,000, from which funds the attorney would receive $250,000. The client informed the attorney that she planned to take $25,000 of the settlement funds and spend the money purchasing lottery tickets. The attorney told the client that he disagreed with this plan and encouraged the client to take some classes on investing money. The client agreed to take the classes, but still insisted on playing the lottery.

The attorney received the check for $1,000,000 three days before the client was to attend the investing classes. The attorney held the check for one week, giving the client at least a few days of classes. The attorney then informed the client of the receipt of the funds, disbursed the funds according to the agreement, and also furnished the client with an accounting. The attorney told the client that he had delayed notice to allow time for the client to come to her senses. The client laughed and said, "I guess your plan worked, because these classes have convinced me to invest my money in the stock market instead of playing the lottery."

Is the attorney subject to discipline?

(A) Yes, because the attorney had a duty to promptly notify the client of the receipt of the $1,000,000.

(B) Yes, because the attorney gave unsolicited advice about nonlegal matters.

(C) No, because the client did not object to the withholding of the notice and funds.

(D) No, because the attorney acted in the client's best interest.

Question 26.

An attorney served two four-year terms as the state's governor immediately prior to reopening his law office in the state. The attorney printed and mailed an announcement of his return to private practice to members of the bar, previous clients, and personal friends whom he had never represented. The printed announcement stated that the attorney had reopened his law office, gave his address and telephone number, and added that he had been the state's governor for the past eight years.

Is the attorney subject to discipline for the announcement?

(A) Yes, because the mailing included persons who had not been his clients.

(B) Yes, because his service as governor is unrelated to his ability as a lawyer.

(C) No, because the information in the announcement was true.

(D) No, because all of the information was already in the public domain.

Question 27.

An attorney has tried many contested cases before a certain judge. The attorney believes the judge is lacking both in knowledge of the law and in good judgment and that another attorney would make an excellent judge. The attorney wishes to help defeat the judge and assist the other attorney in getting elected.

The attorney intends to contribute an anonymous $5,000 donation to other attorney's campaign. Is it proper for the attorney to do so?

(A) Yes, the attorney may give $5,000 to the other attorney personally for his campaign.

- (B) Yes, because the attorney's contribution to the other attorney is made anonymously.

(C) No, because the attorney is practicing before the court to which the other attorney seeks election.

— (D) No, because the attorney is not giving the $5,000 to a committee formed to further the other attorney's election.

Question 28.

An attorney practices law in the same community as a lawyer who is running for election as a state judge. The attorney has frequently observed the judicial candidate's courtroom demeanor in litigated cases. Based on those experiences, the attorney believes that the judicial candidate does not have a proper judicial temperament. A local news reporter asked the attorney how he would rate the candidate, and the attorney responded in good faith that he believed the candidate was unsuited for the bench and lacked the proper judicial temperament for a judge. A local newspaper with a wide circulation quoted the attorney's remarks.

Were the attorney's remarks proper?

(A) Yes, because the attorney was not seeking judicial office.

— (B) Yes, because the attorney believed the candidate was unsuited for the bench.

(C) No, because the remarks serve to bring the judiciary into disrepute.

(D) No, because a lawyer should not publicly comment on candidates for judicial office.

Question 29.

An attorney was retained by a passenger on a bus who was injured in a collision between the bus and a truck. Although he was busy, his time was not completely occupied with work for other clients. The passenger paid the attorney a retainer of $1,000, and agreed further that the attorney should have a fee of 25 percent of any recovery before filing suit, 30 percent of any recovery after suit was filed but before judgment, and 35 percent of any recovery after trial and judgment. The attorney promptly called the lawyer for the bus company and told him she was representing the passenger and would like to talk about a settlement. The attorney made an appointment to talk to the lawyer for the bus company, but did not keep the appointment. The attorney continued to put off talking to the lawyer for the bus company. Meanwhile, the passenger became concerned because she had heard nothing from her attorney. The passenger called the attorney's office, but was told the attorney was not in and would not call back. The passenger was told not to worry because the attorney would look after her interests. After 10 months had passed, the passenger went to another attorney for advice. The other attorney advised the passenger that the statute of limitations would run in one week and, with the passenger's consent, immediately filed suit for the passenger. Upon the passenger's demand, the attorney refunded the $1,000 the passenger had paid.

Is the attorney subject to discipline?

(A) Yes, because the attorney's time was not completely occupied with work for other clients.

(B) Yes, because the attorney neglected the representation of the passenger.

(C) No, because the passenger's suit was filed before the statute of limitations ran.

(D) No, because the attorney returned the $1,000 retainer to the passenger.

Question 30.

An attorney filed a personal injury suit on behalf of a plaintiff. The defendant was personally served with process. The attorney knows that the defendant is insured by an insurance company and that another attorney has been retained by the insurance company to represent the defendant. No responsive pleading has been filed on behalf of the defendant, and the time for filing expired over 10 days ago.

Is the attorney subject to discipline if the attorney proceeds to have a default judgment entered?

(A) Yes, because the attorney knows that another attorney had been retained by the insurance company to represent the defendant.

(B) Yes, because the attorney failed to extend professional courtesy to another lawyer.

(C) No, because the attorney is properly representing her client's interests.

(D) No, because any judgment will be satisfied by the insurance company.

Question 31.

An attorney is a candidate in a contested election for judicial office. Her opponent is the incumbent judge and has occupied the bench for many years. The director of the state commission on judicial conduct, upon inquiry by the attorney, erroneously told the attorney that the judge had been reprimanded by the commission for misconduct in office. The attorney, who had confidence in the director, believed him. In fact, the judge had not been reprimanded by the commission; the commission had conducted hearings on the judge's alleged misconduct in office and, by a three-to-two vote, declined to reprimand the judge.

Decisions of the commission, including reprimands, are not confidential. Is the attorney subject to discipline for publicly stating that the judge had been reprimanded for misconduct?

(A) Yes, because the official records of the commission would have disclosed the truth.

(B) Yes, because the judge had not been reprimanded.

(C) No, because the attorney reasonably relied on the director's information.

(D) No, because the judge was a candidate in a contested election.

Question 32.

An attorney is a well-known, highly skilled litigator. The attorney's practice is in an area of law in which the trial proceedings are heard by the court without a jury.

In an interview with a prospective client, the attorney said, "I make certain that I give the campaign committee of every candidate for elective judicial office more money than any other lawyer gives, whether it's $500 or $5,000. Judges know who helps them get elected." The prospective client did not retain the attorney.

Is the attorney subject to discipline?

(A) Yes, because the attorney's contributions are made without consideration of candidates' merits.

(B) Yes, because the attorney implied that the attorney receives favored treatment by judges.

(C) No, because the attorney's statements were true.

(D) No, because the prospective client did not retain the attorney.

Question 33.

A judge is presiding in a case that has, as its main issue, a complicated point of commercial law. The lawyers have not presented the case to the judge's satisfaction, and the judge believes she needs additional legal advice. The judge's former partner in law practice is an attorney and an expert in the field of law that is at issue. The attorney has no interest in the case. The judge believes the advice is necessary, so she contacts the attorney without telling any of the parties involved.

Was it proper for the judge to consult the attorney?

(A) Yes, because the attorney has no interest in the case.

(B) Yes, because the judge believes that the attorney's advice is needed to serve the interests of justice.

(C) No, because all parties in the case did not first give their written consent to the judge's consultation with the attorney.

(D) No, because the judge did not inform the parties of the attorney's identity and the substance of the attorney's advice and asks for responses.

Question 34.

Under a state law, the court's appointment of lawyers as special masters in certain proceedings is discretionary with the court. A judge decided to appoint special masters in all such proceedings, regardless of their nature and complexity, and decided that compensation for such appointees would be at a reasonable hourly rate. The judge believed that this practice would ensure competent and impartial handling of every proceeding. The judge further decided to use published law directories to compile a list of qualified prospective appointees.

Is the judge's proposed practice proper?

— (A) Yes, because it results in competent and impartial handling of the proceedings.

(B) Yes, because the appointees will be compensated at a reasonable hourly rate.

—(C) No, because the practice may result in unnecessary appointments.

(D) No, because the judge cannot use law directories to compile a list of qualified prospective appointees.

Question 35.

A trust company entered into the following arrangement with an attorney who was newly admitted to the bar:

The trust company would provide the attorney with free office space in the building in which the trust company had its offices. If a customer of the trust company contacted the trust company about a trust or will, an officer of the trust company, who would not be a lawyer, would advise the customer and help the customer work out the details of the trust or will. The customer would be informed that the necessary documents would be prepared by the trust company's staff. The completed documents would be submitted by an officer of the trust company to the customer for execution.

The attorney, in accordance with a memorandum from the trust company's trust officer detailing the plan, would prepare the necessary documents. The attorney would never meet with the customer and would not charge the customer for these services. The attorney would be free to engage in private practice, subject only to the limitation that the attorney could not accept employment adverse to the trust company.

Is the attorney subject to discipline for entering into the arrangement with the trust company?

(A) Yes, because the attorney is restricting his right to practice.

(B) Yes, because the attorney is aiding the trust company in the practice of law.

(C) No, because the attorney is not charging the customer for his services.

(D) No, because the attorney is not giving advice to the trust company's customers.

Question 36.

An attorney represented a husband and wife in the purchase of a business financed by contributions from their respective separate funds. The business was jointly operated by the husband and wife after acquisition. After several years, a dispute arose over the management of the business. The husband and wife sought the attorney's advice, and the matter was settled on the basis of an agreement drawn by the attorney and signed by the husband and wife. Later, the wife asked the attorney to represent her in litigation against her husband based on the claim that her husband was guilty of fraud and misrepresentation in the negotiations for the prior settlement agreement. The husband has not retained counsel in the matter.

Is it proper for the attorney to represent the wife in this matter?

(A) Yes, because all information relevant to the litigation was received by the attorney in the presence of both the husband and wife.

(B) Yes, because there is reason to believe the husband misled both the wife and the attorney at the time of the prior agreement.

(C) No, because the attorney had previously acted for both parties in reaching the agreement now in dispute.

(D) No, because the husband is not now represented by independent counsel.

Question 37.

A client retained an attorney to recover for a personal injury. In the retainer agreement signed by the client and the attorney, the client agreed to cooperate fully and pay the attorney a contingent fee computed as a percentage of the amount of recovery after expenses: 25 percent if settled before trial, 30 percent if settled before verdict, 35 percent after verdict, and 40 percent after appeal.

The attorney's representation of the client in the matter extended over a three-year period, during which the attorney advanced a large amount for litigation expenses. After trial, the client obtained a jury verdict for an amount larger than either the attorney or the client had anticipated.

However, the defendant filed an appeal based on questions of evidence and the measure of damages. Meanwhile, the defendant made an offer of settlement for approximately the amount the attorney had originally projected as reasonable to expect. The client, who was hard-pressed financially, directed the attorney to accept the offer and settle. The attorney refused, because she was confident that there was no reversible error in the trial and that the appeal was without merit. The attorney reasonably believed that the appeal was filed solely to gain negotiating advantage in settlement negotiations.

Is the attorney subject to discipline?

(A) Yes, because the attorney's percentage under the fee contract increased after appeal.

(B) Yes, because the client directed the attorney to accept the settlement offer.

(C) No, because the decision whether to settle or defend an appeal is a tactical matter for the attorney to determine.

(D) No, because evaluation of the merits of an appeal requires the exercise of independent professional judgment.

Question 38.

An attorney advertises on the local television station. In the advertisements, a professional actor says:

"Do you need a lawyer? Call 555-555-5555. Her fees might be lower than you think."

The attorney approved the prerecorded advertisement and is keeping in her office files a copy of the recording of the actual transmission and a record of when each transmission was made. For those responding to the advertisement, she charges for the initial consultation.

Is the advertisement proper?

(A) Yes.

(B) No, because it is not clear the attorney's fees are lower than those generally charged in the area where she practices.

(C) No, because she used a professional actor for the television advertisement.

(D) No, because she makes a charge for the initial consultation.

Question 39.

An attorney represented both the owner of an art gallery and a publisher. The gallery owner and the publisher each made a practice of paying the attorney's fees in cash. The attorney received separate cash payments from the gallery owner and the publisher on the same day. Each payment consisted of 10 $100 bills, which the attorney immediately deposited in her bank account. One week later, the attorney was contacted by United States Treasury agents, who informed her that four of the bills had been identified as counterfeit. The agents did not accuse the attorney of knowingly passing the counterfeit money, but asked her who had given her the bills. The attorney was subpoenaed to testify before a grand jury and was asked who could have given her the counterfeit money.

Is it proper for the attorney to provide the grand jury with the names of the gallery owner and the publisher?

(A) Yes, because negotiation of a counterfeit bill is a criminal act.

(B) Yes, because under the circumstances neither client's identity is privileged.

(C) No, because counterfeiting is not a crime that involves an imminent threat of death or serious bodily harm.

(D) No, because the attorney has no way of knowing which of the two clients gave her the counterfeit bills.

Question 40.

A corporation has applied to a bank for a $900,000 loan to be secured by a lien on the corporation's inventory. The inventory, consisting of small items, constantly turns over. The security documents are complex and if improperly drawn they could result in an invalid lien. The bank has approved the loan on the condition that the corporation and the bank jointly retain an attorney to prepare the necessary security instruments and that the corporation pay the attorney's fees. Both the corporation and the bank gave informed consent in writing to the attorney's representation of both parties. This arrangement is customary in the city in which the attorney's law office and the bank are located. It is obvious to the attorney that he can adequately represent the interests of both the corporation and the bank.

Is it proper for the attorney to prepare the security documents under these circumstances?

(A) Yes, because both the bank and the corporation have given their informed consent to the arrangement.

(B) Yes, because the arrangement is customary in the community.

(C) No, because the attorney's fees are being paid by the corporation, not the bank.

(D) No, because the corporation and the bank have differing interests.

Question 41.

An attorney agreed to represent a client who was being prosecuted for driving while intoxicated in a jurisdiction in which there is an increased penalty for a second offense. The client told the attorney that his driver's license had been obtained under an assumed name because his prior license had been suspended for driving while under the influence of alcohol. Obtaining a license in this way was a felony. The client asked the attorney not to disclose his true name during the course of the representation and told the attorney that, if called as a witness, he would give his assumed name. The attorney informed the client that, in order to properly defend the case, the attorney must call the client as a witness.

The attorney called the client as a witness and, in response to the attorney's question "What is your name?" the client gave his assumed name.

Is the attorney subject to discipline?

(A) Yes, because the attorney knowingly used false testimony.

(B) Yes, because the client committed a felony when he obtained the driver's license under an assumed name.

(C) No, because the attorney's knowledge of the client's true name was obtained during the course of representation.

(D) No, because the client's true name was not an issue in the proceeding.

Question 42.

A judge is one of three trustees of a trust for the educational benefit of her grandchildren. The trust owns 5,000 shares of stock in a large oil company. The stock has been selling for the past year at $10,000 a share. The oil company is suing a refining company for breach of an oil refining agreement, and the case is assigned to the judge for trial. The judge believes that she can be fair and impartial. Additionally, she does not personally own stock in either party to the litigation.

Must the judge disqualify herself from the case?

(A) Yes, because the trust has more than a *de minimis* financial interest in the oil company.

(B) Yes, because the outcome of the lawsuit is likely to affect the value of the stock.

(C) No, because the judge does not personally own stock in either party to the litigation.

(D) No, because the judge believes she can remain impartial.

Question 43.

A judge has served for many years as a director of a charitable organization that maintains a camp for disadvantaged children, although she has not received any compensation for her services. The organization has never been involved in litigation. The charity has decided to sponsor a public testimonial dinner in the judge's honor. As part of the occasion, the local bar association intends to commission and present to the judge her portrait at a cost of $4,000.

The money to pay for the portrait will come from a "public testimonial fund" that will be raised by the city's bar association from contributions of lawyers who are members of the association and who practice in the city's courts.

Is it proper for the judge to accept the gift of the portrait?

(A) Yes, because the gift is incident to a public testimonial for the judge.

(B) Yes, because the judge did not receive compensation for her services to the charitable organization.

(C) No, because the cost of the gift exceeds $1,000.

(D) No, because the funds for the gift are contributed by lawyers who practice in the city's courts.

Question 44.

An attorney, who had represented a client for many years, prepared the client's will and acted as one of the two subscribing witnesses to its execution. The will gave 10 percent of the client's estate to the client's housekeeper, 10 percent to the client's son and sole heir, and the residue to charity. Upon the client's death one year later, the executor of the will asked the attorney to represent him in probating the will and administering the estate. At that time, the executor informed the attorney that the client's son had notified him that he would contest the probate of the will on the grounds that the client lacked the required mental capacity at the time the will was executed. The attorney believes that the client was fully competent at all times and will so testify, if called as a witness. The other subscribing witness to the client's will predeceased the client.

Is it proper for the attorney to represent the executor in the probate of the will?

(A) Yes, because the attorney is the sole surviving witness to the execution of the will.

(B) Yes, because the attorney's testimony will support the validity of the will.

(C) No, because the attorney will be called to testify on a contested issue of fact.

(D) No, because the attorney will be representing an interest adverse to the client's heir at law.

Question 45.

An attorney represented a buyer in a real estate transaction. Due to the attorney's negligence in drafting the purchase agreement, the buyer was required to pay for a survey that should have been paid by the seller. The attorney fully disclosed this negligence to the buyer, and the buyer suggested that he would be satisfied if the attorney simply reimbursed the buyer for the entire cost of the survey.

Although the buyer might have recovered additional damages if a malpractice action were filed, the attorney reasonably believed that the proposed settlement was fair to the buyer. He sent the buyer a letter stating that the buyer should consider seeking independent representation before making a decision. Then, in order to forestall a malpractice action, the attorney readily agreed to make the reimbursement. The attorney drafted a settlement agreement, and it was executed by both the attorney and the buyer.

Was the attorney's conduct proper?

(A) Yes, because the attorney advised the buyer in writing that the buyer should seek independent representation before deciding to enter into the settlement agreement.

(B) Yes, because the attorney reasonably believed that the proposed settlement was fair to the buyer.

(C) No, because the attorney settled a case involving liability for malpractice while the matter was still ongoing.

(D) No, because the buyer was not separately represented in negotiating and finalizing the settlement agreement.

Question 46.

An attorney represented a plaintiff in a civil suit against a defendant who was represented by other counsel. In the course of developing the plaintiff's case, the attorney discovered evidence that she reasonably believed showed that the defendant had committed a crime. The attorney felt that the defendant's crime should be reported to local prosecutorial authorities. After full disclosure, the plaintiff consented to the attorney's doing so. Without advising the defendant's counsel, the attorney informed the local prosecutor of her findings, but she sought no advantage in the civil suit from her actions. The defendant was subsequently indicted, tried, and acquitted of the offense.

Was the attorney's disclosure to prosecutorial authorities proper?

(A) Yes, because the attorney reasonably believed the defendant was guilty of a crime.

(B) Yes, because the attorney was required to report knowledge of criminal conduct when that knowledge was obtained through unprivileged sources.

(C) No, because the attorney did not advise the other counsel of her disclosure before making it.

(D) No, because the plaintiff's civil suit against the defendant was still pending.

Question 47.

A witness was subpoenaed to appear and testify at a state legislative committee hearing. The witness retained an attorney to represent her at the hearing. During the hearing, the attorney, reasonably believing that it was in the witness's best interest not to answer, advised the witness not to answer certain questions on the grounds that she had a constitutional right not to answer. The committee chairperson directed the witness to answer and cautioned her that refusal to answer was a misdemeanor and that criminal prosecution would be instituted if she did not answer.

Upon the attorney's advice, the witness persisted in her refusal to answer. The offense the witness committed did not involve moral turpitude, and the attorney reasonably believed the witness had a legal right to refuse to answer the questions. The witness was subsequently convicted for her refusal to answer.

Is the attorney subject to discipline?

(A) Yes, because his advice to the witness was not legally sound.

(B) Yes, because the witness, in acting on the attorney's advice, committed a crime.

(C) No, because the offense the witness committed did not involve moral turpitude.

(D) No, because the attorney reasonably believed the witness had a legal right to refuse to answer the questions.

Question 48.

An attorney hired a recent law school graduate as an associate. For the first six months, the associate was assigned to draft legal documents that the attorney carefully reviewed and revised before filing. However, shortly after the associate was admitted to the bar, the attorney told the associate that he would be going on vacation the following week and was assigning her the representation of the landlord in a housing case that was going to trial while he was away. The associate had never conducted or observed a trial before and, because she had not previously worked on any housing cases, she was unfamiliar with the relevant law and procedure. She did not believe that she would have enough time to learn everything that she needed to know, but she was reluctant to decline the assignment. Before the trial began, she met with the landlord and disclosed that this would be her first trial, but the landlord did not object. Although the associate prepared diligently, the landlord lost the trial.

Is the attorney subject to discipline?

(A) Yes, because the attorney did not ensure that the associate was competent to conduct the trial on her own.

(B) Yes, because the landlord lost at trial.

(C) No, because the attorney could reasonably assume that, having been admitted to the bar, the associate was capable of conducting the trial.

(D) No, because the landlord did not object to the associate's representation.

Question 49.

An attorney currently represents a builder who is the plaintiff in a suit to recover for breach of a contract to build a house. The builder also has pending before the zoning commission a petition to rezone property the builder owns. However, the builder is represented by another attorney in the zoning matter.

A neighbor who owns property adjoining that of the builder has asked the attorney to represent him in opposing the builder's petition for rezoning. The neighbor knows that the attorney represents the builder in the contract action.

Is it proper for the attorney to represent the neighbor in the zoning matter?

(A) Yes, because there is no common issue of law or fact between the two matters.

(B) Yes, because one matter is a judicial proceeding and the other is an administrative proceeding.

(C) No, because the attorney is currently representing the builder in the contract action.

(D) No, because there is a possibility that both matters will be appealed to the same court.

Question 50.

An elected prosecutor plans to run for reelection in six months. Last year, two teenage girls were kidnapped from a shopping center and sexually assaulted. The community was in an uproar about the crime and put pressure on the prosecutor to indict and convict the assailant. Four months ago, a suspect was arrested and charged with the crimes. The trial is scheduled to begin next week.

The prosecutor met with the police chief last week to review the evidence in the case. At that time, the prosecutor first learned that, before they were interviewed by the detective in charge of sexual assault crimes, the two victims had been tape-recorded discussing the case between themselves in an interview room. Reviewing the tape, the prosecutor realized that the girls' descriptions of the assailant differed significantly in terms of height, weight, and hair color. When officially interviewed, however, their descriptions matched almost perfectly.

The suspect's appointed counsel was busy handling a large caseload of indigent defendants and neglected to seek access to the prosecution's investigative file. The prosecutor was virtually certain that suspect's counsel was unaware of the tape recording. Given the other evidence in the case, the prosecutor reasonably believed that the girls accurately identified the suspect as their assailant. The prosecutor did not reveal the existence of the tape to defense counsel.

Is the prosecutor subject to discipline?

(A) Yes, because the tape raises a legitimate question about the victims' eyewitness identification of the suspect as the assailant.

(B) No, because the prosecutor reasonably believed that the girls accurately identified the suspect as their assailant.

(C) No, because under the adversary system of criminal justice, it is expected that each party will marshal the evidence best supporting its own position.

(D) No, because the suspect's counsel did not submit a request for all mitigating or exculpatory evidence before the start of trial.

Question 51.

An attorney represented the plaintiff in an automobile accident case. Two weeks before the date set for trial, the attorney discovered that there was an eyewitness to the accident. The attorney interviewed the witness. Her version of the accident was contrary to that of the plaintiff and, if believed by the trier of fact, would establish that the plaintiff was at fault. The witness told the attorney that she had not been interviewed by defense counsel.

The witness also told the attorney that she was uncomfortable with testifying and that she had been thinking about taking a vacation to Europe the following week. The attorney told the witness that, since no one had subpoenaed her yet, she had no obligation to appear. He told her that trials were very difficult for witnesses and suggested that she take the vacation so that she would be unavailable to testify.

Is the attorney subject to discipline?

— (A) Yes, because the attorney asked the witness to leave the jurisdiction.

(B) Yes, because the attorney did not subpoena the witness knowing she was an eyewitness.

(∅) No, because the witness had not been subpoenaed by the defense.

(D) No, because the attorney did not offer the witness any inducement not to appear at the trial.

Question 52.

An attorney represented the plaintiff in a personal injury matter. The attorney had heard that the defendant in the matter was anxious to settle the case and reasonably believed that the defendant's lawyer had not informed the defendant about the attorney's recent offer of settlement. The attorney instructed her nonlawyer investigator to tell the defendant about the settlement offer so that the attorney could be sure that the defendant's lawyer did not force the case to trial merely to increase the defendant's lawyer's fee.

Is the attorney subject to discipline?

— (A) Yes, because the defendant was represented by counsel.

(B) Yes, because the attorney was assisting the investigator in the unauthorized practice of law.

(C) No, because the investigator is not a lawyer.

(D) No, because the attorney reasonably believed that the defendant's lawyer was not keeping the defendant informed.

Question 53.

An attorney was approached by a husband and a wife who had decided to dissolve their marriage. They had no children and had worked out a tentative mutual property settlement. They did not want to retain separate lawyers because they hoped to save money and believed that working with one attorney was more likely to result in a reasonably amicable dissolution. Before coming to the attorney, they had drafted and each had signed a written agreement not to run up the costs and increase the adversarial nature of the dissolution by retaining separate lawyers.

The attorney believed that he was able to provide competent and diligent representation to both the husband and the wife. The attorney consulted with both independently concerning the implications of the common representation, including the advantages and risks involved and the effect on their respective attorney-client privileges. The attorney reduced the disclosures to writing in the form of a written retainer agreement and gave them each several days to consult independent legal counsel if they so desired. The husband and the wife each chose not to consult independent counsel.

After six months of reasonably amicable negotiations, the wife announced that she had changed her mind about the representation and had decided to retain her own lawyer. However, after the husband and the attorney insisted that she was obligated to adhere to her prior written agreement, she reluctantly agreed to abide by it. The attorney was then able to draft a property settlement agreement satisfactory to both parties.

Is the attorney subject to discipline for his conduct in the representation?

(A) Yes, because the attorney should not have undertaken to represent both the husband and the wife in the first place.

(B) Yes, because the attorney insisted that the wife not hire another lawyer.

(C) No, because both the husband and the wife initially consented to all aspects of the representation.

(D) No, because the husband and the wife independently made the agreement that neither would retain separate counsel.

Question 54.

An attorney is a well-known tax lawyer and author. During congressional hearings on tax reform, the attorney testified to her personal belief and expert opinion on the pending reform package. She failed to disclose in her testimony that she was being compensated by a private client for her appearance. In her testimony, the attorney took the position favored by her client, but the position was also one that the attorney believed was in the public interest.

Was it proper for the attorney to present this testimony without identifying her private client?

(A) Yes, because the attorney believed that the position she advocated was in the public interest.

(B) Yes, because Congress is interested in the content of the testimony and not who is paying the witness.

(C) No, because a lawyer may not accept a fee for trying to influence legislative action.

(D) No, because a lawyer who appears in a legislative hearing should identify the capacity in which the lawyer appears.

Question 55.

An attorney closed her law practice when she became a state senator. A bank, one of the senator's former private clients, asked her as its senator to try to persuade a state agency to grant the bank a license to open a new branch bank. While the bank's request was pending before the agency, the senator wrote a letter on her legislative letterhead to the agency's chair, asserting that the branch would satisfy a local business need and urging that the bank's application be granted. The senator neither sought nor received any compensation from the bank for her efforts. Eventually the agency granted the bank's application, in part because of the senator's efforts.

Is the senator subject to discipline?

(A) Yes, because the senator used her public position to influence the agency on behalf of the bank.

(B) Yes, because the agency granted the bank's application in part due to the senator's efforts.

(C) No, because the senator's letter to the agency's chair did not express an opinion about the law.

(D) No, because the senator acted on behalf of the bank as a constituent and not as a client.

Question 56.

A county law prohibits stores from selling alcoholic beverages before noon on Sundays. Failure to comply is a misdemeanor punishable by a fine of $150.

An attorney was hired by a client who owns several liquor stores. The client asked the attorney whether any storeowners had been prosecuted for violating the law and whether the fine could be imposed for every sale on a Sunday before noon or only for every Sunday on which alcohol was sold before noon. The client also asked what he could do to minimize the risk that he would be detected.

The attorney accurately told the client that the fine could only be imposed for each Sunday on which he sold alcoholic beverages before noon, not for each transaction, and that no one had been prosecuted under the law as yet. She also told him that she thought it would be improper to advise him about how to avoid detection. The client thanked the attorney for the information and hung up. Several weeks later, the attorney learned that the client had begun to open his store for business on Sundays at 9 a.m.

Is the attorney subject to discipline?

(A) Yes, because the attorney reasonably should have known that the information she gave the client would encourage him to violate the law.

(B) Yes, because the attorney did not discourage her client from breaking the law.

(C) No, because the attorney merely gave the client her honest opinion about the consequences that were likely to result if he violated the law.

(D) No, because the lawyer and the client could have discussed the best way to avoid detection under the criminal law.

Question 57.

A judge has served on a trial court of general jurisdiction for almost three years. During that time, he was assigned criminal cases almost exclusively. Several months ago, however, the judge was assigned an interesting case involving a constitutional challenge to a statute recently passed by the state legislature. The statute permitted any local public school district with an overcrowding problem to purchase educational services for its students in any other public or private school within 15 miles.

Although the briefs submitted by the parties were excellent, the judge was not confident that he had a good grasp of the issues in the case. Accordingly, he took one of his more experienced colleagues on the trial court out to lunch and discussed the case with her in great detail. The colleague was far more conservative than the judge, but he agreed with her and eventually ruled in accord with her views. The case is now on appeal.

Is the judge subject to discipline?

(A) Yes, because the judge sought an ex parte communication on the merits of a case pending before him.

(B) Yes, because the judge initiated a discussion with a colleague that may have influenced his judgment in the case.

(C) No, because the judge is permitted to obtain the advice of a disinterested expert on the law.

(D) No, because the judge was permitted to consult about a pending case with another judge.

Question 58.

An attorney is a senior partner at a law firm in which there are 50 lawyers. The firm pays each of its lawyers a fixed annual salary. In addition, at year's end, each lawyer receives a bonus from the profits of the firm in proportion to the annual salary of each and its relation to the total of the fixed annual salaries of all lawyers.

The attorney plans to introduce a new management plan under which the firm's nonlawyer office administrator would have general charge of all business matters but would not participate in any decisions involving legal judgment. The administrator would be paid a fixed annual salary and would be included as a participant in the firm's bonus plan on the same basis as the lawyers in the firm. This would usually yield a bonus of approximately one-fourth to one-third of the administrator's total annual compensation. The amount paid to the administrator will not exceed the compensation commonly paid to law office administrators within the local legal community.

Is it proper for the attorney to institute such a plan?

(A) Yes, because the amount paid to the administrator does not exceed the compensation commonly paid to law office administrators within the local legal community.

(B) Yes, because an employee of the firm may be compensated based on the profits of the firm.

(C) No, because the administrator's bonus is computed on the same basis as those of the lawyers in the firm.

(D) No, because the administrator's compensation is derived from the legal fees of the firm's lawyers.

Question 59.

An attorney represented a client in an action against the client's former partner to recover damages for breach of contract. During the representation, the client presented the attorney with incontrovertible proof that the former partner had committed perjury in a prior action that was resolved in the partner's favor. Neither the attorney nor the client was involved in any way in the prior action. The attorney believes that it would be detrimental to the client's best interests to reveal the perjury because of the implication that might be drawn from the former close personal and business relationship between the client and the former partner.

Would it be proper for the attorney to fail to disclose the perjury to the tribunal?

(A) No, because the information is unprivileged.

(B) No, because the attorney has knowledge that the former partner perpetrated a fraud on the tribunal.

(C) Yes, because neither the client nor the attorney was involved in the prior action.

(D) Yes, because the attorney believes that the disclosure would be detrimental to the client's best interests.

Question 60.

An attorney represented 10 plaintiffs in a case against a railroad in which the plaintiffs were injured when a train derailed. The railroad offered the attorney a $500,000 lump sum settlement for the 10 plaintiffs. The attorney allocated the $500,000 among the 10 plaintiffs with the amount paid each plaintiff dependent on the nature and extent of that plaintiff's injuries. The attorney reasonably believed the division was fair to each plaintiff.

The railroad would not settle any of the claims unless all were settled. The attorney told each plaintiff the total amount the railroad was prepared to pay, the amount that the individual would receive, and the basis on which that amount was calculated. The attorney did not tell any plaintiff the amount to be received by any other plaintiff. The attorney believed that if she revealed to each plaintiff the amount of each individual settlement, it might jeopardize the settlement.

Each of the plaintiffs agreed to his or her settlement amount and was satisfied with that amount.

Is the attorney subject to discipline for entering into this settlement?

(A) Yes, because the attorney was aiding the lawyer for the railroad in making a lump sum settlement.

(B) Yes, because no individual plaintiff knew the amount to be received by any other plaintiff.

(C) No, because disclosing all settlements to each plaintiff might have jeopardized the entire settlement.

(D) No, because the attorney reasonably believed that the division was fair and each plaintiff agreed to his or her settlement and was satisfied with the amount.

B. Answers to Model Questions

Question 1.

B is the correct answer. A lawyer must provide competent representation to clients. Model Rule 1.1. Competent representation requires having the legal knowledge and skill necessary for the representation. To maintain the required level of knowledge and skill, a lawyer should keep abreast of changes in the law through continuing study and education, as well as comply with any continuing education requirements to which the lawyer is subject. Model Rule 1.1. Independent study is just as valid as continuing legal education courses in maintaining the attorney's competence, although failure to attend continuing legal education courses would be improper if the state required him to do so.

A is incorrect. The attorney must maintain competence without regard to the cost of doing so. Additionally, this answer choice implies that continuing legal education courses are the only way for the attorney to maintain his competence.

C is incorrect. As stated above, continuing legal education courses are not the only way the attorney can maintain his competence.

D is incorrect. Being insured against malpractice has nothing to do with a lawyer's duty to maintain the legal knowledge and skills needed to provide competent representation.

Question 2.

C is the correct answer. Under Model Rule 1.1, an attorney must have the legal knowledge and skill necessary for the representation. In determining whether an attorney has the requisite knowledge and skill in a particular matter, relevant factors include the relative complexity and specialized nature of the matter, the attorney's general experience, the attorney's training and experience in the field in question, the preparation and study the attorney is able to give the matter, and whether it is feasible to refer the matter to, or associate or consult with, an attorney of established competence in the field in question. The standard of competence is usually that of a general practitioner, unless the attorney claims to be an expert in a particular area of law. Here, it appears that the corporation retained the firm because the partner held himself out as an expert in securities regulation law, a complex and specialized area of the law, and the attorney, a newly minted attorney, specifically stated he did not have the time to prepare himself to handle the matter competently. Consequently, the attorney would be in violation of the Rule if he continues to represent the corporation without the required level of competence, and the partner would be in violation of the Rule for directing him to do so and failing to give the attorney proper supervision.

A is incorrect. Although the attorney is a member of the bar and therefore licensed to practice law, he is admittedly incompetent to handle this particular representation without assistance from an attorney who is competent in this area. Consequently, the partner is in violation for directing the attorney to represent the corporation without any assistance.

B is incorrect. Under Model Rule 1.16(b)(6), an attorney may withdraw from a case if working on it would cause unreasonable financial hardship on the attorney. However, the partner willingly accepted the corporation as a client, and the mere fact the partner "prefers" to work on cases with larger fee potential would not meet the standard for withdrawal.

D is incorrect. If the assignment is appropriate, a client generally does not need to give permission for an attorney to assign that representation to an associate. However, because a client's consent does not excuse incompetent representation, the representation would be improper even if the corporation had given permission to assign the matter to the attorney.

Question 3.

A is the correct answer. Model Rule 8.4 defines the acts that constitute misconduct by a lawyer. Model Rule 8.4(c) describes as professional misconduct any conduct "involving dishonesty, fraud, deceit or misrepresentation." The definition is not limited to misconduct in connection with the practice of law but, under Comment [2], extends to all offenses that "indicate lack of those characteristics relevant to law practice," including violence, dishonesty, and breach of trust. Also, misconduct is misconduct wherever it occurs — whether in the state in which the attorney is licensed to practice or elsewhere. Here, the attorney has knowingly filed a false financial statement in connection with a professional license application, a clear violation of the Rule.

B is incorrect. The definition of misconduct extends far beyond conviction for a criminal offense. Comment [2] to Model Rule 8.4 states, "Many kinds of illegal conduct reflect adversely on fitness to practice law, such as offenses involving fraud and the offense of willful failure to file an income tax return."

C is incorrect. A lawyer is judged not only by his or her conduct in his or her capacity as lawyer, but by all conduct that measures his or her honesty, trustworthiness, and fitness as a lawyer. See Model Rule 8.4(b).

D is incorrect. Geography has nothing to do with the concept of misconduct. Misconduct is misconduct wherever it occurs.

Question 4.

D is the correct answer. Lawyers are prohibited from soliciting business from prospective clients by in-person contact or live telephone contact. Model Rule 7.3. The key word is "prospective" — that is, "future" clients. The prohibition against solicitation does not extend to persons with whom the lawyer has had a prior personal or professional relationship. Consequently, the prohibition does not extend to contacts with former clients, personal friends, or family members. Here, the attorney is dealing with a former client whose interests may be adversely affected if the attorney does not advise her of the new IRS regulation.

A is incorrect. The attorney is permitted to contact the woman as a former client whether or not she has reason to believe her former client has another attorney. The attorney has no way of knowing whether her former client has another attorney or if the other attorney is a specialist in tax law or is even aware of the new regulation. The Rule does not require the attorney to inquire into these facts.

B is incorrect. The test is not whether the person is a current client but whether the person is a former client. For purposes of Model Rule 7.3, once a client always a client.

C is incorrect. The attorney is free to offer and supply her services to her client in any way her former client may be willing to utilize them. The issue here is solicitation, not limits on the scope of representation.

Question 5.

D is the correct answer. The answer recognizes the three basic principles a lawyer must observe when dealing with client funds: (1) client funds must always be kept separate from the lawyer's funds in a designated clients' escrow account; (2) as soon as the client's interest in the funds is fixed, the client's money must be delivered to the client; and (3) if both the client and the attorney claim any interest in any part of the funds — for example, if a dispute arises as to the lawyer's fees — the funds must remain in the separate client account until there is an accounting and their respective interests can be severed. Model 1.15. Here, the attorney's maximum claim was for fees totaling 6 hours × $50 = $300. When the bail hearing was completed, the client's interest in the advance was $500. The attorney had a duty to return this promptly. Because the client had demanded $800, the lawyer's fee of $300 was in dispute. Consequently, the money representing the fee had to be retained in the Clients' Fund Account until the dispute was resolved.

A is incorrect. The funds in dispute totaled only $300. The balance of $500 was not in dispute and belonged to the client when it was not applied to the bail costs. The attorney was under a duty to return $500 to the client because the money was not used for the purpose intended.

B is incorrect. Because the fee of $300 was in dispute, the attorney had no right to transfer that sum to his fee account. He was required to retain the funds in his Clients' Fund Account until the dispute was resolved. Further, the attorney had no right to retain the balance of $500 in either account pending the appeal. The money was deposited with the attorney only in connection with the bail application, not the appeal itself.

C is incorrect. The attorney was right to send the $500 to the client, but wrong in transferring $300 to his fee account. So long as his fee was in dispute, the $300 had to be retained in the Clients' Fund Account. Model Rule 1.15(e).

Question 6.

B is the correct answer. A judge is expected to perform his or her duties fairly, impartially, and without prejudice against any litigant. Model Code of Judicial Conduct, Rule 2.2. The test is the judge's mindset as perceived by a reasonable observer. If the judge has a personal bias toward a party or his or her lawyer, or personal knowledge of disputed evidentiary facts concerning the proceeding, he or she must disqualify himself or herself. Also, if he or she or a former law partner has served either side as a lawyer concerning the matter, or if he or she has served as a material witness in the matter, he or she must disqualify himself or herself. B correctly states the issue facing the judge. However, if there is any chance that his prior investigation of the defendant will prejudice his judgment, he must dis-qualify himself.

A is incorrect because it misstates the test for disqualification. It doesn't matter that the prior investigation is unrelated to the present case. The relevant question is whether the judge is adversely influenced by his participation in the investigation.

C is incorrect. Although it states a basis for suspecting prejudice by the judge against the defendant, it is not as good an answer as B, which correctly frames the issue as one of potential prejudice.

D is incorrect. This option does not revolve around the judge's state of mind. It is just as reasonable to conclude that the judge was not prejudiced by the prior investigation as that he was prejudiced. The issue is whether he was and is actually prejudiced against the defendant. B is the best formula for deciding that issue.

Question 7.

B is the correct answer. When a lawyer gives a client advice, he or she may rely on considerations other than those involved in giving purely technical legal advice. Model Rule 2.1. Consequently, it is proper for a lawyer to rely on moral, economic, and social factors in doing so, which is what the attorney did here.

A is incorrect because the issue isn't whether the landlord accepted the attorney's advice — and, in fact, a lawyer should not be deterred from giving candid advice simply because the client might not be happy about it — but whether the attorney acted properly in going beyond the technical legal aspect of the case in advising the landlord.

C is incorrect. An initial, or engagement, letter to the client is concerned with fees. Its purpose is to make clear what services the lawyer will provide and what he or she will charge for them, not in what form he or she will render advice. Model Rule 1.5.

D is incorrect. It raises the issue of a lawyer's responsibility to "act with . . . zeal in advocacy." Model Rule 1.3, Comment [1]. But that isn't really the issue here. The issue is what is the proper scope for the advice a lawyer gives a client. Not only is it proper for a lawyer to refer to considerations other than the law in advising a client, he or she also has a responsibility to exercise independent professional judgment in advising a client and to advise the client in a straightforward, honest manner, in the best interests of the client. Here, the attorney has done exactly that.

Question 8.

B is the correct answer. Basic to the integrity of the legal profession is the principle that only persons admitted to the practice of law may provide legal services to others. Consequently, any person who is not a lawyer but who gives legal advice is said to engage in the unauthorized practice of law, and any lawyer who helps a nonlawyer to engage in the unauthorized practice of law violates Model Rule 5.5(a). Here, the bank is not authorized to practice law, but it is providing legal services through its salaried employee, the attorney. Thus, the attorney is assisting the bank in the unauthorized practice of law.

A is incorrect. A newsletter does not provide legal "advice" to any particular person, but only supplies generalized legal information to the general public. Even so, a lawyer is not prevented from giving advice to a nonclient. However, if the lawyer is representing a client whose interests may be affected by the nonclient's actions, the lawyer is required to avoid stating or implying to the nonclient that the lawyer is disinterested. In that case, if the lawyer knows or reasonably should know that the unrepresented person misunderstands the lawyer's role in the matter, he or she must make reasonable efforts to correct the misunderstanding. Model Rule 4.3.

C is incorrect. Whether the attorney charges a fee or not, he's still assisting the bank in the unauthorized practice of law.

D is incorrect. Only a lawyer is subject to discipline under the Model Rules. Consequently, the attorney is subject to discipline *because* he is a member of the bar.

Question 9.

A is the correct answer. Although the attorney does not have the "requisite knowledge and skill" to competently represent his cousin and knows he doesn't, this scenario would fall under the "emergency" situation discussed in Model Rule 1.1, Comment [3]. When his cousin called, it would have been impractical for the attorney to refer his cousin to another lawyer or to consult with another lawyer, so he gave reasonably necessary assistance to get his cousin out on bail. However, for any additional work, the attorney would have to become competent or find another lawyer to take on the matter, which the attorney did in this case.

B is incorrect. The fact that the attorney and his cousin are related has nothing to do with whether the attorney can represent his cousin competently. The attorney must decide whether he has the requisite knowledge and skill to provide his cousin with competent representation regardless of their relationship.

C is incorrect. It is precisely because of the attorney's inexperience that he made the decision that he did. He acted appropriately in giving assistance in an "emergency" situation, which included finding an experienced criminal lawyer for his cousin.

D is incorrect. The attorney did not accept representation.

Question 10.

A is the correct answer. A lawyer shall not form a partnership with a nonlawyer if any of the activities of the partnership consist of the "practice of law." A lawyer who does so is assisting another in the unauthorized practice of law, and is subject to discipline. Model Rule 5.5(a). Here, the important point is that the *partnership* is delivering the legal services, which choice A states explicitly.

B is incorrect. There is no absolute ban on lawyer and nonlawyer partnerships. As stated above, the issue is whether the partnership delivers legal services. For example, the attorney would not be subject to discipline if this partnership provided only accounting services.

C is incorrect. Again, the important fact is that the partnership is providing legal services. However, as a partner, the accountant is receiving a portion of the entity's profits and has control over the legal aspects of the business. Under Model Rule 5.4(a), a lawyer may not share legal fees with a nonlawyer, which would clearly happen here under the partnership agreement. This Rule is the major deterrent to partnerships like this, and even splitting fees with a charity is not allowed. The only exceptions to this Rule involve paying the estates of deceased attorneys or law firm retirement plans, neither of which apply here. Consequently, what the accountant actually does in terms of work is not important, because, as a partner in this partnership, she is still engaged in the unauthorized practice of law.

D is incorrect. As stated above, the main issues are the creation of a partnership that provides legal services and the sharing of fees with a nonlawyer. Simply keeping the accountant from interfering with the attorney's professional obligations is not enough.

Question 11.

B is the correct answer. As long as the client is fully informed, a lawyer and client may agree to limit the scope of the lawyer's representation so long as the limitation is reasonable under the circumstances. Model Rule 1.2(c). Although clients usually retain a lawyer to take care of all aspects of a particular matter, if the client affirmatively consents after consultation, the client can limit the scope of the representation to only one part of the claim. Consequently, it is clearly permissible under the Rules for the client and the lawyer to agree to a representation that only covers the grand jury proceeding.

A is incorrect. The important issues are whether the client is informed, agrees, and the limitation is reasonable. Whose idea it was is completely irrelevant. While a client will usually be the one to suggest a limit to the scope of representation, if it was the attorney's suggestion, the analysis would still be the same.

C is incorrect. Lawyers are not obligated to provide free legal services, and the limited representation here puts the client in a better position than if he were represented by no lawyer at all. When an attorney and a client agree to limit the scope of a representation, the client's ability to pay is most likely the cause.

D is incorrect. The fact a case is a criminal or civil matter is also irrelevant.

Question 12.

D is the correct answer. A lawyer shall not reveal any information relating to the representation of a client unless the client gives informed consent. Model Rule 1.6(a). This is probably the most important Rule in the Model Rules of Professional Conduct. It is intended to promote candid communications between the client and attorney, so all the aspects of a particular legal problem become known and the lawyer can provide the most competent legal advice. Importantly, if a client knew the attorney could share his or her confidences to third parties, competent representation would become much more difficult, if not impossible, as the client would likely leave the lawyer in the dark on many important facts. Here, although the prior murders are not part of the present case, this information was obtained during the course of the attorney's representation, and consequently "relates" to that representation. Additionally, the prior murders would likely affect the attorney's strategy in the present case, specifically whether his client should plead guilty or testify at trial.

A is incorrect. Although there are several exceptions to the Model Rule 1.6's confidentiality requirement, none of the exceptions requires an attorney to disclose a client's past crimes of violence. Under the major exceptions to the Rule, a lawyer may reveal confidences to the extent necessary to prevent the client from committing a crime causing imminent death or substantial bodily injury (including a client's potential suicide), to the extent necessary to establish a claim or defense in a controversy between the lawyer and the client, or to the extent necessary to prevent or rectify financial harm caused by a crime or fraud involving the lawyer's services. Often, when testing this particular issue, the MPRE uses "as an officer of the court" in its "distracter" answer choices.

B is incorrect. Despite the fact the attorney is impeding the state's access to significant evidence, he still has an obligation to keep the client's information confidential. This answer option is trying to prey on your sympathies to the victims' families. Don't fall for the "sympathy" choice.

C is incorrect. As stated above, although the attorney did not advise the client with respect to the prior crimes, he discovered that information during his representation of the client during this matter. However, if the attorney had advised the client regarding how to commit the prior crimes or how to hide the bodies, he would be subject to discipline and criminal prosecution.

Question 13.

D is the correct answer. A lawyer who was formerly employed by a government agency may not later represent a client "in connection with a matter in which the lawyer participated personally and substantially" as a public employee, unless the government agency consents in writing. Model Rule 1.11(a)(2). If the lawyer is practicing in a firm, this disqualification would cover any other lawyer in the firm unless the firm puts together a screening arrangement and gives written notice to the agency. Model Rule 1.11(b). Here, the attorney participated personally and substantially by conducting a title search on the client's property when he was employed by the government agency. Furthermore, the attorney may not disclose the confidential information he learned while working at the department because a lawyer who was formerly employed by a government agency must not reveal confidential information relating to a former representation. Model Rules 1.11(a)(1) and 1.9(c).

A is incorrect. Because the attorney participated personally and substantially in the matter as a public employee, he cannot now represent the client unless the government agency consents in writing, whether or not he plans to use the confidential information he learned while working there. Importantly, even if he only represents the client on damages, he will still be representing her "in connection with a matter in which the lawyer participated personally and substantially."

B is incorrect. As stated above, he can neither represent the client nor disclose the confidential information.

C is incorrect. Whether or not he represents the client, he still cannot disclose the government's confidential information. Model Rules 1.11(a)(1) and 1.9(c).

Question 14.

D is the correct answer. These facts invoke the concepts of conflicts of interest and imputed disqualification. Model Rule 1.9 deals with the conflict faced by a lawyer who has represented one client, terminates the representation, and then is asked to represent a new client with interests adverse to those of the lawyer's former client. If you simplify these facts, it's clear that the former assistant district attorney could not himself represent the codefendant after he participated in the investigation of the codefendant because the interests of the codefendant are adverse to the former assistant district attorney's interests. Model Rule 1.9(a). But the question asks about the attorney's representation of the codefendant, not the former assistant district attorney's. Model Rule 1.10(a) extends the former assistant district attorney's disqualification to the attorney under the imputed disqualification rule: "While lawyers are associated in a firm, none of them shall knowingly represent a client when any one of them practicing alone would be prohibited from doing so by Model Rules 1.7. or 1.9."

A is incorrect. Model Rule 1.9 doesn't give the lawyer with the prohibited conflict the discretion to decide that he or she can protect the interests of the new client by protecting confidences. Under these circumstances, the lawyer may not represent the new client if (1) the lawyer himself or herself formerly represented a client in a substantially related matter with interests adverse to the new client's interests (Model Rule 1.9 (a)) or (2) the lawyer was associated with a firm representing a client with interests adverse to his or her present client, about whom the lawyer acquired information protected by the confidentiality rules that is material to the new client's matter (Model Rule 1.9(b)(2)).

B is incorrect. It states correctly a basic rule that prosecutors must follow, but it is not responsive to the question. The facts do not suggest that there was any exculpatory evidence, or that the former assistant district attorney knew of or withheld any. Also, the statement in B is irrelevant to the facts because the former assistant district attorney is no longer a prosecutor.

C is incorrect. The initial prohibition is directed at the former assistant district attorney because he's the lawyer with the conflict between the former and present clients. But the prohibition extends to the attorney under the imputed disqualification rule, whether or not the former assistant district attorney participates. Model Rule 1.10.

Question 15.

A is the correct answer. The question deals with the general obligation of a lawyer not to reveal any information relating to representation of a client without the client's consent after consultation. The obligation is defined in Model Rule 1.6(a). Model Rule 1.6(b) creates three exceptions to the general rule. One of the exceptions permits a lawyer to reveal a client confidence to defend him- or herself in a controversy with the client or against a criminal charge or civil claim for conduct involving the client, or to respond to allegations in any proceeding concerning the representation. Because the defendant has made a serious charge that would have grave consequences for the attorney if accepted as true, the attorney has a right to reveal the contents of the client's letter.

B is incorrect. Although the client has indeed committed a fraud on the court, the attorney would be obligated not to reveal the fraud except for the need to protect himself against the false accusation of complicity. General client fraud does not fall within one of the exceptions to the general duty of confidentiality.

C is incorrect. Whether or not the attorney learned the facts in confidences, he has a right to disclose them to protect himself in the disciplinary proceeding.

D is incorrect. When a lawyer is accused of a disciplinary infraction, he or she has a right to disclose a client's confidences to defend him- or herself. In the balance between the lawyer's right to defend himself or herself and the consequences to the client of revealing the client's confidence, the Rules have tipped the scales in favor of the lawyer, whose livelihood and reputation are at stake. Otherwise, the lawyer would be unable to defend him- or herself.

Question 16.

C is the correct answer. Under Model Rule 1.18, a prospective client is a person who discusses with the lawyer the possibility of forming a client-lawyer relationship with respect to a certain matter. The Comment to the Rule recognizes that prospective clients should receive some but not all of the protection afforded clients. Here, the attorney talked to the prospective client, declined the representation, gave the man another lawyer's name, and urged him to contact the other lawyer in a timely manner. Under the Rule, the attorney did not owe the prospective client any other duty, except that he must not mislead the prospective client into believing the attorney will represent him, and he must also protect any confidential information revealed by the prospective client. Model Rules 3.3 and 1.6.

A is incorrect because the attorney did not advertise falsely. The advertisement did not state, either expressly or impliedly, that he would take every case presented to him. Importantly, advertising in and of itself does not create an attorney-client relationship. False or misleading advertising is improper, but a lawyer may communicate that he or she practices certain types of law. Model Rules 7.1 and 7.4. However, with certain historical exceptions (such as "patent attorney"), a lawyer may not state or imply he or she is a specialist in a particular field of law unless the lawyer has been certified as a specialist by an organization that has been approved by an appropriate state authority or the American Bar Association. Model Rule 7.4. The name of any certifying organization must be clearly identified in the communication.

B is incorrect. Under these circumstances, the attorney was not required to give the man the exact date the statute of limitations would run. However, if that date had been within a very short time, such as one to two days instead of the six months here, the attorney may have had a duty to warn him.

D is incorrect. This answer implies that the reason the attorney is not subject to civil liability is because he offered to give the man a referral. However, as stated above, the reason the attorney is not subject to liability is because he did everything that was required under Model Rule 1.18. Always pick the answer that addresses the exact requirements and concerns of the particular Rule being tested.

Question 17.

C is the correct answer. A lawyer may not knowingly counsel or assist a client in conduct the lawyer knows is criminal or fraudulent. Model Rule 1.2(d). When the client's course of action has already begun and is continuing, the lawyer is required to avoid assisting the client in the criminal act, such as by suggesting how the wrongdoing can be concealed. Here, although the client is engaged in continuing illegal conduct by remaining a fugitive, the attorney is not actually counseling or assisting the client in doing so (in fact, he encouraged the client to surrender). The important point in the Rule is "counsel or assist" in the criminal act. Consequently, the attorney is acting correctly under the Rules.

A is incorrect. While the client is engaging in continuing illegal conduct, the client is nevertheless entitled to the advice of a lawyer, and the attorney is not helping her to remain in hiding. Importantly, the attorney may discuss the legal consequences of any proposed course of conduct and may counsel or assist the client in making a good faith effort to determine the validity, scope, meaning, or application of the law. Model Rule 1.2(d).

B is incorrect. If a lawyer gives appropriate advice, he or she cannot be disciplined simply because his or her client refuses to listen.

D is incorrect. Whether or not the indictment is defective, the attorney is still acting appropriately here.

Question 18.

C is the correct answer. "In representing a client, a lawyer shall not communicate about the subject of the representation with a person the lawyer knows to be represented by another lawyer in the matter, unless the lawyer has the consent of the other lawyer or is authorized to do so by law or a court order." Model Rule 4.2. This Rule applies even though the represented person initiates or consents to the communication.

A is incorrect. The represented person's lawyer is the one who must consent, not the represented person. Consequently, as stated above, Rule 4.2 applies even if the represented person initiates or consents to the communication.

B is incorrect. The prohibition is on any communication, and is not based on the signing of any documents.

D is incorrect. Under Rule 4.2, communication is prohibited only when the lawyer knows that the person is represented by another lawyer. This means that the lawyer must have actual knowledge of the representation, but such knowledge may be inferred from the circumstances. Thus, although the Rule imposes no duty on the lawyer to investigate, the lawyer cannot evade the Rule by ignoring the obvious.

Question 19.

D is the correct answer. The guiding Rule is Model Rule 1.7, which deals with conflicts of interest. Unless the son is able to prove fraud and undue influence, you must assume that the client intended to cut his son's bequest in half. Thus, his son's position is directly adverse to the client's. If the client were still alive, Model Rule 1.7(a) would preclude representation of his son by the attorney because the interests of two clients would be directly adverse to each other. Now that the client is dead, the attorney is still constrained by Model Rule 1.7(a)(2), which also directs a lawyer not to represent a client if representation of that client may be materially limited by the lawyer's responsibilities to another client or to a third person. (A deceased client is still a client for purpose of this Rule.) Note also that the attorney will necessarily be called as witness to execution of the will and the behavior and circumstances of the deceased client. Because a lawyer may not act as advocate at a trial in which the lawyer is likely to be a necessary witness on a disputed issue (Model Rule 3.7), the attorney should not agree to represent the son in this will contest.

A is incorrect. The client's death does not trigger a release of the attorney from her duty of loyalty to the client. The second will is assumed to express the client's intent. The loyalty that the attorney owed to the client is transferred to the client's will, which the attorney prepared and witnessed.

B is incorrect. Although it correctly states one fact, that fact is immaterial to the issue raised by the entire fact pattern. The issue is the ability of a lawyer to represent two clients with directly adverse interests at the same time.

C is incorrect. First of all, it is incorrect on the law. A lawyer is not a guarantor of the validity of a will that he or she prepares. His or her job is to restate in legally sufficient form the intent of the testator and, if asked to do so, to supervise the proper execution of the will. Also, the statement is irrelevant to the issue raised by the facts.

Question 20.

C is the correct answer. The essence of our judicial system is the open and public development of facts and issues before jury and judge. Consequently, neither lawyer may communicate with the judge or any juror who is not simultaneously or equally available to the other lawyer. The intent is to prevent undue influence by either side. Further, Model Rule 3.5(b) says specifically, "A lawyer shall not ... communicate ex parte with such a person [judge, juror, prospective juror or other official] during the proceeding unless authorized to do so by law or court order." Here, however noble his intent, the attorney called the judge without advising his adversary that he would do. This was a direct violation of the Rules.

A is incorrect. Ex parte contact with a judge is not permitted even if it ultimately leads to an argument by both sides. Obviously, an ex parte conversation between a lawyer and the judge is not monitored for content. Although it may lead to open argument, it's always possible that some nuance or some ingredient in the original conversation has already worked its influence on the judge.

B is incorrect for the same basic reason as A. Ex parte contacts with judge or jury are prohibited, period.

D is incorrect. Whether or not the ex parte contact leads to a better result, it is prohibited. If it were not, one could never be certain that the record of a trial correctly reflected the testimony or the arguments that influenced the outcome.

Question 21.

D is the correct answer. A lawyer is prohibited from knowingly making a false statement of material fact or law to a third person in the course of representing a client. Model Rule 4.1. Omissions that rise to the level of an affirmative false statement are also improper. Importantly, the Rule applies only to statements of *material fact.* Under generally accepted standards of negotiation, certain types of statements ordinarily are not taken as statements of material fact. Model Rule 4.1, Comment [2]. Estimates of price, value, or settlement maximums are ordinarily placed in this category, and are considered mere "puffing" on the part of the attorney. Here, the attorney's comments as to "steady profits" amounted to mere "puffing."

A is incorrect. Here, although the lawyer may have exaggerated the value of his client's business, this exaggeration would not be considered a statement of material fact for the reasons stated above.

B is incorrect. This answer choice is basically the same choice as A, except choice A is stating a suggested legal reason for discipline, while choice B is stating the factual way the attorney might be violating that legal reason (that is, the attorney is making a false statement of fact by exaggerating the profitability of the business). Because only one answer choice can be correct, recognizing the similarity between the two choices cancels out both answer choices.

C is incorrect. Under Model Rule 4.1, it is irrelevant which party the lawyer represents.

Question 22.

C is the correct answer. It is clear that a lawyer may advertise his or her services. Under Model Rule 7.2, a lawyer may advertise by any public medium or through written or recorded communication. The right is subject, however, to Model Rules 7.1 and 7.3. Model Rule 7.1 imposes the requirement that the advertisement not be false or misleading. Generally, so long as the statements in the advertisement are truthful, the ad passes muster. Model Rule 7.3 forbids direct solicitation either in person or by telephone. Here, no part of the attorney's ad would seem to be anything more than a statement of simple facts about the attorney.

A is incorrect. The advertisement need not state the lawyer's qualifications. On the contrary, a lawyer who ventures to state his or her qualifications risks the possibility that he or she will overstate them.

Comment [2] to Model Rule 7.2 lists some of the matters a lawyer may list with impunity: name, address, telephone number, range of services, basis for fees, foreign language ability, references and, with their consent, names of clients regularly represented.

B is incorrect. Nothing in this ad can reasonably be construed as encouraging litigation.

D is incorrect. Many radio and television stations can be heard across state lines. As long as a lawyer licensed in one state does not state that he or she is able to practice in a state in which he or she is not licensed, it will be assumed that his or her ad is directed only at listeners and viewers in the state in which he or she is licensed.

Question 23.

C is the correct answer. Under Model Rule 7.2, lawyers are permitted to advertise, subject to Model Rule 7.1, which prohibits a lawyer from making false or misleading statements about his or her services, and Model Rule 7.3, which limits direct contact with prospective clients. So long as there are no false or misleading statements in the attorney's advertisement, he would not be subject to discipline for placing this ad.

A is incorrect. Option A refers to Model Rule 7.3(a), which prohibits a lawyer from making *an in-person or live telephone or real-time electronic contact* with a prospective client unless the lawyer has had a prior relationship with the prospective client. This question deals with written advertising.

B is incorrect. There is no reason the attorney shouldn't use a coupon in his advertisement.

D is incorrect. The issue here is whether the advertisement meets the requirements of the Rules. The attorney is placing a general written advertisement and has no way of knowing whether a person is currently represented by another lawyer.

Question 24.

D is the correct answer. Ordinarily, a lawyer is duty bound to report another lawyer's violation of the Model Rules of Professional Conduct if the violation raises a substantial question as to that lawyer's honesty, trustworthiness, or fitness as a lawyer. Model Rule 8.3. However, when the information about the violation is protected under the client-confidentiality rules of Model Rule 1.6, this duty becomes discretionary. Even so Comment [2] to Model Rule 8.3 advises: "However, a lawyer should encourage a client to consent to disclosure where prosecution would not substantially prejudice the client's interests." On these facts, which show that the client would be reluctant to report the other attorney because he is an old friend, the attorney would probably be wasting her breath to encourage the disclosure of the other attorney's neglect of the client's interests. Ultimately, because the information about the violation is protected under client-confidentiality rules (because the client told the attorney about the violation during the course of her representation of him), the attorney will not be subject to discipline if she chooses not to report the other attorney without the client's consent.

A is incorrect. Whether or not the attorney believes the other attorney was guilty of professional misconduct, she will not be subject to discipline if she chooses not to report the other attorney without the client's consent.

B is incorrect. If there is no Model Rule 1.6 confidentiality issue, the attorney's belief as to the other attorney's usual conduct would be immaterial. The duty to report another lawyer's misconduct of which a lawyer has knowledge is absolute, not discretionary. Once an act of misconduct is known, it becomes a matter for the "appropriate professional authority," not for the lawyer. Only when the client tells the lawyer in confidence and does not consent to disclosure can the lawyer choose not to report another attorney.

C is incorrect. The trigger that converts the attorney's duty from an absolute duty to a discretionary option is the lack of the client's consent, not the level of the client's satisfaction with the other attorney or the fact that the client was not out of money.

Question 25.

A is the correct answer. A lawyer must promptly notify the client on receiving funds, securities, or other properties in which the client has an interest. Model Rule 1.15(d). In addition, except as otherwise permitted by law or by agreement with the client, a lawyer shall promptly deliver to the client any funds or property the client is entitled to receive and, on request by the client, promptly render a full accounting regarding such property. Here, the attorney deliberately delayed notifying the client for a week so the client could take investing classes. The fact that the attorney was arguably doing so in the client's best interest is irrelevant.

B is incorrect. The lawyer was permitted to give this unsolicited advice. Under Model Rule 2.1, a lawyer who is advising a client "shall exercise independent professional judgment and render candid advice." In doing so, the lawyer may "refer not only to law but to other considerations such as moral, economic, social, and political factors that may be relevant to the client's situation."

C is incorrect. The lawyer's failure to promptly notify the client of the lawyer's receipt of the client funds is not excused by the client's later failure to object. Many times, the MPRE will try to conceal a wrong answer by having the client later consent to the attorney's violation of the Rules.

D is incorrect. Under Rule 1.15(d), as stated above, there is no exception when the lawyer thinks it would be in the client's best interest to delay notification.

Question 26.

C is the correct answer. Even though this is a somewhat limited communication, it is clearly an advertisement for the attorney's new law office, and as such is covered by Model Rule 7.1. Model Rule 7.1 forbids only false or misleading communications, and this communication was neither false nor misleading. Here, all the communication did was state the simple facts regarding the reopening of the office, its location and phone number, and the fact that the attorney had been the state's governor for eight years.

A is incorrect. A lawyer is prohibited from making in-person, live telephone, or real-time electronic contact with prospective clients to solicit employment when the lawyer's motive for doing so is the lawyer's financial gain. Model Rule 7.3(a). This Rule seeks to address the fact that "the person, who may already feel overwhelmed by the circumstances giving rise to the need for legal services, may find it difficult to fully evaluate all available alternatives with reasoned judgment and appropriate self-interest in the face of the lawyer's presence and insistence upon being retained immediately." Model Rule 7.3, Comment [2]. However, there is an exception for contacts with former clients, friends, other lawyers, or relatives, which is what this answer choice is trying to get you to think of, since this communication is only going out to those people who fall within this exception. However, as the communication here is simply a printed announcement, it does not fall within this type of banned behavior, so the exception does not apply.

B is incorrect. Model Rule 7.1 forbids only false or misleading communications in lawyer advertising. However, an advertisement can be misleading if it creates an unjustified expectation as to the results the lawyer may achieve. Here, a truthful statement about the attorney's prior service as governor is unlikely to create any unjustified expectations as to what the attorney can achieve and is therefore not misleading.

D is incorrect. Depending on how it is used in the advertisement, information in the public domain can still be either false or misleading.

Question 27.

D is the correct answer. In construing the propriety of a lawyer's contribution in a judicial election campaign, the ABA Model Rules and the ABA Model Code of Judicial Conduct must be read in tandem. Model Rule 3.5(a) prohibits a lawyer from seeking to influence a judge or juror. Although the other attorney is not a judge yet, he soon could be. Comment [1] to Model Rule 3.5 says: "Many forms of improper influence upon a tribunal [. . .] are specified in the ABA Model Code of Judicial Conduct, with which an advocate should be familiar." The cases and the disciplinary rulings in all states almost invariably construe a loan or gift to a judge by a lawyer who appears before him or her as an attempt to influence the judge. Thus, a contribution to the other attorney's campaign may not be made by a gift to the other attorney personally under Model Rule 3.5. Further, Rule 4.1(A)(8) of the Model Code of Judicial Conduct states, a candidate shall not "personally solicit or accept campaign contributions other than through a campaign committee authorized by Rule 4.4."

D correctly recognizes that the attorney may make his contribution to the other attorney's campaign committee.

A is incorrect. The attorney may not give the contribution to the other attorney personally. The underlying reason for the rule prohibiting giving personal gifts directly to the candidate is that it will lead to excessive influence by the donor lawyer when he or she appears before that person if that person in fact becomes a judge.

B is incorrect. The Rules do not require that the gift be made anonymously, only that it not be made to the person running for judge personally. A donation to the judge's duly constituted campaign committee is perfectly proper.

C is incorrect. A lawyer may contribute to a judge's campaign committee whether or not he or she appears before the judge. This recognizes the fact that lawyers who appear before a judge are better able than others to determine whether the judge is really qualified.

Question 28.

B is the correct answer. "A lawyer shall not make a statement that the lawyer knows to be false or with reckless disregard as to its truth or falsity concerning the qualifications or integrity of a judge, adjudicatory officer, or public legal officer, or of a candidate for election or appointment to judicial or legal office." Model Rule 8.2(a). However, lawyers' assessments are necessarily relied on in determining the fitness of persons being considered for election or appointment to judicial offices. Model Rule 8.2, Comment [1]. Consequently, the attorney's expression of good faith views about a judicial candidate's qualifications was proper, because "[e]xpressing honest and candid opinions on such matters contributes to improving the administration of justice." Model Rule 8.2, Comment [1]. The Rule targets false statements, not honest opinions.

A is incorrect. Even if the attorney was seeking judicial office, it was still proper for him to provide good faith opinions about the judicial candidate's qualifications because such opinions promote the administration of justice by assisting the voters in making informed electoral decisions. Model Rule 8.2, Comment [1]. If he were a candidate for public office, the attorney would be required to comply with the applicable provisions of the Model Code of Judicial Conduct. Model Rule 8.2(b). However, the Model Code does not forbid comments such as those made by the attorney.

C is incorrect. Although false statements about judicial candidates can unfairly undermine public confidence in the administration of justice, a lawyer's good faith expressions of opinion about a judicial candidate's temperament, based on the lawyer's experience, promotes the administration of justice by helping voters make informed decisions. Model Rule 8.2. Also, the lawyer running for election has not yet served in the judiciary, so any comments regarding his ability and temperament would say nothing regarding the judiciary.

D is incorrect. As stated above, although false public statements about a judicial candidate's qualifications are improper, lawyers are entitled to make truthful public statements about judicial candidates.

Question 29.

B is the correct answer. Model Rule 1.3 states: "A lawyer shall act with reasonable diligence and promptness in representing a client." Comment [2] states: "A lawyer's work load must be controlled so that each matter can be handled competently." Comment [3] states: "Perhaps no

professional shortcoming is more widely resented than procrastination."
The facts here show the typical way a lawyer can end up subject to
discipline: (1) make appointments and ignore them, (2) ignore the client's
phone calls and requests for information and progress reports, (3) fail to
keep the client advised, (4) work on other matters to the exclusion or
neglect of the client, and (5) ignore the passage of time and the inevitable
running of the statute of limitations. The key word in Answer B is
"neglect." Here, the attorney has been guilty of professional neglect.
After misuse of client funds, this is the most common basis for lawyer
discipline.

A is incorrect. Commitment to one or several clients to the neglect of
another is exactly what Model Rule 1.3 was intended to prevent.

C is incorrect. The attorney is not relieved of the consequences of her
neglect because the passenger avoided the running of the statute. The
passenger has already suffered in other ways. First, if the attorney had
pursued her settlement negotiations, the passenger might have enjoyed the
proceeds of settlement many months earlier. Second, the attitude of the bus
company may have hardened in the interim and made settlement more
difficult. Third, the passenger could have been spared the anguish and
frustration caused by unanswered phone calls and worry about her claim.

D is incorrect. The issue is not the retainer, but rather the attorney's neglect
of the passenger's interests.

Question 30.

C is the correct answer. Model Rule 3.2 directs a lawyer to make reasonable efforts to expedite litigation consistent with the interests of the
client. Model Rule 1.3 directs a lawyer to act with reasonable diligence and
promptness in representing a client. Model Rule 3.4 covers fairness to
opposing counsel, specifically issues such as falsifying evidence and
inducing witnesses to give false testimony. Even though the attorney
knows the insurance company is represented by another attorney, nothing
in Model Rule 3.4 states that the attorney must warn the opposing attorney
of a possible default judgment. Importantly, such a requirement could
force a lawyer to violate Model Rules 3.2 and 1.3.

A is incorrect. For the same reasons as above, the attorney's knowledge
that another attorney represented the insurance company did not give the
attorney an obligation to inform the other attorney of the default judgment.

B is incorrect. If the attorney knew the other attorney and had dealt with him in other matters, it might have been preferable to advise the other attorney before entering the default in order to avoid the other attorney's anger, but nothing required the attorney to do so.

D is incorrect. First, this answer choice is not responsive to the question. Second, each step in a litigation requires prompt action by a lawyer. Whether or not the insurance company will pay, the attorney must protect her client's interests at every step.

Question 31.

C is the correct answer. Candidates for judicial office must observe the provisions of the Model Code of Judicial Conduct governing judicial campaigns and elections. Most of these provisions are contained in Canon 4. Rule 4.1(A)(11) provides that a candidate shall not "knowingly or with reckless disregard for the truth, make any false or misleading statement." Importantly, a person's knowledge may be inferred from the circumstances. Here, the attorney does not have actual knowledge that the judge was not reprimanded for misconduct in office. Nor was it unreasonable for her to rely on the statement of an official directly responsible for maintaining the information at issue.

A is incorrect. It assumes that the attorney had a duty to inquire into the records themselves after getting a response to her inquiry from the director of the commission himself. This was not a reasonable requirement to impose on the attorney.

B is incorrect. The test is not the truth of the statement but whether the attorney has knowledge of the truth.

D is incorrect. The answer suggests that judges are held to a different standard in contested elections than in noncontested elections.

However, even in a contested judicial election, there are constraints on the candidates that do not apply to candidates for nonjudicial offices. See Canon 4.

Question 32.

B is the correct answer. Lawyers are officers of the court and are charged with the responsibility not to make statements with reckless disregard for the truth concerning the qualifications or integrity of a judge. Model Rule 8.2. Comment [1] points out that false statements by a lawyer can undermine public confidence in the administration of justice. Here, the attorney has attacked the integrity not only of one judge, but of the entire judiciary. Especially because his work as a skilled litigator brings him before these very judges, who decide both fact and law, the inescapable inference is that he has special influence over them.

A is incorrect. A lawyer may contribute to a judge's campaign committee without accounting for his or her motivation in doing so. The Model Code of Judicial Conduct permits the campaign committees of judges to solicit funds from lawyers, but the funds may not be used for the private benefit of the candidates.

C is incorrect. If the statements are indeed true, then the attorney is subject to discipline under Model Rule 3.5 for seeking "to influence a judge, juror, prospective juror or other official by means prohibited by law."

D is incorrect. It's immaterial to the attorney's misconduct that the prospective client did not retain him.

Question 33.

D is the correct answer. Each side is entitled to know and to respond to every fact and every argument presented by the other side. If a judge could consult any legal source he or she wished without identifying it and giving each side the right to respond, the adversarial nature of the judicial system would collapse. At the same time, there are instances in which a judge will need to get advice on the law, especially when, as in these facts, the lawyers have not cleared up all the issues. To enable the judge to do this without subverting the adversarial process, Model Code of Judicial Conduct, Rule 2.9(A)(2) permits a judge to "obtain the written advice of a disinterested expert on the law applicable to a proceeding before the judge, if the judge gives advance notice to the parties of the person to be consulted and the subject matter of the advice to be solicited, and affords the parties a reasonable opportunity to object and respond to the notice and to the advice received."

A is incorrect. It's not enough that the expert consulted by the judge be impartial. The parties are entitled to know what the expert has been asked and what he or she has advised. After all, the expert may be wrong or the judge may not have communicated the issues correctly. The parties may want to respond, and they must be given the opportunity to do so.

B is incorrect. What's at issue here is not the judge's integrity, but the very process by which adversarial issues are determined under the judicial process.

C is incorrect only because it doesn't correspond with how the Model Code of Judicial Conduct resolves this issue. Under the Model Code, it is possible for the judge to ask for advice so long as he or she tells the parties what he or she is doing and gives them the opportunity to respond.

Question 34.

C is the correct answer. "In making administrative appointments, a judge: (1) shall exercise the power of appointment impartially and on the basis of merit; and (2) shall avoid nepotism, favoritism, and unnecessary appointments." Model Code of Judicial Conduct, Rule 2.13(A). Here, the judge is violating the Rule by unnecessarily appointing special masters regardless of the nature and complexity of a proceeding. Additionally, the underlying theme of the Model Code of Judicial Conduct is to avoid creating the *appearance* of impropriety. Here, the decision of the judge to appoint special masters without reference to need arguably creates such an appearance.

A is incorrect. Achieving competence and impartiality does not justify making special master appointments in all cases before a judge. As stated above, the important point is that the judge must avoid making unnecessary appointments.

B is incorrect. Even if a special master charges a reasonable rate, the judge is still violating the Rule by making unnecessary appointments.

D is incorrect. Nothing in the Model Code prohibits a judge from using a law directory to make appointments. In fact, using general law directories in compiling the list is a logical way for the judge to avoid the appearance of either nepotism or favoritism.

Question 35.

B is the correct answer. Because the attorney is newly admitted, he may not realize that he's become party to a scheme that enables the trust company to engage in the unauthorized practice of law. Model Rule 5.5(a) says quite simply, "A lawyer shall not practice law in a jurisdiction in violation of the regulation of the legal profession in that jurisdiction, or assist another in doing so." The attorney is enabling the trust company to discuss and "work out" the details of trusts and wills, functions that clearly fall within the parameters of law practice. The attorney is also aiding the trust company and its officer to misrepresent to the customer the way in which the documents are being prepared. The arrangement between the attorney and the trust company is in the nature of a partnership, and Model Rule 5.4(b) prevents a lawyer from forming a partnership with a nonlawyer if the function of the partnership is the practice of law. Also, even if the attorney is not sharing in the trust company's fees directly, he is in effect doing so by getting free office space. Importantly, Model Rule 5.4(a) prohibits fee splitting with nonlawyers. Ultimately, the attorney is subject to discipline for his actions.

A is incorrect. Don't be confused by the phrase "restricting the right to practice." It may suggest to you the restrictions against a lawyer's right to practice that are contained in Model Rule 5.6. But Model Rule 5.6 deals with restrictions imposed by restrictive employment agreements between a lawyer and his or her partners or law firm and by settlement agreements resolving controversies between private parties. Except for these provisions, which are intended to prevent economic pressure on a lawyer either to gain or keep employment or to settle a pending matter, there are no rules preventing a lawyer from restricting the range or extent of his or her practice.

C is incorrect. A lawyer is not required to charge a client for his or her services. The problem here is not the failure to charge, but the fact that the attorney is helping the trust company engage in the unauthorized practice of law.

D is incorrect. The important point is that the attorney is participating in an arrangement that enables persons who are not authorized to practice law to give legal advice.

Question 36.

C is the correct answer. Here, the attorney has represented both husband and wife in a business transaction, and then in resolving a business dispute between them. Each is a former client. As such, each is entitled to the protective umbrella of Model Rule 1.9. Model Rule 1.9(a) states that a lawyer who has formerly represented a client in a matter shall not thereafter represent another person in the same or a substantially related matter in which that person's interests are materially adverse to the interests of the former client, unless the former client consents after consultation. Further, a lawyer who has formerly represented a client in a matter may not use information relating to the former representation to the disadvantage of the former client (with exceptions not relevant here). Model Rule 1.9(c)(1). Under these facts, the attorney may not represent the wife in litigation against her husband.

A is incorrect. The important point is that the attorney represented both parties in the past, not that the husband may have lied to the attorney as well.

B is incorrect. The rule against representing a current client in an action adverse to the interests of a former client protects all former clients, whatever the facts.

D is incorrect. Again, Model Rule 1.9 is designed to protect a former client against an adverse action on behalf of a current or prospective client. That the former client is now represented by new counsel is irrelevant to the application of the Rule.

Question 37.

B is the correct answer. Subject to prior limitations on the scope of representation and the lawyer's duty not to assist a client in criminal conduct, a lawyer "shall abide by a client's decisions concerning the objectives of representation." Model Rule 1.2(a). Specifically, a lawyer must abide by a client's decision to settle a matter, or, in a criminal case, the client's decision as to the "plea to be entered, whether to waive jury trial, and whether the client will testify." Model Rule 1.2(a). However, the lawyer has implied authorization to decide what actions are required to achieve the client's goals, as long as the lawyer consults with the client. Model Rule 1.4(a)(2). Here, once the client decided to settle, the attorney was required to accept the offer, whether or not the attorney reasonably believed the appeal was filed to gain an advantage in the settlement negotiations.

A is incorrect. Although the percentage increase gives the attorney an incentive to favor going through the appeal, this incentive does not create an impermissible conflict of interest. The important point in this question is that the client directed the attorney to settle.

C is incorrect. As stated above, the client makes any decision regarding settlement. A settlement is an objective of representation. Tactical matters are things such as the extent of discovery and what witnesses will be presented at trial.

D is incorrect. Although it is true that evaluating the merits of an appeal requires the exercise of independent professional judgment, this does not change the fact that the client has the ultimate authority in deciding whether to settle a matter.

Question 38.

A is the correct answer. A lawyer may advertise his or her services in the same media as any other professional or merchant. Model Rule 7.2. There are, however, special limitations that apply only to lawyers. The most important is embodied in Model Rule 7.1. Model Rule 7.1 requires that the lawyer not make a misleading statement about himself or herself or his or her services. A statement is misleading if it contains a material misrepresentation of fact or law, omits a fact that will make the statement not misleading, is likely to create unjustified expectations about the results the lawyer is likely to achieve, or compares the lawyer's services with other lawyers' services without substantiation in fact. Here, the ad televised by the attorney meets all of these requirements on its face. Even the last sentence is not objectionable. It suggests only that the attorney may have a relatively low fee schedule, or that potential clients may have a mistaken notion about the level of legal fees in the attorney's area. Also, the attorney is complying with the requirement to maintain copies of all of her ads.

B is incorrect. The ad does not state that the attorney's fees are lower than those generally charged in her area, only that the potential client may have a mistaken notion about legal fees in general. Further, a statement that the attorney's fees were lower than those generally charged in her area would not be improper if the statement could be supported by the facts.

C is incorrect. Nothing in the Rules prevents a lawyer from using professional actors to read a radio or TV ad. The actor is obviously not pretending to be the attorney; he is simply conveying her message in the same way as in other TV ads. If a lawyer did instruct an actor to pretend to be the lawyer when reading the ad, that, of course, would represent a material misrepresentation of fact and could lead to discipline.

D is incorrect. Nothing in the Rules prohibits a lawyer from charging for an initial consultation and nothing in the ad suggests that the attorney will not charge for the consultation.

Question 39.

B is the correct answer. Although Model Rule 1.6 protects a client's confidential information under the attorney-client privilege, one of the exceptions is that "a lawyer may reveal information relating to the representation of a client to the extent the lawyer reasonably believes necessary . . . to comply with other law or a court order." Model Rule 1.6(b)(6). In this case, the attorney has been subpoenaed to testify before a grand jury. Importantly, the clients' names may be confidential under Rule 1.6, but they are not protected by the attorney-client privilege. The attorney-client privilege protects only confidential communications between a lawyer and a client. It does not protect clients' identities unless disclosing their identities will implicitly reveal their confidential communications, which does not appear to be the case here. Thus, the attorney may provide the grand jury with the clients' names.

A is incorrect. Because the information isn't protected by the attorney-client privilege, it is irrelevant that negotiating a counterfeit bill is a crime.

C is incorrect. As stated above, the information is not confidential under Model Rule 1.6, so it is irrelevant whether it would fall under the exception that allows the disclosure of confidences to prevent imminent death or substantial bodily harm.

D is incorrect. As stated above, the information in this case is not privileged. However, if the attorney's information in this case were in fact privileged, it is true that the attorney could not disclose it under the "crime-fraud" exception, even though passing counterfeit money is a crime, because the attorney does not know which client paid with counterfeit bills, and also does not know whether the client who did so was aware the bills were counterfeit. Thus, if the attorney were to reveal confidential information, the attorney would be violating the Rule as to at least one innocent client who does not fall under the exception.

Question 40.

A is the correct answer. Under Model Rule 1.7(a), a lawyer shall not represent a client if the representation of one client will be directly adverse to the representation of another client. Here, the attorney has a conflict of interest arising from the representation of two clients in the same transaction — the bank, which is the lender, and the corporation, which is the borrower. However, Model Rule 1.7(b) allows the attorney to represent both clients if he reasonably believes that he will be able to provide competent and diligent representation to each client, the representation is not prohibited by law, the representation does not involve the assertion of a claim by one client against the other, and each client gives informed consent in writing. Here, because the proposed representation meets all the requirements of Model Rule 1.7(b), the joint representation is proper.

B is incorrect. Because the attorney has a conflict of interest under Model Rule 1.7(a), the fact that the arrangement is customary in the community is irrelevant. The important question is whether the proposed representation meets the requirements of Model Rule 1.7(b).

C is incorrect. "A lawyer shall not accept compensation for representing a client from other than the client unless: (1) the client gives informed consent; (2) there is no interference with the lawyer's independence of professional judgment or with the client-lawyer relationship; and (3) information relating to representation of a client is protected as required by Rule 1.6." Model Rule 1.8(f). The Rule recognizes the fact that third-party payers frequently have interests that differ from the client, such as minimizing the amount spent on the representation. The classic example of an arrangement violating this Rule is when a defendant's insurance company is responsible for the ultimate damage claim and is also paying the defendant's legal defense expenses. Here, in a joint representation such as this one, there is no restriction against the payment of legal fees by one of the two clients with informed consent. Model Rule 1.8(f).

D is incorrect. Although there is a conflict of interest, the attorney can represent clients with differing interests as long as the requirements of Model Rule 1.7(b) are met.

Question 41.

A is the correct answer. A lawyer may not counsel or assist a client in conduct that is criminal or fraudulent. Model Rule 1.2(d). Similarly, a lawyer has a duty under Model Rule 3.3(a)(3) not to use false evidence. When the attorney asked the client for his name, he knew that the response would be a falsehood that would mislead the court in its judgment of the client's offense.

B is incorrect. It's immaterial to the attorney's duty to the court whether the client committed a felony or a lesser crime. The point is the testimony would mislead the court into administering a lighter sentence than the law required.

C is incorrect. While the information would ordinarily be protected because it was disclosed to the attorney as a confidence during the course of representation, it cannot be protected if it results in the presentation of testimony that the attorney knows is false.

D is incorrect. The client's name is an issue in the trial. If the client's true name is used, he's subject to the heavier penalty. If the court doesn't learn his true name, the client gets the lighter penalty.

Question 42.

A is the correct answer. If a judge personally or as a fiduciary (trustee of a trust) has more than a *de minimis* economic interest in the subject matter in controversy, disqualification is required. Model Code of Judicial Conduct, Rule 2.11(A)(3). A financial interest disqualification can be remitted if the judge fully discloses the potential impartiality conflict on the record, all the parties and lawyers agree that the conflict is immaterial in a proceeding outside the presence of the judge, and the agreement is then incorporated into the record. Model Code of Judicial Conduct, Rule 2.11(C). However, considering the large size of the financial interest ($50,000,000), a remittance here is likely inappropriate. Also, the potential for remittance was not included among any of the answer choices, making A the best answer.

B is incorrect. Even if the value of the stock is unlikely to be affected, disqualification is still necessary to prevent the appearance of judicial impropriety and the judge's impartiality can reasonably be questioned under the circumstances. The overarching goal of the Model Code of Judicial Conduct is to make sure judges act in a manner that promotes public confidence in the integrity, fairness, and impartiality of the judiciary. Consequently, members of the judiciary must avoid creating even an appearance of bias.

C is incorrect. Even if the judge does not personally own stock in either party to the litigation, she is a trustee who owns a legal interest in the stock while acting as a fiduciary for others with an equitable interest. Under these circumstances, the judge's impartiality can still be reasonably questioned by others. Further adding to the appearance of impropriety, the trust is set up for the educational benefit of the judge's grandchildren, and disqualification is similarly required in circumstances where a member of the judge's family has an economic interest in the matter.

D is incorrect. Although the judge believes she can be fair and impartial (and she might, in fact, be correct in this belief), that impartiality could be reasonably questioned by others. Consequently, she should disqualify herself for the same reasons as in B.

Question 43.

A is the correct answer. A judge's extrajudicial activities are always subject to scrutiny to "minimize the risk of conflict with judicial obligations." Model Code of Judicial Conduct, Canon 3. Rule 3.7(A) permits a judge to serve as an officer, director, trustee, or nonlegal advisor of "educational, religious, charitable, fraternal, or civic organizations not conducted for profit . . . ." (Note that the judge is precluded from giving any legal advice to the organization.) But the judge may not serve an organization that is engaged in a proceeding that is likely to come before the judge or that is engaged frequently in adversarial proceedings in the court of which the judge is a member. Rule 3.7(A)(6). Rule 3.13 permits a judge to accept gifts incident to a public testimonial. However, there are limitations on testimonials. Importantly, the gift must not be one that would "appear to a reasonable person to undermine the judge's independence, integrity, or impartiality." Rule 3.13(A). On these facts, the judge may accept the portrait.

B is incorrect. The fact that the judge did not receive compensation is only one piece of the puzzle. Other pieces are also required to make the gift proper: (a) that it is a public testimonial, (b) by a charitable organization, (c) that does not engage in litigation before the judge's court. (Note: a judge may receive compensation for activities permitted under Canon 3 if the source of payment does not give the appearance of influencing the judge in his or her judicial duties and if the compensation is reasonable and does not exceed what a nonjudge would receive for the same activity. Rule 3.12.)

C is incorrect. There is no specific limit in the Model Code for the cost of a testimonial gift. The test is whether the value of the gift is so excessive as to suggest undue influence either in a specific matter or generally, and, also, whether the source of the gift is suspect. (On this issue, see the next paragraph.)

D is incorrect. A testimonial gift from lawyers to a judge is not prohibited per se.

Question 44.

C is the correct answer. A lawyer in litigation is expected to be a zealous advocate of his or her client's position. If he or she is called to testify on a contested issue of fact, his or her role as advocate becomes confused. Also, his or her testimony may create an irreconcilable conflict of interest between the client and the attorney. For these reasons, a lawyer is prohibited from acting as advocate in a matter if he or she is likely to be called as a witness. Model Rule 3.7. However, there are three exceptions: (1) if the testimony relates to an uncontested issue, (2) if the testimony relates to the nature and value of the lawyer's services rendered in the case, or (3) if the lawyer's disqualification would work substantial hardship on the client. Model Rule 3.7. Because the facts here do not present an exception to the general rule, the attorney may not represent the executor. The executor may retain other counsel and the attorney will then be free to testify about the client's competence. This question illustrates why a lawyer should never act as subscribing witness to a will he or she prepares. When a lawyer prepares a will and then acts as subscribing witness, he or she knows that he or she may later be called to appear as a witness in a contest of the will.

A is incorrect. It restates the problem, not the solution. It's exactly because the attorney is likely to be called as a witness that he may not represent the executor. True, there is some hardship on the executor in forcing him to find and retain other counsel to prove the will, but the problem is not insurmountable. On balance, the need to forestall participation by the lawyer as both advocate and witness is paramount.

B is incorrect. The rule against the lawyer as witness assumes that the lawyer would testify in support of his or her client. "The problem can arise whether the lawyer is called as a witness on behalf of his client or is called by the opposing party." Model Rule 3.7, Comment [6].

D is incorrect. It states correctly the underlying rationale for the Rule, but not the Rule itself. Whether or not the attorney's testimony supports one side or another, he may not represent either side if he is likely to be called as a necessary witness.

Question 45.

A is the correct answer. In settling a claim or potential claim for malpractice, a lawyer must advise an unrepresented client in writing of the desirability of seeking independent legal counsel. Model Rule 1.8(h)(2).

B is incorrect. The attorney's belief, or even whether the agreement is fair or unfair to the buyer, is not the issue. In this situation, under the Rules, the lawyer must advise the client in writing of the appropriateness of independent representation and must give the client ample time to find and consult with another lawyer.

C is incorrect. There is no prohibition on settling a potential malpractice claim, whether or not a related matter is ongoing.

D is incorrect. The Rules do not require that the buyer actually be separately represented, only that he be advised in writing of the desirability of seeking independent legal counsel and given time to consult with another lawyer.

Question 46.

A is the correct answer. If a lawyer identifies criminal behavior on the part of an opposing party, upon consent of the client, the lawyer may disclose such information to the prosecutor. Once the lawyer has the client's consent, disclosure of the information would be permissive, not mandatory.

B is incorrect. As stated above, the lawyer is not required to report an opposing party's criminal activity to the prosecutor. Additionally, the decision to report the defendant to the criminal authorities does not depend on whether the information discovered is privileged or not.

C is incorrect. There is no duty to inform the defendant's lawyer before reporting the information.

D is incorrect. It was permissible to report even though the civil suit was pending because the attorney was not trying to gain an advantage by making a complaint to the prosecutor. Had she been seeking an advantage, it might have been impermissible under Model Rule 3.4, which covers fairness to opposing party and counsel.

Question 47.

D is the correct answer. In making decisions and exercising options, a lawyer is required to act with competence. Model Rule 1.1. This means that he or she must employ "the legal knowledge, skill, thoroughness and preparation reasonably necessary for the representation." In other words, the lawyer is not a guarantor of a successful outcome or even of a consequence-free result. He or she is required, however, to exercise his or her judgment in a manner that would be considered reasonable by other lawyers under all the circumstances. There are circumstances in which a lawyer may reasonably advise a client not to respond to questions by a legislative fact-finding committee, even when the client is faced by the risk of imprisonment. These facts do not tell us what the underlying facts were, but they do state clearly that the attorney "reasonably believed" that it was in the best interests of the witness not to answer. Ultimately, the attorney is not subject to discipline so long as he acted reasonably.

A is incorrect. Whether or not the attorney ultimately made the right decision, he cannot be disciplined because he acted on a reasonable belief that he was protecting the witness. There is no suggestion in the facts that the attorney was not competent to represent the witness before the committee or to exercise his reasonable discretion to advise the witness not to answer.

B is incorrect. The facts do not disclose the constitutional basis for the refusal by the witness to answer the committee's questions. Obviously, however, the consequences to the witness in failing to exercise her constitutional rights were deemed by the attorney to be more serious and severe than the refusal to answer. Although the general rule is that an attorney may not counsel a client to engage, or assist a client, in conduct that the lawyer knows is criminal (Model Rule 1.2), most courts would support the witness' right to refuse to answer if her constitutional rights were in jeopardy.

C is incorrect. Model Rule 1.2 does not distinguish between crimes involving moral turpitude and other crimes. A lawyer may not assist a client in any crime, however characterized. However, the conflict between the need to protect a constitutional right not to answer and the obligation to observe a law requiring an answer is irreconcilable. The lawyer's obligation under these circumstances is to advise the client of the consequences of each alternative.

Question 48.

A is the correct answer. A newly admitted lawyer in a firm must have his or her work properly supervised by a more experienced lawyer to ensure that all lawyers in the firm conform to the Model Rules of Professional Conduct. Model Rule 5.1. Under Model Rule 1.1, a law firm owes a client a duty of competence, specifically the appropriate "legal knowledge, skill, thoroughness and preparation reasonably necessary for the representation." Consequently, when a firm uses less-experienced lawyers to perform client work, the partners must supervise that work. In this case, the associate, who had never conducted or observed a trial and had not worked on landlord-tenant cases before, needed supervision. There was not enough time for the associate to become familiar with the relevant law and procedure, nor did she have the experience to competently handle the case.

Importantly, the attorney did not take the proper precautions to make sure that the associate was adequately prepared to carry out the assignment.

B is incorrect. The outcome of the trial is irrelevant to whether the associate was properly supervised. In particular, be wary of answer choices where a good outcome "fixes" the violation.

C is incorrect. The associate's admission to the bar did not relieve the attorney of the responsibility to properly supervise and train her. The question of a lawyer's competence revolves around that lawyer's training and experience, not the simple fact that the lawyer has passed a bar exam.

D is incorrect. The consent of the landlord to this representation would not mitigate the fact that the attorney failed to properly supervise the associate. Also be wary of answer choices where a client consents to the Rule violation.

Question 49.

C is the correct answer. There is definitely a conflict of interest involved if the attorney represents the builder and the neighbor. A lawyer may not represent one client if it will be directly adverse to another client without the client's informed consent. Model Rule 1.7. This is true even if the lawyer would be acting as advocate against the client in a matter unrelated to the one in which the lawyer represents the client. Model Rule 1.7, Comment [6]. It is possible the attorney could undertake the representation of the neighbor with informed written consent from the builder, but since that option is not offered, C remains the best answer.

A is incorrect. The conflict of interest rule speaks to a lawyer's loyalty to a client, so it doesn't matter whether there are common issues in the two matters. If the attorney represents the neighbor in opposing the builder's petition for rezoning, the builder would likely feel betrayed, which would likely damage the attorney's and the builder's lawyer-client relationship and interfere with the attorney's representation of the builder in the contract suit.

B is incorrect for the same reasons that A is incorrect. Loyalty to the client is the issue, and again, it doesn't matter what types of proceedings are involved.

D is incorrect. The issue is dealing with a concurrent conflict; what might or might not happen in the future has nothing to do with the attorney's decision whether it is proper to undertake representation of the neighbor.

Question 50.

A is the correct answer. With regard to *civil cases,* the adversary system contemplates that the evidence in a case is to be marshaled competitively by the parties. Model Rule 3.4, Comment [1]. Likewise, a lawyer's duty not to conceal evidence in a civil case does not carry with it a duty to report or volunteer all relevant information. Prosecutors, however, have special responsibilities. Model Rule 3.8. "A prosecutor has the responsibility of a minister of justice and not simply that of an advocate" (Model Rule 3.8, Comment [1]) and as such, must "make timely disclosure to the defense of all evidence or information known to the prosecutor that tends to negate the guilt of the accused . . . ." Model Rule 3.8(d). The fact that the girls' descriptions varied significantly at one point, but later matched almost perfectly, raises a definite question as to the accuracy of their identification and "tends to negate the guilt" of the suspect. Here, the prosecutor has a duty to reveal the existence of the tape to the suspect's counsel.

B is incorrect. What the prosecutor believes is not the point. If there is evidence or information that would raise a question as to the guilt of the suspect, the prosecutor must disclose the existence of that information or evidence in a timely manner.

C is incorrect. This is a true statement with regard to civil cases. See Model Rule 3.4. However, as discussed above, a prosecutor has special responsibilities in a criminal case. Model Rule 3.8.

D is incorrect. The prosecutor's responsibilities under Model Rule 3.8 exist independently of a request by defense counsel. The prosecutor's responsibility "carries with it specific obligations to see . . . that guilt is decided upon the basis of sufficient evidence." Model Rule 3.8, Comment [1].

Question 51.

A is the correct answer. A lawyer is prohibited from asking a person other than the client to refrain from voluntarily giving relevant information to another party unless that person is a relative, employee, or agent of the client and the lawyer reasonably believes that the person's interests will not be adversely affected by refraining to give that information. Model Rule 3.4(f). In that case, the attorney may instruct the person to refrain from giving information unless subpoenaed. Here, the eyewitness did not fall under any of the exceptions to the Rule.

B is incorrect. A lawyer is under no obligation to subpoena a witness that the lawyer does not intend to call at trial.

C is incorrect. Even if a witness has not yet been subpoenaed, Model Rule 3.4(f) prohibits an attorney from asking that witness to refrain from giving relevant information to another party, unless that witness falls within one of the three exceptions.

D is incorrect. Even though the attorney did not offer the witness any inducement not to appear at trial, Model Rule 3.4(f) prohibits the attorney from making any "request" to refrain from voluntarily giving relevant information.

Question 52.

A is the correct answer. A lawyer is prohibited from communicating about a matter with a person known to be represented in the matter unless the person's lawyer consents to the communication or the communication is authorized by law. Model Rule 4.2. The important point is that it is the *lawyer's* consent that is necessary, not the client's. In addition, a lawyer may not violate the Rules directly or through the acts of another. Model Rule 8.4(a). Here, the attorney used a nonlawyer agent, the investigator, to violate the no-contact rule.

B is incorrect. The investigator merely relayed a communication from the attorney to the defendant and did not thereby engage in the unauthorized practice of law.

C is incorrect. As stated above, a lawyer is prohibited from communicating with a represented person whether the communication is performed by the attorney or an agent of the attorney. Here, the attorney cannot get around the Rule by using a nonlawyer in making the communication.

D is incorrect. Here, the defendant's lawyer did not consent to the communication, and the fact the defendant's lawyer might not have relayed the settlement offer did not otherwise justify the communication.

Question 53.

B is the correct answer. A client who has given consent to a potential conflict of interest may revoke the consent and, like any other client, terminate the lawyer's representation at any time. Model Rule 1.7, Comment [21]. Here, it was improper for the attorney to insist that the wife adhere to the prior agreement since she had an absolute right to terminate the joint representation.

A is incorrect. Under Model Rule 1.7, the initial representation was proper because it was reasonable for the attorney to believe that he was able to provide competent and diligent representation to both the husband and the wife, and both clients' consent was informed and in writing.

C is incorrect. Even though the clients initially consented to the joint representation, each had an absolute right at any time to revoke the consent and terminate the attorney's representation. Here, it was improper for the attorney to insist that the wife gave up that right. However, in some cases, a client's revocation of consent to a joint representation can effect whether the attorney can continue to represent the other client. Whether a client's revoked consent precludes the lawyer from continuing to represent other clients depends on the circumstances, "including the nature of the conflict, whether the client revoked consent because of a material change in circumstances, the reasonable expectations of the other client, and whether material detriment to the other clients or the lawyer would result." Model Rule 1.7, Comment [21].

D is incorrect. As stated above, whether the husband and wife independently made the agreement or not, they still had an absolute right to revoke their consent to the joint representation at any time.

Question 54.

D is the correct answer. A lawyer appearing before a legislative body must disclose that the appearance is in a representative capacity. Model Rule 3.9. This Rule recognizes the fact that a legislative body will likely give great weight to a lawyer's opinions on a question of law or legislative rule making. Requiring a lawyer to disclose the client relationship allows the legislative body to assess any potential bias of the lawyer.

A is incorrect. Here, the fact that the attorney believes her client's position is in the public interest does not cure the Rule violation. Always be wary of answer choices that imply a Rule was not violated because the attorney would have said or done the same thing despite the Rule violation.

B is incorrect. As stated above, the congressional members at the hearing would be very interested in knowing whether a witness is possibly biased in his or her testimony; therefore, Model Rule 3.9 requires a lawyer appearing in a representative capacity to disclose that fact to the legislative body.

C is incorrect. Lawyers frequently serve as paid lobbyists. This activity is permissible so long as the lawyer-lobbyist complies with applicable rules, such as the requirement to disclose his or her representative capacity when appearing before a legislative body.

Question 55.

D is the correct answer. A practicing lawyer who is also a legislator may not use his or her official authority for the benefit of a private client. However, a legislator who is a lawyer but who is no longer practicing law may assist a constituent in its dealings with a state agency. Here, the facts show that the senator is helping the bank as a constituent, not a client. Consequently, the senator's action would not subject her to discipline.

A is incorrect. Because the senator was assisting the bank as a constituent and not a client, she did not misuse her official position.

B is incorrect. The senator's efforts as a legislator on behalf of a constituent were proper because she was no longer practicing law and was not seeking to assist the bank as a private client. Therefore, it does not matter that the senator in fact influenced the agency in her former client's favor.

C is incorrect. The Rules do not prohibit a legislator who is also a lawyer from expressing opinions about the law.

Question 56.

C is the correct answer. Although a lawyer is not allowed to counsel or assist a client in criminal or fraudulent conduct, a lawyer may help a client determine the validity, scope, meaning, or application of the law to a client's particular situation. Model Rule 1.2(d). Here, the attorney is not helping the client break the law; she is simply delineating the law's boundaries.

A is incorrect. As long as a lawyer is not helping a client to violate the law, he or she is not required to make a guess as to how that client is going to use the lawyer's advice, nor is the attorney subject to discipline if the client decides to use the lawyer's advice to break the law. Here, the attorney simply gave her opinion regarding the parameters of the law.

B is incorrect. Here, the attorney specifically told the client that she would not tell him how to avoid detection. All she did was tell him about the law and its history. Although discouraging a client from violating the law might have been the best practice, failing to discourage him from violating the law is not cause for discipline.

D is incorrect. As stated above, lawyers may not assist clients in violating the law, and this includes discussing the best way to avoid detection.

Question 57.

D is the correct answer. Judges are permitted to consult with other judges on the court about pending cases as long as any consultation does not affect their responsibilities to personally decide the matters and as long as they make "reasonable efforts to avoid receiving factual information that is not part of the record." Model Code of Judicial Conduct, Rule 2.9(A)(3).

A is incorrect. A conversation with another judge on the court about a pending matter does not count as an inappropriate ex parte communication.

B is incorrect. As stated above, a judge may consult with another judge in the court about a case, as long as the judge does not thereby give up his or her responsibility to personally decide the matter.

C is incorrect. Under the Model Code of Judicial Conduct, Rule 2.9(A)(2), a judge may obtain written advice from a disinterested expert provided that the judge gives advance notice to the parties about details of the consultation and the opportunity to object and respond to the advice. This Rule, however, is not applicable to a situation in which a judge consults with another judge in the court.

Question 58.

B is the correct answer. This plan for part of the administrator's compensation to be based upon the net profits of the firm is expressly permitted under Model Rule 5.4(a) as long as the nonlawyer is an employee of the firm. Importantly, the other aspects of the arrangement do not give the administrator an inappropriate ownership interest in the firm, nor in any right to control the legal work done in the law firm, thus avoiding any violation of the Rule.

A is incorrect. The plan is proper, but the reason why it is proper has nothing to do with the compensation paid to other law office administrators in the community. This answer wrongly refers to Model Rule 1.5(a)'s guidelines on reasonable fees for lawyers, which lists as one factor fees paid to other similarly situated lawyers in the community. Be wary of answer choices referring to standards in the local community, as these are often wrong.

C is incorrect. The Rules do not address the basis on which net profits may be divided and distributed to nonlawyer employees. Such decisions are properly made by the firm.

D is incorrect. Although lawyers may not share legal fees with nonlawyers, Model Rule 5.4(a) contains an exception for compensation plans that involve the sharing of net profits with nonlawyer employees.

Question 59.

D is the correct answer. The information regarding the perjury committed by the client's former partner is "information relating to the representation" of the client, which generally may not be disclosed without client consent. Model Rule 1.6(a). Confidential information may be disclosed without client consent under Model Rule 1.6(a) when "the disclosure is impliedly authorized in order to carry out the representation," but there would be no implied authorization where, as here, the disclosure would likely harm the client.

A is incorrect. The lawyer's duty to protect client information under Model Rule 1.6(a) covers more than just privileged information. It covers all "information relating to the representation of a client." Thus, it doesn't matter whether the information is privileged or not.

B is incorrect. Under Model Rule 3.3(b), if a lawyer is representing a client and offers material evidence (such as a person's testimony) that is later discovered to be false, that lawyer must "take reasonable remedial measures, including, if necessary, disclosure to the tribunal." However, that duty does not apply here because the attorney did not represent the client in the proceeding where the client's former partner committed the perjury. Therefore, the attorney has no duty to disclose the perjury under Model Rule 3.3(b).

C is incorrect. The duties created by Model Rule 3.3(b) last only to the end of the case. Here, the case in which the former partner committed perjury is over. Consequently, even if the attorney had represented the client in that proceeding, the attorney would have no duty at this time to disclose the former partner's perjury. Importantly, if a lawyer first learns of the false evidence after the case is over, the duty of confidentiality under Model Rule 1.6 prohibits disclosure.

Question 60.

B is the correct answer. Because this is an aggregate settlement of all of the clients' claims, the attorney must obtain the clients' informed consent after disclosing "the existence and nature of all the claims" and "the participation of each person in the settlement." Model Rule 1.8(g). The necessary disclosure must include information about "all the material terms of the settlement, including what the other clients will receive or pay if the settlement or plea offer is accepted." Model Rule 1.8(g), Comment [13]. Even if the settlement could be jeopardized, Model Rule 1.2(a) protects each client's right to have the final say in deciding whether to accept or reject a settlement. Ultimately, it is not the lawyer's place to decide what is the best outcome for the clients.

A is incorrect. A lawyer may participate in an aggregate settlement of civil claims as long as the lawyer complies with the requirement of informed consent by all clients. Model Rule 1.8(g). Here, by not giving the clients all the information regarding what each one of them would receive under the settlement, the attorney failed to do so.

C is incorrect. As stated above, regardless of whether the settlement will be jeopardized, the clients need to know all the material terms of the settlement.

D is incorrect. The lawyer must still make a full disclosure to the clients whether or not the lawyer believes the aggregate settlement offer is fair, or whether or not the clients are satisfied with the amount. Always be wary of such "no-harm, no-foul" answer options.

Part Three
Three Practice MPREs

Part Two contained Model Answers to 60 of the Model Questions taken from the National Conference of Bar Examiner's MPRE Sample Questions VI and MPRE — Online Practice Exam 1 (although some questions were modified to match recent changes in test format). Below are three practice MPREs also made up of questions taken from these two sources (also modified as necessary and to provide enough unique questions for this book).

Taking the three practice MPREs below under timed conditions (give yourself two hours for each exam) will complete your preparation for the MPRE. Read each question carefully and circle the answer you think is correct. After completing each exam, check your answers against the answers in Part B, which not only identify the correct answer, but explain why the other answers are not correct.

If you selected the right answer, make sure you can articulate the reasons that led you to that answer (too often students check only their wrong answers, and fail to discover that they got a question right for the wrong reasons or simply made a lucky guess). Importantly, write down which of the Rules in the Model Rules or the Model Code of Judicial Conduct you relied on in reasoning your way to your answer.

If you selected one of the three wrong answers, you have some work to do. Ask yourself: Why am I wrong? What did I miss in the facts? How do I avoid making this mistake again? Importantly, figure out what Rule the question was testing you on, and write that down on a list. Highlight the ones you miss. Also highlight anything you didn't know or didn't understand that threw off your analysis.

Once you've made this list of Rules and "things you didn't know" or "things you didn't understand," you should memorize it. The best way to do so (and educational studies going back to the 1960s support this) is to memorize the list, put it away, and then try to write it again from memory. Keep repeating this exercise until you can write out the entire sheet without a mistake (and you will likely never make those mistakes again).

Basically, if you review and re-review these questions and your own answers, there's a good chance you'll recognize essentially the same facts and issues in the questions when you sit for the real MPRE exam.

A. Practice MPREs

1. Practice MPRE 1

Question 1.

An attorney and a restaurant owner entered into a reciprocal referral arrangement. The attorney agreed to prominently display ads for the restaurant in her office, and to mention the restaurant to all of her clients who requested a recommendation of a nearby place to eat. In return, the owner agreed to prominently display ads for the attorney's firm in the restaurant and to recommend the attorney to any of his customers who indicated a need for the services provided by the attorney. The reciprocal referral agreement was not exclusive, and the clients and customers would be informed of the existence and nature of the agreement.

Is the attorney subject to discipline for entering into this agreement?

(A) Yes, because she asked the owner to place ads for the firm in the restaurant.

(B) Yes, because the agreement provided something of value to the restaurant owner in return for recommending the attorney's services.

(C) No, because she did not pay the restaurant owner for the referrals.

(D) No, because the agreement is not exclusive, and the clients and customers will be informed of the existence and nature of the agreement.

Question 2.

Attorneys Alpha and Beta practiced law under the firm name of Alpha and Beta. When Beta died, Alpha did not change the firm name. Thereafter, Alpha entered into an arrangement with another attorney, Gamma. Gamma pays Alpha a certain sum each month for office space and use of Alpha's law library and for secretarial services, but Alpha and Gamma each has his own clients, and neither participates in the representation of the other's clients or shares in fees paid. On the entrance to the suite of offices shared by Alpha and Gamma are the words "Law Firm of Alpha, Beta, and Gamma."

Is Alpha subject to discipline?

(A) Yes, because Beta was deceased when Alpha made the arrangement with Gamma.

(B) Yes, because Gamma is not a partner of Alpha.

(C) No, because Alpha and Beta were partners at the time of Beta's death.

(D) No, because Gamma is paying a share of the rent and office expenses.

Question 3.

An attorney was employed as a lawyer by the state Environmental Control Commission (ECC) for 10 years. During the last two years of her employment, the attorney spent most of her time in the preparation, trial, and appeal of a case involving the discharge by a corporation of industrial effluent into a river in the state. The judgment in the case, which is now final, contained a finding of a continuing and knowing discharge of a dangerous substance into a major stream by the corporation and assessed a penalty of $25,000.

The governing statute also provides for private actions for damages by persons injured by the discharge of the effluent.

The attorney recently left the employment of ECC and went into private practice. Three landowners have brought private damage actions against the corporation. They claim their farms were contaminated because they irrigated them with water that contained dangerous chemicals discharged by the corporation. The corporation has asked the attorney to represent it in defense of the three pending actions. The judgment in the prior case was not determinative of the corporation's liability, and all of the information acquired by the attorney when representing the ECC is now a matter of public record.

Is the attorney subject to discipline if she represents the corporation in these actions?

(A) Yes, because the judgment in the prior case is not determinative of the corporation's liability.

(B) Yes, because the attorney had substantial responsibility in the matter while employed by ECC.

(C) No, because the attorney has acquired special competence in the matter.

(D) No, because all information acquired by the attorney while representing ECC is now a matter of public record.

Question 4.

An attorney is skilled in trying personal injury cases. The attorney accepted the representation of a plaintiff in a personal injury case on a contingent fee basis. While preparing the case for trial, the attorney realized that the direct examination and cross-examination of the medical experts would involve medical issues with which the attorney was not familiar and, as a consequence, the attorney might not be able to represent the plaintiff competently.

Without informing the plaintiff, the attorney consulted another attorney who is also a medical doctor and a recognized specialist in the care and treatment of injuries of the type sustained by the plaintiff. The two attorneys agreed that the other attorney would participate in the trial to the limited extent of conducting the direct examination and cross-examination of the medical experts and that the attorneys would divide the fee in proportion to the services performed and the responsibility assumed by each. Upon conclusion of the matter, the attorney provided the plaintiff with a written statement explaining the relevant fees.

Was the arrangement between the two attorneys proper?

(A) Yes, because the fee to be paid by the plaintiff was not increased by reason of the other attorney's association.

(B) Yes, because the fee would be divided in proportion to the services performed and the responsibility assumed by each.

(C) No, because the plaintiff was not advised of the association of the other attorney.

(D) No, because, upon conclusion of the matter, the attorney provided the plaintiff with a written statement setting forth the method of determining both the fee and the division of the fee with the other attorney.

Question 5.

An attorney represents a famous politician in an action against a newspaper for libel. The case has attracted much publicity, and a jury trial has been demanded. After one of the pretrial hearings, as the attorney left the courthouse, news reporters interviewed the attorney. In responding to questions, the attorney revealed the identity of the reporter.

Is the attorney subject to discipline for making this statement?

(A) Yes, because the attorney identified a prospective witness in the case.

(B) Yes, because prospective jurors might learn of the attorney's remarks.

(C) No, because the statement relates to a matter of public record.

(D) No, because the trial has not commenced.

Question 6.

An attorney was employed as an assistant prosecutor in the district attorney's office during the time that an investigation of a suspect was being conducted by that office. The attorney took no part in the investigation and had no knowledge of the facts other than those disclosed in the press. Two months ago, the attorney left the district attorney's office and formed a partnership with another attorney.

Last week, the suspect was indicted for offenses allegedly disclosed by the prior investigation. The suspect asked the attorney to represent him. The attorney declined to do so, but suggested his new partner. The district attorney's office was promptly notified and consented to the representation. The attorney did not participate in the representation or share in the fee.

Is the new partner subject to discipline if he represents the suspect?

(A) Yes, because the attorney was employed in the district attorney's office while the investigation of the suspect was being conducted.

(B) Yes, because the district attorney's office was promptly notified and consented to the representation.

(C) No, because the attorney did not participate in the representation or share in the fee.

(D) No, because the attorney had no responsibility for or knowledge of the facts of the investigation of the suspect.

Question 7.

An attorney represents a plaintiff in a civil action that was filed a year ago and is about to be set for trial. The plaintiff informed the attorney that he could be available at any time during the months of October, November, and December. In discussing possible trial dates with opposing counsel and the court clerk, the attorney was advised that a trial date on October 5 was available and that the next available trial date would be December 10. Without first consulting the plaintiff, the attorney requested the December 10 trial date because she was representing a defendant in a felony criminal trial that was set for October 20 and she wanted as much time as possible to prepare for that trial. She was not court-appointed counsel in the criminal case. The later trial date will not prejudice the client.

Was it proper for the attorney to agree to the December trial date without obtaining the plaintiff's consent?

(A) Yes, because the plaintiff will not be prejudiced by the delay.

(B) Yes, because a criminal trial takes precedence over a civil trial.

(C) No, because the attorney should manage her calendar so that her cases can be tried promptly.

(D) No, because the attorney was not court-appointed counsel in the criminal case.

Question 8.

Three men were indicted for the armed robbery of the cashier of a grocery store. Together, two of them met with an attorney and asked the attorney to represent them. The attorney then interviewed the two of them separately. Each told the attorney that the robbery had been committed by the third man while they sat in the third man's car outside the store. They also said that the third man had said he needed some cigarettes, and that neither knew of the man's plan to rob the cashier. The attorney agreed to the joint representation. One week prior to the trial date, one of the men represented by the attorney told the attorney that he wanted to plea bargain and that he was prepared to turn state's evidence against both of the other two suspects.

It is proper for attorney to:

(A) request court approval to withdraw as lawyer for both men.

(B) continue to represent the man who had not stated that he wanted to plea bargain and, with the other man's consent and court approval, withdraw as his lawyer.

(C) continue to represent the man who wanted to plea bargain and, with the other man's consent and court approval, withdraw as that man's lawyer.

(D) continue to represent both men, but not call the man who wanted to plea bargain as a witness.

Question 9.

While presiding over the trial of a highly publicized antitrust case, a judge received in the mail a lengthy letter from a local attorney. The letter discussed the law applicable to the case. The judge knew that the attorney did not represent either party or any client whose interests could be affected by the outcome. The judge read the letter and, without mentioning its receipt to the lawyers in the pending case, filed the letter in his general file on antitrust litigation.

Later, after reading the trial briefs in the case, the judge concluded that the attorney's letter better explained the law applicable to the case pending before him than either of the trial briefs. The judge followed the attorney's reasoning in formulating his decision. Prior to rendering his decision, the judge did not tell the attorneys anything about the letter.

Was it proper for the judge to consider the attorney's letter?

(A) Yes, because the judge did not initiate the communication with the attorney.

(B) Yes, because the attorney did not represent any client whose interests could be affected by the outcome.

(C) No, because the judge, prior to rendering his decision, did not communicate its contents to all counsel and give them an opportunity to respond.

(D) No, because the attorney is not of record as counsel in the case.

Question 10.

An attorney's recorded radio advertisement stated:

"For a fee of $600 I will represent a party to a divorce that does not result in a court trial of a contested issue of fact."

The attorney had the advertisement prerecorded and approved by the appropriate bar agency for broadcast. The attorney retained a recording of the actual transmission in her office. A woman who had previously agreed with her husband to an uncontested dissolution of their marriage heard the broadcast and called on the attorney in the attorney's office. She told the attorney that she had heard the broadcast and asked the attorney to represent her. The attorney agreed to the representation. Because of the nature of the parties' property, the attorney spent more time on the tax aspects of the case than the attorney anticipated. The time expended by the attorney, if charged at a reasonable hourly rate, would have resulted in a fee of $2,000. After the decree was entered, the attorney billed his client for $2,000. The client paid the fee.

Is the attorney subject to discipline?

(A) No, because the attorney's fee was a reasonable charge for the time expended.

(B) No, because the attorney, when the representation was accepted, did not anticipate the tax problems.

(C) Yes, because the client paid the fee without protest.

(D) Yes, because the attorney charged a fee in excess of the advertised fee.

Question 11.

A certified public accountant proposed to an attorney who is a recognized specialist in the field of tax law, that the accountant and the attorney form a partnership for the purpose of providing clients with tax-related legal and accounting services. Both the accountant and the attorney have deserved reputations of being competent, honest, and trustworthy. The accountant further proposes that the announcement of the proposed partnership, the firm stationery, and all public directory listings clearly state that the accountant is a certified public accountant and that the attorney is a lawyer. The attorney will be the only person in the partnership who gives legal advice.

Is the attorney subject to discipline if he enters into the proposed partnership with the accountant?

(A) Yes, because one of the activities of the partnership would be providing legal services to clients.

(B) Yes, because the attorney would be receiving fees paid for other than legal services.

(C) No, because the partnership will assure to the public high-quality services in the fields of tax law and accounting.

(D) No, because the attorney is the only person in the partnership who gives advice on legal matters.

Question 12.

A client retained an attorney to appeal his criminal conviction and to seek bail pending appeal. The agreed-upon fee for the appearance on the bail hearing was $100 per hour. The attorney received $1,600 from the client, of which $600 was a deposit to secure the attorney's fee and $1,000 was for bail costs in the event that bail was obtained. The attorney maintained two office bank accounts: a fee account, in which all fees collected from clients were deposited and from which all office expenses were paid, and a clients' trust account. The attorney deposited the $1,600 in the clients' trust account the week before the bail hearing. She expended six hours of her time preparing for and appearing at the hearing. The effort to obtain bail was unsuccessful. Dissatisfied, the client immediately demanded return of the $1,600.

What should the attorney do with the $1,600?

(A) Transfer the $1,600 to the fee account.

(B) Transfer the $600 to the fee account and leave $1,000 in the clients' trust account until the attorney's fee for the final appeal is determined.

(C) Transfer $600 to the fee account and send the client a $1,000 check on the clients' trust account.

(D) Send the client a $1,000 check and leave $600 in the clients' trust account until the matter is resolved with the client.

Question 13.

An attorney represents a client in commercial litigation that is scheduled to go to trial in two months. Over the past several weeks, the client has disagreed with almost every tactical decision that the attorney has made. Frustrated, the attorney finally said to the client that if she didn't like the way he was handling the lawsuit, perhaps she should get another lawyer. The client was upset at the suggestion and accused the attorney of trying to get out of the case. Reasonably believing that he could no longer work effectively with the client, the attorney sought the client's permission to withdraw from the representation, and the client reluctantly agreed. After giving the client sufficient notice to obtain replacement counsel, the attorney requested the court's permission to withdraw from the litigation, but the court denied the request.

May the attorney withdraw from the representation?

(A) Yes, because the client agreed, and the attorney gave the client sufficient notice to obtain replacement counsel.

(B) Yes, because the client had made it unreasonably difficult for the attorney to carry out the representation effectively.

(C) No, because the court denied the attorney's request to withdraw.

(D) No, because the attorney's withdrawal would cause material prejudice to the client, and the client's agreement was not voluntary.

Question 14.

An attorney is employed in the legal department of a public utility company and represents that company in litigation. The company has been sued by a consumer group that has accused the company of various acts in violation of its charter. Through its general counsel, the company has instructed the attorney not to negotiate a settlement but to go to trial under any circumstances because a precedent needs to be established. The attorney believes the defense can be supported by a good faith argument, but also believes the case should be settled if possible.

Must the attorney withdraw as counsel in this case?

(A) Yes, because the company is controlling the attorney's judgment in refusing to settle the case.

(B) Yes, because a lawyer should endeavor to avoid litigation.

(C) No, because the company's defense can be supported by a good faith argument.

(D) No, because as an employee, the attorney is bound by the instruction of the general counsel.

Question 15.

A defendant was on trial for murder. The victim was killed during a barroom brawl. In the course of closing arguments to the jury, the prosecutor said,

"The defendant's whole defense is based on the testimony of his friend, who said that the victim attacked the defendant with a knife before the defendant struck him. No other witness testified to such an attack by the victim. I don't believe the defendant's friend was telling the truth, and I don't think you believe him either."

The prosecutor accurately stated the testimony, and truly believed the defendant's friend was lying.

Was the prosecutor's statement proper?

(A) Yes, because the prosecutor accurately stated the testimony in the case.

(B) Yes, because the prosecutor, in fact, believed the defendant's friend was lying.

(C) No, because the prosecutor alluded to the beliefs of the jurors.

(D) No, because the prosecutor asserted his personal opinion about the defendant's credibility.

Question 16.

An attorney represented a plaintiff in an action for defamation against a defendant. After the defendant's lawyer had filed and served an answer, the attorney, at the plaintiff's direction, hired a licensed private investigator and instructed him to attempt to interview the defendant without revealing his employment. The investigator succeeded in interviewing the defendant privately and obtained an admission from the defendant that the statements the defendant had made were based solely on unsubstantiated gossip.

Is the attorney subject to discipline for obtaining the statement from the defendant in this matter?

(A) No, because the attorney was following the plaintiff's instructions.

(B) No, because the statement obtained was evidence that the defendant's allegations were unfounded.

(C) Yes, because the attorney should have interviewed the defendant personally.

(D) Yes, because the attorney instructed the investigator to interview the defendant.

Question 17.

An attorney was retained by a woman to advise her in negotiating a separation agreement with her husband. The husband, who was not a lawyer, had decided to act on his own behalf in the matter. The attorney never met or communicated with the husband during the negotiations.

After several months, the woman advised the attorney that the parties had reached agreement and presented him with the terms. The attorney prepared a proposed agreement that contained all of the agreed-upon terms. The attorney mailed the proposed agreement to the husband, with a cover letter stating:

> "As you know, I represent your wife in this matter and I do not represent your interests. I enclose two copies of the separation agreement that I have drafted in accordance with my client's directions. Please read the agreement and, if it meets with your approval, sign both copies before a notary and return them to me. I will then have your wife sign them and will furnish you with a fully executed copy."

Is the attorney subject to discipline?

A. Yes, because the attorney did not suggest that the husband seek the advice of independent counsel before signing the agreement.

B. Yes, because the attorney directly communicated with an unrepresented person.

C. No, because the attorney acted only as a scrivener.

D. No, because the attorney's letter did not imply that the attorney was disinterested and the attorney did not give legal advice to the husband.

Question 18.

A judge, prior to her appointment to the probate court, was a partner in a law firm. The law firm had an extensive probate practice. At the time of the judge's appointment, the law firm had pending before the court to which the judge was appointed numerous matters in which requests were being made for allowances for attorney's fees. The judge did not note her association on the record. When the judge left the law firm, she was paid a cash settlement. She has no further financial interest in any matter handled by the law firm. The judge is now being asked to rule on these requests for allowances for attorney's fees. The requests are not contested.

Is it proper for the judge to rule on these requests?

A. Yes, because the judge has no financial interest in the outcome of these cases.

B. Yes, because these requests are not contested.

C. No, because the judge did not note on the record in each case her prior association with the law firm.

D. No, because the judge was associated with the law firm when these matters were pending.

Question 19.

An attorney's law firm regularly represented a large company in its international business transactions. The company became involved in a contractual dispute with a foreign government. The company invoked a mandatory arbitration procedure contained in the contract. Under the arbitration clause, each party was allowed to choose a partisan arbitrator and the partisan arbitrators were to choose an additional arbitrator to sit on the panel. The company selected the attorney to be on the arbitration panel. Neither the attorney nor his law firm had represented the company in connection with the contract with the foreign government. The arbitration was completed, and the company was awarded the sum of $100,000. The company then hired the attorney to enforce the award. The attorney obtained the consent of the other arbitrators before accepting the representation. He was successful in enforcing the award.

Is the attorney subject to discipline?

(A) Yes, because the attorney should not have represented the company in a matter in which the attorney had been an arbitrator.

(B) Yes, because the attorney should have declined the arbitration assignment in view of his law firm's regular representation of the company.

(C) No, because the attorney obtained the consent of the other arbitrators before accepting the representation.

(D) No, because the attorney was appointed to the arbitration panel as a partisan arbitrator.

Question 20.

An attorney represented a client who was injured when the television antenna he was attempting to erect in his yard came in contact with a power line. As part of its defense, the manufacturer of the antenna claimed that the antenna came with a warning label advising against erecting the antenna near power lines. The client told the attorney that he had not seen a warning label. The client's wife told the attorney that she had kept the antenna and the box it came in and that she saw no warning label anywhere.

When called by the attorney as witnesses, both the client and his wife testified that they had never seen a warning label. After their testimony, but while the trial was still in progress, the attorney learned from the wife's sister that there indeed had been a warning label on the box, but that the wife had removed and destroyed it. When the attorney confronted the wife with her sister's statement, the wife admitted destroying the label but insisted that her husband knew nothing about it. The attorney continued the trial, but made no reference to the absence of a warning label in his summation to the jury. Instead, the attorney argued that the warning label, even if seen, was insufficient to advise his client of the serious consequences that would ensue if the warning was not heeded. The jury found in favor of the manufacturer.

Is the attorney subject to discipline?

(A) Yes, because the attorney called the wife as a witness and she gave perjured testimony.

(B) Yes, because the attorney failed to take reasonable remedial action after he realized that the wife had given perjured testimony.

(C) No, because the jury apparently disbelieved the wife's testimony.

(D) No, because the attorney did not rely on the wife's testimony once he discovered the perjury.

Question 21.

The attorney represented a client in a claim involving a breach of the client's employment contract. The case was settled without suit being filed. The proceeds of the settlement were paid directly to the client, who subsequently paid the attorney in full for the attorney's fee and expenses. Thereafter, the attorney did no other work for the client.

The client is now being audited by the Internal Revenue Service (IRS). The IRS has asked the attorney for details of the settlement, including the amount claimed for each item of damage and the amounts paid for the items. The attorney reported the request to the client, who told the attorney not to provide the information to the IRS. The attorney believed the disclosure could hurt his client.

Is it proper for the attorney to furnish the information to the IRS?

(A) Yes, because the information does not involve the attorney's work product.

(B) Yes, because the attorney no longer represents the client.

(C) No, because the client told the attorney not to provide the information.

(D) No, because the attorney did not believe the disclosure would be beneficial to the client.

Question 22.

An attorney and a licensed real estate broker entered into an agreement whereby the broker was to recommend the attorney to any customer of the broker who needed legal services, and the attorney was to recommend the broker to any client of the attorney who wished to buy or sell real estate. The attorney's practice is limited almost entirely to real estate law. The attorney and the broker do not share fees with each other, and their prices are reasonable.

Is the attorney subject to discipline for entering into the agreement with the broker?

(A) Yes, because the attorney is compensating the broker for recommending the attorney's legal services.

(B) Yes, because the arrangement constitutes the practice of law in association with a nonlawyer.

(C) No, because neither the attorney nor the broker shares in the other's fees.

(D) No, because the fees of the attorney and the broker do not clearly exceed reasonable fees for the services rendered by each.

Question 23.

An attorney represented a respondent in proceedings instituted by a child protection services agency to establish the paternity of a child and to recover past-due child support. The mother of the child had refused to file a complaint, had refused to retain a lawyer, and in fact had asked that the agency not file any action whatsoever. However, state law permitted the agency to commence paternity and support proceedings in its own name in such circumstances.

The attorney contacted the mother without the knowledge or consent of the agency or its lawyers. The attorney identified himself to the mother as "an officer of the court" and told the mother that he was investigating the matter. Based upon what she told him, the attorney prepared and the mother signed an affidavit truthfully stating that the respondent was not the father of the child.

Is the attorney subject to discipline?

(A) Yes, because the attorney acted without the knowledge or consent of the agency or its lawyers.

(B) Yes, because the attorney implied that he was disinterested in the matter.

(C) No, because all of the attorney's statements to the mother were true.

(D) No, because the attorney did not give the mother legal advice.

Question 24.

An attorney in his capacity as part-time assistant county attorney represented the county in a criminal nonsupport proceeding against a defendant. This proceeding concluded with an order directing the defendant to pay or be jailed. The defendant refused to pay.

The attorney, pursuant to applicable rules, is permitted to maintain a private law practice. The defendant's ex-wife has discovered some assets of the defendant. The attorney now has accepted employment from the defendant's ex-wife to maintain a civil action against the defendant to recover out of those assets arrearages due to the ex-wife under the ex-wife's support decree. The attorney did not obtain consent from the county attorney or from the defendant to represent the ex-wife in the civil action.

Is the attorney subject to discipline for accepting employment in the ex-wife's civil action against the defendant?

(A) Yes, because the attorney did not obtain the defendant's consent to the representation.

(B) Yes, because the attorney had personal and substantial responsibility in the first proceeding.

(C) No, because the attorney's responsibility in his public employment has terminated.

(D) No, because the attorney is representing the ex-wife's interest in both the criminal and the civil proceedings.

Question 25.

An attorney is a lawyer for the city and advises the city on all tort claims filed against it. The attorney's advice is limited to recommending settlement and the amount thereof. If a claim is not settled and suit is filed, defense of the suit is handled either by lawyers for the city's insurance carrier or by outside counsel specially retained for that purpose. In connection with any notice of claim and before suit is filed, the attorney arranges for an investigator to call upon the claimant at the claimant's home and, with no one else present, to interview the claimant and endeavor to obtain a signed statement of the claimant's version of the facts.

A claimant has filed a notice of claim against the city. The attorney knows the claimant is represented by counsel and has sent an investigator to interview the claimant. The attorney is planning to use the claimant's statements against him.

Is the attorney subject to discipline for arranging an interview with the claimant?

(A) Yes, because the claimant was known by the attorney to be represented by counsel.

(B) Yes, because the statement taken will be used to the claimant's disadvantage.

(C) No, because the claimant had not filed suit at the time of the interview.

(D) No, because the attorney would not be representing the city in any subsequent litigation on the claimant's claim.

Question 26.

An attorney joined a professional corporation engaged solely in the practice of law. As a salaried associate, she is not a member or shareholder of the professional corporation. The spouse of one of the partners, who is not a lawyer, is vice-president of the corporation and office manager. She does not participate in any decision regarding a client or a client's case. All of the other officers are lawyers in the firm. All of the corporate shares are held by lawyers in the corporation, except for 10 shares held by an executor under the will of a lawyer-member who died one month previously and whose will is now being probated. The attorney knows that the partner's wife is an officer and not a lawyer.

Is the attorney subject to discipline?

(A) Yes, because the partner's wife is an officer of the corporation.

(B) Yes, because a nonlawyer holds the stock as the executor of the will of the deceased member.

(C) No, because the attorney is a salaried employee and not a member or shareholder of the corporation.

(D) No, because the partner's wife does not participate in any decision regarding a client or a client's case.

Question 27.

An attorney is representing a plaintiff in a paternity suit against a defendant. Both the plaintiff and the defendant are well-known public figures, and the suit has attracted much publicity. The attorney has been billing the plaintiff at an agreed hourly fee for his services. Recently, the plaintiff told the attorney,

"I'm going broke paying you. Why don't you let me assign you all media rights to books, movies, or television programs based on my suit as full payment for all services you will render me between now and the conclusion of the suit?"

The attorney replied,

"I'll consider it, but first you should seek independent advice about whether such an arrangement is in your own best interests. Why don't you do so and call me next week?"

The plaintiff received independent advice and entered into the agreement soon thereafter.

Is the attorney subject to discipline if he agrees to the plaintiff's offer?

(A) Yes, because the amount received by the attorney would be contingent on the receipts from the sale of media rights.

(B) Yes, because the attorney has not concluded the representation of the plaintiff.

(C) No, because the paternity suit is a civil and not a criminal matter.

(D) No, because the plaintiff received independent advice before entering into the agreement.

Question 28.

Four years ago, an attorney represented a husband and wife, both high school teachers, in the purchase of a new home. Since then, the attorney prepared their tax returns and drafted their wills.

Recently, the husband called the attorney and told her that he and his wife had decided to divorce, but wanted the matter to be resolved amicably. The husband stated that they were planning to file and process their own divorce case, utilizing the state's new streamlined divorce procedure, applicable in "no-fault" cases where there are no minor children. The husband asked if the attorney would agree to work with them to prepare a financial settlement agreement that could be presented to the divorce court, reminding the attorney that the couple's assets were modest and that they wanted to "split it all down the middle."

After considering the risks of a conflict of interest arising in this limited representation, the attorney wrote to the couple separately, and advised each that he or she might be better off with separate lawyers, but that the attorney would assist with the financial settlement agreement, charging an hourly fee of $140 per hour, provided that they were in complete agreement and remained so. The attorney advised that if a conflict developed, or if either party was dissatisfied or uncomfortable about continuing with the joint representation, the attorney would withdraw and would not represent either party from that point forward, forcing them to start all over again with separate lawyers. Finally, the attorney cautioned the husband and wife that the attorney would be representing both of them equally, would not and could not favor one or the other, and that their separate communications to her could not be kept confidential from the other party. Both the husband and the wife signed their individual copy of the letter, consenting to the joint representation, and returned them to the attorney.

Was it proper for the attorney to accept the representation on these terms?

(A) Yes, because there was little risk that the interests of either the husband or the wife would be materially prejudiced if no settlement was reached.

(B) Yes, because the attorney had previously represented the husband and the wife in their joint affairs.

(C) No, because the attorney conditioned representation upon receiving a waiver of client confidentially.

(D) No, because the attorney did not advise both the husband and the wife, in writing, that they should seek independent counsel before agreeing to enter into the financial settlement on the terms proposed.

Question 29.

An attorney represented a client in negotiating a large real estate trans-action. The buyer who purchased the real estate from the client has filed suit against both the client and the attorney, alleging fraud and violation of the state unfair trade practices statute. The attorney had advised the client by letter against making the statements that are the basis for the buyer's claim. The attorney and the client are each represented by separate counsel. In responding to a deposition under subpoena, the attorney wishes to reveal, to the extent the attorney reasonably believes necessary to defend herself, confidential information imparted to the attorney by the client that will be favorable to the attorney but damaging to the client. The client did not object to the disclosure. At this point, no criminal charges have been brought against the attorney.

Is it proper for the attorney to reveal such information?

(A) Yes, because the client did not object to the disclosure.

(B) Yes, because the attorney may reveal such information to defend herself against a civil claim.

(C) No, because criminal charges have not also been brought against the attorney.

(D) No, because the disclosure will be detrimental to the client.

Question 30.

An attorney, who is corporate counsel for a company, is investigating a possible theft ring in the parts department of the company. The attorney knows that an employee has worked in the parts department a long time and believes that the employee is a suspect in the thefts. The attorney believes that if the employee were questioned, the employee would not answer truthfully if she knew the real purpose of the questions. The attorney plans to question the employee and falsely tell her that she is not a suspect and that her answers to the questions will be held in confidence.

Is the attorney subject to discipline if she so questions the employee?

(A) Yes, because the attorney's conduct involves misrepresentation.

(B) Yes, because the attorney did not first advise the employee to obtain counsel.

(C) No, because no legal proceedings are now pending.

(D) No, because the attorney did not give legal advice to the employee.

Question 31.

A manufacturer sued a parts company for breach of warranty regarding machine components furnished by the parts company. A judge, who presided at the nonjury trial, sent her law clerk to the manufacturer's plant to observe the machine that was malfunctioning due to the allegedly defective parts. The clerk returned and told the judge that the machine was indeed malfunctioning and that one of the manufacturer's engineers had explained to the clerk how the parts delivered by the parts company caused the malfunction. There was testimony at the trial that supported what the clerk learned on his visit, although the engineer was not a witness. The judge rendered a judgment for the manufacturer.

Was the judge's conduct proper?

(A) Yes, because the judge's judgment was supported by evidence at the trial.

(B) Yes, because the judge has the right to gather facts concerning the trial.

(C) No, because the judge has engaged in ex parte contacts that might influence the outcome of litigation.

(D) No, because the engineer was not a witness at the trial and subject to cross-examination by the parts company.

Question 32.

When one of an attorney's regular clients planned to leave on a world tour, the client delivered to the attorney sufficient money to pay the client's property taxes when they became due. The attorney placed the money in her Clients' Trust Account. When the tax payment date arrived, the attorney was in need of a temporary loan to close the purchase of a new personal residence. Because the penalty for late payment of taxes was only 2 percent while the rate for a personal loan was 6 percent, the attorney withdrew the client's funds from the trust account to cover the attorney's personal check for the closing. The attorney was confident that the client would not object. Ten days later, after the receipt of a large fee previously earned, the attorney paid the client's property taxes and the 2 percent penalty, fully satisfying the client's tax obligation. After the client returned, the attorney told the client what she had done, and the client approved the attorney's conduct.

Is the attorney subject to discipline?

(A) Yes, because the attorney failed to pay the client the 10 days of interest at the fair market rate.

(B) Yes, because the attorney used the client's funds for a personal purpose.

(C) No, because the client was not harmed and the attorney reasonably believed at the time she withdrew the money that the client would not object.

(D) No, because when the attorney told the client what she had done, the client approved the attorney's conduct.

Question 33.

An attorney entered into a written retainer agreement with a defendant in a criminal case. The defendant agreed in writing to transfer title to the defendant's automobile to the attorney if the attorney successfully prevented him from going to prison. Later, the charges against the defendant were dismissed.

Is the attorney subject to discipline for entering into this retainer agreement?

(A) Yes, because the attorney agreed to a fee contingent on the outcome of a criminal case.

(B) Yes, because a lawyer may not acquire a proprietary interest in a client's property.

(C) No, because the charges against the defendant were dismissed.

(D) No, because the retainer agreement is in writing.

Question 34.

An attorney filed a complaint on behalf of her client against a corporation, alleging that the corporation had breached a valid oral contract entered into on the corporation's behalf by its president and chief executive officer. The attorney representing the corporation has filed an answer denying the contract and asserting the statute of frauds as a defense.

The corporation's attorney has given notice that he will take the deposition of the corporation's president on the grounds that he will be out of the country on the date the case is set for trial. The corporation's president is not a shareholder of the corporation. The attorney would like to interview the corporation's president prior to the taking of the deposition in order to better prepare her cross-examination.

Is the attorney subject to discipline if she interviews the corporation's president without the corporation's attorney's knowledge and consent?

(A) No, because the corporation president will not be personally liable to the corporation for damages in the event judgment is rendered against the corporation.

(B) No, because the corporation's president allegedly entered into the contract on behalf of the corporation.

(C) Yes, because the corporation's president is being called as an adverse witness.

(D) Yes, because the corporation's president is president of the corporation.

Question 35.

An attorney agreed to represent a client in a lawsuit. The attorney and the client executed the attorney's preprinted retainer form that provides, in part:

"The client agrees to pay promptly the attorney's fee for services. In addition, the client and the attorney agree to release each other from any and all liability arising from the representation. The client agrees that the attorney need not return the client's file prior to receiving the client's executed release. Upon full payment, the attorney will return the file to the client."

Although the attorney recommended that the client consult independent counsel before signing the retainer agreement, the client chose not to do so. The attorney reasonably believes that his fee is fair and that the quality of his work will be competent.

Is the attorney's retainer agreement with the client proper?

(A) Yes, because the attorney furnished consideration by agreeing to return the client's file.

(B) Yes, because the attorney reasonably believes that his fee is fair and that the quality of his work will be competent.

(C) No, because the attorney is attempting to limit his liability for malpractice.

(D) No, because the attorney uses a preprinted form for all retainers.

Question 36.

An attorney serves on a bar association committee established to counsel and rehabilitate lawyers who suffer from substance abuse. The day before the attorney was to leave on a fishing trip, the attorney's close friend, another attorney, disclosed to the attorney that, over the preceding two years, he had become heavily addicted to cocaine and was afraid he had committed criminal offenses in his banking activities as a result of his addiction. He then asked the attorney to represent him. The attorney agreed, but explained that he could do little for two weeks and would consult with his friend immediately upon his return. While on the fishing trip, an accountant who knew that the attorney was going to represent his friend told him that the accountant had been retained by the trust department of a commercial bank to audit several substantial trust accounts in which the bank and the attorney's friend are cotrustees. The accountant also told the attorney that the audit furnished incontrovertible proof that the attorney's friend had embezzled more than $100,000 from the trust accounts.

Must the attorney report his friend's embezzlement to the appropriate disciplinary authority?

(A) Yes, because the attorney learned of his friend's embezzlement from the accountant.

(B) Yes, because the attorney's failure to report would assist the concealment of his friend's breach of trust.

(C) No, because the attorney gained the information while representing his friend.

(D) No, because the information will probably be made public by the bank.

Question 37.

The following advertisement appeared in a daily newspaper in a state in which both parties are members of the bar:

A. ALPHA, M.D., J.D.

and

B. BETA, J.D.

Attorneys at Law

1000 "A" Street, City, State, 00000

Telephone (555) 555-5555

Are Alpha and Beta subject to discipline?

(A) No, because both law and medicine are licensed professions.

(B) No, because they possess the degree(s) stated.

(C) Yes, because the reference to the M.D. degree is self-laudatory.

(D) Yes, unless they limit their practice to areas in which a medical degree is relevant.

Question 38.

While working on a complex matter for her client, an attorney, a partner in a law firm, identified a particularly difficult issue of law that could prove decisive in the dispute. The attorney had not encountered this issue before and was uncertain of its effect. The attorney asked her partner for assistance. The attorney planned on including the consultation cost in her fee, and she did not identify the client to her partner.

Was it proper for the attorney to consult with her partner?

(A) No, because the total fee is increased by the consultation.

(B) No, because the client's consent was not previously obtained.

(C) Yes, because the attorney did not identify the client to her partner.

(D) Yes, because the attorney and her partner are partners in the same firm.

Question 39.

A state court judge has presided over the pretrial proceedings in a case involving a novel contract question under the Uniform Commercial Code.

During the pretrial proceedings, the judge has acquired considerable background knowledge of the facts and law of the matter and, therefore, is particularly well qualified to preside at the trial. Shortly before the trial date, the judge discovered that his brother owns a substantial block of stock in the defendant corporation. He determined that his brother's financial interests would be substantially affected by the outcome of the case.

Although the judge believed he would be impartial, he disclosed to the parties, on the record, his brother's interest.

Is it proper for the judge to hear the case?

(A) Yes, because the judge is particularly well qualified to preside at the trial.

(B) Yes, because the judge believes his judgment will not be affected by his brother's stockholding.

(C) No, because disqualification based on a relative's financial interest cannot be waived.

(D) No, because there have not yet been proceedings in which the judge did not participate, where all parties and their lawyers consent in writing that the judge may hear the case.

Question 40.

An attorney is representing a client on a charge of armed robbery. The client claims that the prosecution witness is mistaken in her identification. The client has produced a witness who will testify that the client was in another city 500 miles away when the robbery occurred. The attorney knows that the witness is lying, but the client insists that the witness be called on the client's behalf. The attorney is not planning on relying on the alibi defense in her argument before the jury.

Is the attorney subject to discipline if she calls the witness?

(A) Yes, because before calling the witness, the attorney did not inform the court of her belief.

(B) Yes, because the attorney knows the witness will be testifying falsely.

(C) No, because the attorney will not rely on the alibi defense in her argument before the jury.

(D) No, because the client has insisted that the witness be called as a witness on the client's behalf.

Question 41.

A recently graduated attorney began a plaintiffs' personal injury practice, but was having a difficult time attracting clients. The attorney hired an advertising agency to prepare a television commercial in which the attorney appeared to be arguing a case before a jury. In the commercial, the jury brought back a large award for the attorney's client. The voice-over stated that results would vary depending upon particular legal and factual circumstances. The attorney's only experience at the time the commercial was filmed was in moot court. As a result of airing the commercial, the attorney received several significant cases.

Is the attorney subject to discipline?

(A) Yes, because the commercial created an unjustified expectation about the results that could be achieved in court.

(B) Yes, because the commercial implied that the attorney had success-fully argued a case to a jury.

(C) No, because commercial speech is protected under the First Amendment.

(D) No, because the commercial contained an express disclaimer about the results a client could expect.

Question 42.

The state bar association has offered a judge and her spouse free transportation and lodging to attend its institute on judicial reform. The judge is expected to deliver a banquet speech. Members of the bar association regularly appear in the judge's court. The value of the transportation and lodging is less than $500.

Is it proper for the judge to accept this offer?

(A) Yes, because the value of the transportation and lodging does not exceed $500.

(B) Yes, because the activity is devoted to the improvement of law.

(C) No, because members of the bar association regularly appear in the judge's court.

(D) No, because the bar association is offering free transportation to the judge's spouse.

Question 43.

An attorney regularly appears before a trial court judge who is running for reelection in six months. Over the past year, the attorney has noticed that the judge has become increasingly ill tempered on the bench. Not only is the judge abrupt and critical of lawyers appearing before him, he is also rude and abusive to litigants. On more than one occasion, the judge has thrown his gavel across the courtroom in a fit of temper. The judge's conduct on the bench is often the subject of discussion whenever a group of lawyers meets. Some lawyers are automatically filing requests for judicial substitution whenever a case in which they are to appear is assigned to the judge.

The attorney discussed the matter with her law partners, who rarely make court appearances. The attorney's law partners suggested that she also file a request for judicial substitution whenever one of her cases is assigned to the judge. In addition, the attorney and her law partners discussed the possibility of reporting the judge to the appropriate disciplinary authority but are concerned that this would alienate the other judges to whom their cases are assigned. The attorney has reluctantly started filing for substitution of the judge in every one of her cases to which the judge is assigned, but she has taken no further action.

Is the attorney subject to discipline?

(A) Yes, because the attorney failed to inform the appropriate authorities about the judge's conduct.

(B) Yes, because, by filing automatic requests for substitution of the judge, the attorney undermined public confidence in the administration of justice.

(C) No, because the attorney has a duty to represent her clients zealously.

(D) No, because the judge is running for reelection and may not be reelected.

Question 44.

Leaving an airport, an attorney who primarily practices criminal law shared a cab with a medical doctor. The cab was involved in a collision, and the doctor was seriously injured, while the attorney was only shaken up. The attorney accompanied the doctor to the hospital in the ambulance. The doctor believed that she was dying and asked the attorney to prepare a simple will for her. The attorney told the doctor, "I have never prepared a will, but hope that I can remember the basics from law school." The attorney then complied with the doctor's request. The doctor signed the will, and the two paramedics in the ambulance signed as witnesses. The will was ultimately found valid.

Was it proper for the attorney to prepare the will?

(A) Yes, because the attorney did not omit some required formality that rendered the will invalid.

(B) Yes, because the attorney provided legal services that were reasonably necessary under the circumstances.

(C) No, because the doctor did not waive the attorney's malpractice liability.

(D) No, because the attorney did not have the skill required for the representation.

Question 45.

An attorney has recently started her own law firm with four other lawyers as associates. The law firm has moved into offices in a new building which is owned by a bank. The attorney has borrowed heavily from the bank to finance her new law firm. In addition, the bank provides the law firm with accounting services through its computer.

At the bank's suggestion, an employee of the bank, who is not a lawyer, serves as a part-time office manager for the law firm without compensation from the firm. The duties of the office manager are to advise the firm generally on fees and time charges, program matters for the computer services, and consult with the attorney on accounting and billing practices to ensure solvency. The attorney and the bank do not discuss client confidences.

Is the arrangement with the bank proper?

(A) Yes, because secrets or confidences of clients will not be disclosed to the bank.

(B) Yes, because the office manager is paid by the bank.

(C) No, because a nonlawyer will be advising the law firm on fees and time charges.

(D) No, because the bank will be involved in the practice of law.

Question 46.

An attorney is representing the plaintiff in a personal injury case, on a contingent fee basis. The client is without resources to pay for the expenses of the investigation and the medical examinations necessary to prepare for trial. The client asked the attorney to pay for these expenses. The attorney declined to advance the funds but offered to guarantee the client's promissory note to a local bank in order to secure the funds needed to cover those expenses. The client has agreed to reimburse the attorney in the event the attorney incurs liability on the guaranty.

Is the attorney subject to discipline if she guarantees the client's promissory note?

(A) Yes, because the attorney is lending her credit to the client.

(B) Yes, because the attorney is helping to finance litigation.

(C) No, because the funds will be used for trial preparation.

(D) No, because the attorney took the case on a contingent fee basis.

Question 47.

An attorney represents a defendant in an action for personal injuries. The attorney, pursuant to the defendant's authorization, made an offer of settlement to the attorney who represents the plaintiff. The plaintiff's attorney has not responded to the offer, and the attorney is convinced that the plaintiff's attorney has not communicated the offer to the plaintiff. State law authorizes a defendant to move for a settlement conference and to tender an offer of settlement. If such a motion is made and the offer is rejected by the plaintiff and the eventual judgment does not exceed the amount of the offer, the plaintiff must bear all costs of litigation, including reasonable fees, as determined by the court, for the defendant's counsel.

The attorney, with the defendant's consent, filed a motion requesting a settlement conference, tendered an offer to settle for $25,000, and served copies of the motion and tender on the plaintiff's attorney and on the plaintiff personally.

Is the attorney subject to discipline for serving the plaintiff with a copy of the motion and tender?

(A) Yes, because service of copies of the motion and tender on the plaintiff were not authorized by statute or rule of court.

(B) Yes, because the attorney did not first inform the plaintiff's attorney of the attorney's intention to serve copies of the motion and tender on the plaintiff.

(C) No, because the decision to accept or reject a settlement offer rests with the client.

(D) No, because the motion and tender became public documents when they were filed in court.

Question 48.

An attorney represents a wife in a marriage dissolution proceeding that involves bitterly contested issues of property division and child custody. After one day of trial, the husband, through his attorney, made a settlement offer. Because of the husband's intense dislike for the attorney, the proposed settlement requires that the attorney agree not to represent the wife in any subsequent proceeding, brought by either party, to modify or enforce the provisions of the decree. The wife wants to accept the offer, and the attorney believes that the settlement offer made by the husband is better than any award the wife would get if the case went to judgment. Although the attorney thought it was in the wife's best interest to accept the offer, he was concerned that another attorney may not be able to adequately protect the wife's interests in the future.

Is it proper for the attorney to agree that he will not represent the wife in any subsequent proceeding?

(A) Yes, because the restriction on the attorney is limited to subsequent proceedings in the same matter.

(B) Yes, because the attorney believes that it is in the wife's best interests to accept the proposed settlement.

(C) No, because the proposed settlement would restrict the attorney's right to represent the wife in the future.

(D) No, because the attorney did not believe that the wife's interests can be adequately protected by another lawyer in the future.

Question 49.

A company's president telephoned his city's best-known employment attorney and asked her to represent the company in a dispute that had just arisen with the company's chief financial officer. The attorney, who had never previously represented the company, agreed. At the president's insistence, she immediately commenced the representation. A few days later, during a meeting with the president, the attorney first revealed the amount of her customary hourly fee and then explained that the company would also be responsible for reimbursing her expenses. The president responded that her fee was higher than he had expected but that he would be happy for the company to pay it, given her excellent work to date. Although the attorney intended to follow up with a confirming letter, she never did so. For several more months, she assisted the company in resolving its employment dispute. Afterward, she sent the company a bill accurately reflecting her hourly fee and expenses, which were reasonable.

Is the attorney subject to discipline?

(A) Yes, because she did not disclose the basis of her fee before commencing the representation.

(B) Yes, because she did not confirm her fee agreement in writing.

(C) No, because she disclosed the basis of her fee within a reasonable time after commencing the representation.

(D) No, because she was not required to advise the client of her customary hourly fee, unless requested to do so.

Question 50.

In the attorney's closing statement to the court in a bench trial, the attorney said,

> "Your honor, I drive on the street in question every day and I know that a driver cannot see cars backing out of driveways as the one did in this case. I believe that my client was not negligent, and I ask you to so find."

The attorney was not trying to deceive the court with his statement. There was no other evidence in the record regarding the facts asserted by the attorney.

Was the attorney's closing argument proper?

(A) Yes, because the attorney was speaking truthfully and not trying to deceive the court.

(B) Yes, because the rules of evidence are very liberal when the trial is before a judge without a jury.

(C) No, because the attorney asserted her personal knowledge of facts in issue.

(D) No, because there is no other evidence in the record about the facts asserted by the attorney.

Question 51.

A plaintiff who is not a lawyer is representing himself in small claims court in an action to recover his security deposit from his former landlord. The plaintiff told an attorney, a close friend who lived near him, about this case, but did not ask the attorney for any advice. The attorney said,

> "I'll give you some free advice. It would help your case if the new tenants would testify that the apartment was in good shape when they

moved in, and, contrary to the allegations of your former landlord, it was not, in fact, repainted for them."

The plaintiff followed the attorney's advice and won his case.

Is the attorney subject to discipline for assisting the plaintiff in preparing for his court appearance?

(A) Yes, because the attorney assisted the plaintiff in the practice of law.

(B) Yes, because the attorney offered unsolicited, in-person legal advice.

(C) No, because the plaintiff was representing himself in the proceedings.

(D) No, because the attorney was not compensated for his advice.

Question 52.

An attorney is defending a client who has been indicted for burglary. During an interview, the client stated to the attorney that before he had consulted the attorney, the client had committed perjury while testifying before the grand jury that indicted him.

The attorney is subject to discipline if she:

(A) continues to represent the client.

(B) continues to represent the client unless he admits his perjury.

(C) does not inform the authorities of the perjury.

(D) informs the authorities of the perjury.

Question 53.

Attorney Alpha, a sole practitioner, recently suffered a heart attack and was advised that she could not return to work for six months. Alpha delivered all of her clients' files to Attorney Beta, who is also a sole practitioner. Beta agreed to review each client's file promptly, take any action necessary to protect each client's interests, and treat the information in the files as confidential. Alpha then wrote her clients, advising each client that the client's file had been delivered to Beta for review and for any action necessary to protect the client's interest, and that the client was free to select another lawyer.

Alpha knows that Beta is a competent attorney. Beta did not accept the file of any person whose interests were, or could be, adverse to the interests of any of Beta's own clients.

Was it proper for Alpha to deliver the files to Beta for review?

(A) Yes, because Alpha knows that Beta is competent to protect the clients' interests.

(B) Yes, because Beta agreed to treat the information in the files as confidential.

(C) Yes, because given her medical condition, Alpha's delivery of the files was necessary to protect the clients' interests.

(D) No, because Alpha did not obtain the prior consent of each client whose file was delivered to Beta.

Question 54.

A judge has recently resigned from the state trial court bench. When she was a judge, she supervised activity in cases pending before another judge while he was on vacation. In one pending case, she entered an administrative order changing the courtroom in which a particular case was to be tried. After trial and appeal, the case was remanded for a new trial. The plaintiff in that case decided to change lawyers and has asked the recently resigned judge to try the case.

Will the judge be subject to discipline if she tries this case on behalf of the plaintiff?

(A) Yes, because the judge acted officially as a judge with respect to an aspect of the case.

(B) Yes, because the judge would try the case before a judge of the court on which she previously sat.

(C) No, because the judge did not act as a judge with respect to a substantial matter in or the merits of the case.

(D) No, because any information that the judge learned about the case while acting as a judge was a matter of public record.

Question 55.

An attorney decided to obtain a master's degree in taxation, but lacked the funds required for tuition and expenses. The attorney consulted one of his clients, a wealthy banker, for advice about obtaining a loan. To the attorney's surprise, the client offered the attorney a personal loan of $10,000. The attorney told the client that he would prepare the required note without charge.

Without further consultation with the client, the attorney prepared and signed a promissory note bearing interest at the current bank rate. The note provided for repayment in the form of legal services to be rendered by the attorney to the client without charge until the value of the attorney's services equaled the principal and interest due. The note further provided that if the client died before the note was fully repaid, any remaining principal and interest would be forgiven as a gift.

The attorney mailed the executed note to the client with a transmittal letter encouraging the client to look it over and call with any questions. The client accepted the note and sent the attorney a personal check for $10,000, which the attorney used to obtain his master's degree. A month after the degree was awarded, the client was killed in a car accident. The attorney had not rendered any legal services to the client from the date of the note's execution to the date of the client's death. Thereafter, in an action brought by the client's estate to recover on the note, the court ruled that the note was discharged as a gift.

Was the attorney's conduct proper?

(A) Yes, because the client, without being requested by the attorney to do so, voluntarily made the loan.

(B) Yes, because the court ruled that the note had been discharged as a gift.

(C) No, because a lawyer may never accept a loan from a client.

(D) No, because the attorney did not comply with the requirements for entering into a business transaction with a client.

Question 56.

An attorney served as a state congressman immediately prior to reopening his law office in the state. The attorney printed and mailed an announcement of his return to private practice to members of the bar, persons who had previously been his clients, and personal friends whom he had never represented. The printed announcement stated that the attorney had reopened his law office, gave his address and telephone number, and added that he had recently served as a state congressman.

Is the attorney subject to discipline for the announcement?

(A) Yes, because it was mailed to persons who had not been his clients.

(B) Yes, because his service as a congressman is unrelated to his ability as a lawyer.

(C) No, because the information in the announcement is true.

(D) No, because all of the information was already in the public domain.

Question 57.

An attorney placed an associate, recently admitted to the bar, in complete charge of the work of the paralegals in the attorney's office. That work consisted of searching titles to real property, an area in which the associate had no familiarity. The attorney instructed the associate to review the searches prepared by the paralegals, and thereafter to sign the attorney's name to the required certifications of title if the associate was satisfied that the search accurately reflected the condition of the title. This arrangement enabled the attorney to lower office operating expenses. The attorney told the associate that the associate should resolve any legal questions that might arise and not to bother the attorney because the attorney was too busy handling major litigation.

Is it proper for the attorney to assign the associate this responsibility?

(A) Yes, because the paralegals are experienced in searching titles.

(B) Yes, because the attorney is ultimately liable for the accuracy of the title searches.

(C) Yes, because it enables the attorney to charge lower fees for title certification.

(D) No, because the attorney is not adequately supervising the work of the associate.

Question 58.

A law firm agreed to represent a client in various business matters. The written retainer agreement called for the client to pay hourly rates of $180 per hour for a partner's time and $110 per hour for an associate's time. The representation proceeded and the firm submitted monthly bills, which the client paid promptly, After two years, the firm decided to increase their hourly rates by $10. The firm thereafter billed the client at their new rates, but did not specifically inform the client of the increase. The client continued to pay monthly bills promptly.

Are the firm's partners subject to discipline?

(A) Yes, because the entire original fee agreement was required to be in writing.

(B) Yes, because the client did not consent to the increase.

(C) No, because the $10 hourly increase is reasonable.

(D) No, because the client agreed in writing to pay the firm's hourly rate.

Question 59.

A sole practitioner was appointed to represent a criminal defendant on appeal. A recently admitted lawyer who shared office space with the sole practitioner agreed to write the brief if the sole practitioner would pay him one-half of the statutory fee. The defendant agreed to the arrangement in writing, after full consultation. The recently admitted lawyer entered an appearance as co-counsel for the defendant and, with the sole practitioner's knowledge, applied for and received several extensions of time to file the brief. Subsequently, the appellate court dismissed the appeal for failure to pursue the appeal. A third lawyer was later appointed to represent the defendant, whose conviction was affirmed after the appeal was reinstated.

Is the sole practitioner subject to discipline?

(A) Yes, because he neglected the defendant's case.

(B) Yes, because he shared fees with the recently admitted lawyer.

(C) No, because the defendant agreed in writing to the co-counsel arrangement.

(D) No, because the affirmance by the appellate court indicated that the defendant's appeal was without merit.

Question 60.

An attorney's standard retainer contract in divorce cases provides for the payment of a fee of one-third of the amount of alimony or property settlement secured by the attorney. The attorney declines to represent clients who do not agree to this arrangement.

Is the attorney's standard retainer contract proper?

(A) Yes, because clients often prefer to pay a lawyer a fee based on the outcome of the case.

(B) Yes, if a fee of one-third is not excessive.

(C) No, because a lawyer may not acquire a proprietary interest in a cause of action.

(D) No, because the fee is contingent.

2. Practice MPRE 2

Question 1.

An attorney was retained to represent the client in defense of an action brought against the client by a plaintiff. In order to obtain ample time for settlement negotiations, the attorney immediately requested and obtained from opposing counsel a stipulation extending the client's time to answer the complaint until 10 days after receipt of written demand from the plaintiff's attorney. Four months later, no settlement had been reached, and on May 1, the plaintiff's attorney wrote to the attorney demanding that an answer be filed within 10 days. When no answer was filed by May 15, the plaintiff's attorney had a default judgment entered in favor of the plaintiff.

The attorney was away on a two-month vacation when the plaintiff's attorney's letter was received in her office. When the attorney returned on June 15, she promptly moved to have the default set aside and her motion was granted.

Is the attorney subject to discipline?

(A) Yes, because she did not make restitution to the client for any loss sustained by the client.

(B) Yes, because she did not make provision for the handling of her pending cases while she was away.

(C) No, because the default judgment was set aside.

(D) No, because she did not know that the plaintiff's attorney had demanded that an answer be filed within 10 days.

Question 2.

An attorney represented a plaintiff in an action against a manufacturer of a drain cleaner. The plaintiff's complaint alleged that the manufacturer's product exploded in use and caused her serious and permanent injuries. The jury agreed and awarded the plaintiff $5,000,000 in actual damages and an additional $5,000,000 in punitive damages. The manufacturer paid the judgment.

The attorney made this recovery the cornerstone of an aggressive television advertising campaign for his law practice. In those ads, a voice-over discussed the $10,000,000 recovery obtained in the plaintiff's case. The plaintiff praised the attorney's legal skills in an on-camera statement, saying that no one would work harder on a case than the attorney.

The plaintiff prepared her on-camera statement in response to the attorney's request, but without any further involvement by the attorney, and she believed it to be entirely true.

Is the attorney subject to discipline for using the television advertisement described above?

(A) Yes, because the advertisement is likely to create an unjustified expectation about the results the attorney will be able to achieve and is therefore misleading.

(B) Yes, because the attorney's advertisement contains a client testimonial.

(C) No, because the plaintiff prepared the entire statement without any involvement by the attorney.

(D) No, because the result obtained in the plaintiff's case was reported accurately, and the plaintiff believed that everything she said about the attorney was true.

Question 3.

A corporation hired a law firm to handle all of its corporate work. The firm had not previously represented a corporation on an ongoing basis, but decided that it wanted to attract additional corporate clients. Accordingly, the partners handling the corporation's work began a practice of giving to all lawyers in the firm, on a monthly basis, detailed descriptions of the work they were doing for the corporation for the purpose of illustrating what the firm could do for corporate clients. One of the partners mentioned this practice to the corporation's management, and the corporation complained that its confidences had been violated.

Was it proper for the partners to give detailed descriptions of the work being done for the corporation to other lawyers in the firm?

(A) Yes, because, absent client instructions to the contrary, lawyers may discuss client information with other lawyers in the firm.

(B) Yes, because lawyers may discuss client information with other lawyers in the firm, regardless of client instructions to the contrary, so long as the disclosure does not disadvantage the client.

(C) No, because sharing the information increased the risk that it might be improperly disclosed to third parties outside the firm.

(D) No, because lawyers may not disclose client information, even to other firm lawyers, unless the disclosure is in furtherance of the representation.

Question 4.

An attorney has been representing the client in a matter in litigation. During protracted pretrial proceedings, the client complained bitterly about the time and expense involved and insisted that the attorney take steps to terminate the pretrial proceedings. The attorney believes that to do so would jeopardize the client's interests and has so informed the client. The attorney believes that the case cannot be adequately prepared for trial without further pretrial proceedings that will require an additional six months' delay and involve further expense. The client insists that the attorney forgo any further pretrial proceedings and set the case for trial at the earliest available date. There are several other competent lawyers who are willing to undertake the representation.

Is it proper for the attorney to ask leave of the court to withdraw?

(A) Yes, because a lawyer may discontinue representation in a civil case at any time before trial.

(B) Yes, because the client's conduct makes it unreasonably difficult for the attorney to represent the client effectively and competently.

(C) No, because the attorney must follow the client's instructions.

(D) No, because the client did not consent to the attorney's withdrawal.

Question 5.

The judicial district in which a judge sits has a rule that allows litigants two postponements as a matter of right. After that, a litigant who moves for a postponement must convince the presiding judge that a postponement is appropriate. The judge routinely grants additional postponements because, in her view,

"What harm is done if one of the litigants wants a postponement? The worst that can happen is that the parties have more time to negotiate and thus are more likely to settle."

Are the judge's actions proper?

(A) Yes, because the judge is exercising her judicial discretion.

(B) Yes, because a party objecting to a postponement can seek appellate review.

(C) No, because judges have no official obligation to encourage private settlements.

(D) No, because the judge should expedite the determination of matters before her.

Question 6.

A trial court judge had instructed his court clerk and his secretary that one of them should be present in the office during working hours to answer the telephone. One day, however, the secretary was out sick. The judge was in his office when his court clerk was at lunch, and when the telephone rang, the judge answered it. The call was from a lawyer in a case presently pending before the judge. The lawyer was calling to attempt to reschedule a pretrial conference set for the next day because of a sudden family emergency. The lawyer had tried to call opposing counsel on the case, but she was not answering his calls. The judge agreed to reschedule the pretrial conference for the following week. When the judge's court clerk returned from lunch, the judge instructed the clerk to contact opposing counsel to inform her of the telephone call and the fact that the pretrial conference had been rescheduled.

Did the judge act properly?

(A) No, because the judge participated in an ex parte communication.

(B) No, because there was still time for the calling lawyer to notify opposing counsel in order to reach agreement on rescheduling the pretrial conference.

(C) Yes, because the ex parte communication was for scheduling purposes only and did not deal with substantive matters or issues.

(D) Yes, because there was no one else in the office to take the lawyer's call.

Question 7.

An attorney, who had represented a client for many years, prepared the client's will and acted as one of the two subscribing witnesses to its execution. The client's sister and brother were his sole heirs. The will left the client's entire estate to his sister and nothing to his brother. Upon the client's death two years later the executor named in the will asked the attorney to act as his lawyer in the probate of the will and the administration of the estate. At that time, the executor informed the attorney that the client's brother would concede that the will was properly executed but intended to contest the will on the ground that he had been excluded because of fraud previously practiced on the client by the client's sister. The other subscribing witness to the will predeceased the client, and the attorney will be called as a witness solely for the purpose of establishing the due execution of the will.

Is it proper for the attorney to accept the representation?

(A) Yes, because there is no contested issue of fact with respect to the formal execution of the will.

(B) Yes, because the executor has no beneficial interest under the will.

(C) No, because the attorney's services are not necessary to avoid substantial hardship to the executor.

(D) No, because the attorney will be called as a witness in the case.

Question 8.

An attorney has been retained to defend an adult charged with a sex offense involving a minor. The attorney believes that, in order to win the case, she must keep parents of minor children off the jury. The attorney instructed her investigator as follows:

> "Visit the neighborhood of those prospective jurors on the panel with minor children. Ask the neighbors if they know of any kind of unusual sex activity of the prospective juror or any member of the family. This talk will get back to the prospective jurors, and they will think of excuses not to serve. But don't under any circumstances talk directly with any prospective juror or member of the family."

Many of the prospective jurors investigated were, in fact, selected to serve on the jury.

Is the attorney subject to discipline for so instructing her investigator?

(A) Yes, because the prospective jurors investigated were, in fact, selected to serve on the jury in the case.

(B) Yes, because the investigation is intended to harass prospective jurors and members of their families.

(C) No, because the matters inquired into might be relevant to a prospective juror's qualifications to serve in the case.

(D) No, because no prospective juror was directly contacted.

Question 9.

A client telephoned an attorney who had previously represented him. The client described a problem on which he needed advice and made an appointment for the following week to discuss the matter with the attorney. Prior to the appointment, the attorney performed five hours of preliminary research on the client's problem. At the end of the appointment the client agreed that the attorney should pursue the matter and agreed to a fee of $100 per hour. The client then gave the attorney a check for $5,000 to cover the five hours already worked and as an advance on additional fees and expenses.

The attorney gave the check to the office bookkeeper with directions to deposit the check into the client trust account and immediately transfer $3,000 to the general office account to cover the five hours of research already conducted plus the 25 additional hours she would spend on the matter the following week. At that time, the attorney reasonably believed that she would spend 25 additional hours on the case.

The bookkeeper followed these directions. The next week, the attorney worked diligently on the matter for 23 hours. Reasonably believing that no significant work remained to be done on the matter, the attorney directed the bookkeeper to transfer $200 from the general office account to the client trust account. The attorney then called the client and made an appointment to discuss the status of the matter.

Is the attorney subject to discipline?

(A) Yes, because the attorney accepted legal fees in advance of performing the work.

(B) Yes, because the attorney transferred funds for unearned fees to the general office account.

(C) No, because the attorney transferred the $200 owed to the client from the general office account to the client trust account.

(D) No, because the attorney reasonably believed that she would spend 25 additional hours on the case.

Question 10.

An attorney represented a plaintiff in an action against several defendants. The retainer agreement provided that the plaintiff would pay all costs and expenses of litigation and would, on demand, reimburse the attorney for any costs or expenses advanced by the attorney. After serving process on two defendants, the attorney had difficulty locating and serving the remaining defendants. The plaintiff approved the hiring of an investigator to locate and serve the defendants, and the attorney advanced the costs for the investigator. When the attorney asked the plaintiff for reimbursement, the plaintiff refused to pay. The attorney then told the plaintiff that the attorney would do no more work on the case until the attorney was reimbursed for the amount advanced.

Thereafter, one of the defendants filed a counterclaim that required a responsive pleading within 30 days. Because the attorney had not been paid, the attorney permitted the time to respond to the counterclaim to expire without filing a responsive pleading, and a default was entered on the counterclaim. Later, the plaintiff reimbursed the attorney for the costs the attorney had advanced, and the attorney was successful in having the default on the counterclaim set aside. The case was tried, and the plaintiff prevailed on the plaintiff's complaint, and the counterclaimant recovered nothing.

Is the attorney subject to discipline for not initially filing a responsive pleading to the counterclaim?

(A) Yes, because the attorney neglected the plaintiff's cause.

(B) Yes, because the attorney had not asked leave of court to withdraw.

(C) No, because the plaintiff breached the agreement to reimburse the attorney.

(D) No, because the plaintiff did not sustain any prejudice as a result of the attorney's action.

Question 11.

A judge, prior to her recent appointment to the federal court, had been an outspoken and effective opponent of the racial segregation policies of a foreign country's government. As part of its worldwide tour, that country's national soccer team scheduled a soccer match with a team in this country. Several civil rights groups have applied to the judge for an order enjoining the playing of the proposed match. The matter is now pending. Only legal issues are presented. The judge, after painstaking consideration, has privately concluded that she cannot decide the legal questions without bias against the representatives of the country's government. However, no one has made a motion to disqualify the judge. The judge does not believe she has any greater expertise in racial matters than other judges on the court.

Must the judge recuse herself in the pending matter?

(A) Yes, because the judge does not believe she has greater expertise than other judges on the court in legal issues involving racial segregation.

(B) Yes, because the judge believes that she cannot be impartial.

(C) No, because the only issues presented for decision are legal questions.

(D) No, because none of the interested parties has moved to disqualify the judge.

Question 12.

An attorney agreed to represent a plaintiff in a personal injury matter. The original agreement between the attorney and the plaintiff specified a 30 percent contingent fee, which was a reasonable fee for the type of cases the attorney handled. One year into the litigation, the attorney noted that he was extremely busy and that many potential clients sought his services. As a result, the attorney raised his standard fee to a 35 percent contingent fee, which was also a reasonable fee. The attorney's agreement with the plaintiff was silent on the possibility of a fee increase. He approached the plaintiff and proposed that she agree to modify the contingent fee percentage from 30 percent to 35 percent. The attorney informed the plaintiff that if she did not agree, the attorney would find her another experienced personal injury lawyer at the original fee, but that the attorney was unwilling to continue the representation unless the fee was modified. The plaintiff reluctantly agreed to modify the fee agreement as the attorney proposed.

Subsequently, the plaintiff's case was settled. The plaintiff, however, refused to pay the attorney more than a 30 percent contingent fee, and the attorney sued the plaintiff to recover under the modified fee agreement.

Is the attorney likely to prevail?

(A) Yes, because the attorney offered to find the plaintiff another experienced personal injury lawyer at the original rate.

(B) Yes, because a contingent fee of 35 percent constituted a reasonable fee.

(C) No, because the attorney did not suggest that the plaintiff seek the advice of independent counsel before accepting the increased fee.

(D) No, because there were no special circumstances justifying the attorney's insistence on a fee increase.

Question 13.

A member of the bar is a candidate for judicial office in an election. The candidate personally asked several of his friends to contribute $1,000 each to kick off his campaign. After the candidate's friends made the contributions, the candidate, who was elated by the support, formed a committee to collect more contributions. The committee does not include lawyers likely to practice before the candidate. The candidate then turned over the contributions to the committee and began campaigning in earnest.

Is the candidate subject to discipline?

(A) No, because the candidate turned over the funds to his committee.

(B) No, because the committee does not include lawyers likely to practice before the candidate.

(C) Yes, because at least one of the original contributors was a lawyer.

(D) Yes, because the candidate personally solicited funds.

Question 14.

An attorney was hired to file a lawsuit against the client's former employer, a corporation, for wrongful discharge. The attorney filed the suit in federal district court based upon three grounds. It turned out that a unanimous U.S. Supreme Court decision had recently eliminated the third ground as a theory available to plaintiffs in wrongful discharge cases. The corporation filed a motion alleging that the complaint was based upon a theory (the third ground) that is no longer supported by existing law and cited the new decision. Within 10 days after the filing of the complaint, the attorney withdrew the third ground and continued with the litigation.

Is the attorney subject to litigation sanction?

(A) Yes, because the attorney did not discuss the adverse legal authority with the client before filing the complaint.

(B) Yes, because the client should have cited the U.S. Supreme Court decision in the complaint.

(C) No, because the attorney withdrew the third ground within 10 days after filing the complaint.

(D) No, because the attorney did not know or should not have known of the recent decision when the complaint was filed.

Question 15.

Although licensed to practice law in the state, an attorney does not practice law but works as an investment broker. The attorney could have elected inactive status as a member of the bar, but chose not to do so. Recently, in connection with a sale of worthless securities, the attorney made materially false representations to an investment customer.

The customer sued the attorney for civil fraud, and a jury returned a verdict in the customer's favor. The attorney did not appeal. The standard of proof in the state was not the same in lawyer disciplinary cases and civil cases.

Is the attorney subject to discipline?

(A) Yes, because the attorney was pursuing a nonlegal occupation while an active member of the bar.

(B) Yes, because the attorney's conduct was fraudulent.

(C) No, because the attorney was not convicted of a crime.

(D) No, because the standard of proof in the state was not the same in lawyer disciplinary cases and civil cases.

Question 16.

A client was an experienced oil and gas developer. The client asked an attorney for representation in a suit to establish the client's ownership of certain oil and gas royalties. The client did not have available the necessary funds to pay the attorney's reasonable hourly rate for undertaking the case. The client proposed instead to pay the attorney an amount in cash equal to 20 percent of the value of the proceeds received from the first year royalties the client might recover as a result of the suit. The attorney accepted the proposal and took the case. The fee will likely not exceed the fee the attorney would have earned from his hourly rate.

Is the attorney subject to discipline?

(A) Yes, because the agreement gave the attorney a proprietary interest in the client's cause of action.

(B) Yes, because the fee the attorney receives will likely exceed that which the attorney would have received by charging a reasonable hourly rate.

(C) No, because the client rather than the attorney proposed the fee arrangement.

(D) No, because the attorney may contract with the client for a reasonable contingent fee.

Question 17.

An attorney has been hired by a client to represent the client in a civil commitment proceeding initiated by the state. The client is now undergoing psychiatric evaluation to determine whether civil commitment should be ordered. The client told the attorney that the client intends to commit suicide as soon as the tests are completed, and the attorney believes that the client will carry out this threat. Suicide and attempted suicide are crimes in the state.

Is it proper for the attorney to disclose the client's intentions to the authorities?

(A) Yes, because the information concerns a future crime and is not protected by the attorney-client evidentiary privilege.

(B) Yes, because the information concerns a future crime that is likely to result in the client's imminent death.

(C) No, because the attorney does not know whether the client has attempted suicide in the past.

(D) No, because disclosure would aid the state in its civil commitment case against the client.

Question 18.

An attorney is a long-time member of the state legislature and serves on the legislative budget committee that funds the local trial courts in the state. The attorney also maintains a part-time law practice as is permitted in the state. An influential businessperson who regularly makes significant contributions to the attorney's political campaigns asked the attorney to help his uncle, who was involved in a bitter divorce. The attorney called the trial judge sitting on the uncle's case, a personal friend of the attorney. In discussing some upcoming votes of the budget committee with the judge, the attorney mentioned that the uncle was the type of solid citizen and influential person who could help garner support for the budget and thus ensure the economic health of the judicial system. The trial judge ultimately ruled in the uncle's favor.

Is the attorney subject to discipline?

(A) Yes, because the trial judge ruled in the uncle's favor.

(B) Yes, because the attorney used her public position to attempt to influence a tribunal in a pending matter.

(C) No, because the attorney called the trial judge in her capacity as a legislator and not as the uncle's lawyer.

(D) No, because members of the state legislature are permitted by law to engage in part-time legal practice.

Question 19.

A judge in a criminal trial court of the state wishes to serve as guardian of her father, who has been declared incompetent. Accepting the responsibilities of the position would not interfere with the performance of the judge's official duties. Although the position in all likelihood would not involve contested litigation, it would be necessary for the judge to prepare and sign various pleadings, motions, and other papers and to appear in civil court on her father's behalf.

Would it be proper for the judge to undertake this guardianship?

(A) Yes, because the judge does not receive compensation for her services as guardian.

(B) Yes, because the position involves a close family member and will not interfere with the judge's performance of her judicial duties.

(C) No, because the position will require the judge to appear in court.

(D) No, because the position will require the judge to prepare and sign pleadings, motions, and other papers.

Question 20.

An attorney represents a corporation that is a defendant in a product liability case. An engineer who is a corporation employee and nearing retirement was likely to be a key witness in the case, as she had been in charge of all of the corporation's product safety testing during the relevant period. The engineer had been very critical of the corporation's safety testing procedures during that period and had repeatedly complained that the product at issue had not been adequately tested. The engineer's views were reduced to writing and were well known to many employees of the corporation. Because of the early stage of the case, however, plaintiff's counsel was not yet aware of the engineer's existence or her views.

Aware of the engineer's views, the attorney approached the corporation's officials and recommended that it offer the engineer a special package of severance benefits if she would retire immediately and move to the Bahamas. The attorney believed that if the engineer accepted this offer, she would be beyond the subpoena power of the court in which the suit against the corporation was pending. The corporation adopted the attorney's recommendation and made the offer. The engineer accepted it. The attorney did not disclose the engineer's identity to plaintiff's counsel.

Is the attorney subject to discipline?

(A) Yes, because the attorney caused the engineer to leave the jurisdiction of the court for the purpose of making her unavailable as a witness.

(B) Yes, because opposing counsel had not yet had a reasonable opportunity to learn of the engineer's views.

(C) No, because the engineer's views were reduced to writing and are well known to many other employees of the corporation.

(D) No, because there was no pending request for the engineer's testimony at the time the retirement offer was made to the engineer.

Question 21.

An attorney represented a client in a personal injury action against the driver of the car in which the client was injured while a passenger. The personal injury action was settled, and the attorney received a check in the amount of $10,000 payable to the attorney. The attorney deposited the check in her Clients' Trust Account.

One day later, the attorney received a letter from a bank that had heard of the settlement of the personal injury lawsuit. The bank informed the attorney that the client had failed to make his monthly mortgage payments for the last three months and demanded that the attorney immediately release $900 of the proceeds of the settlement to the bank or the bank would institute mortgage foreclosure proceedings against the client. The attorney informed the client of the bank's letter. The client responded:

"I don't care what the bank does. The property is essentially worthless, so let the bank foreclose. If the bank wants to sue me, I'll be easy enough to find. I don't think they'll even bother. You just take your legal fees and turn the rest of the proceeds over to me."

Is the attorney subject to discipline if she follows the client's instructions?

(A) Yes, because the client does not dispute the $900 debt to the bank.

(B) Yes, because the attorney knew that the client was planning to force the bank to sue him.

(C) No, because the attorney had no reason to believe that the client would not have sufficient funds to pay any subsequent judgment obtained by the bank.

(D) No, because the bank has no established right to the specific proceeds of the client's personal injury judgment.

Question 22.

Three lawyers, Alpha, Beta, and Delta, formed a partnership to practice law with offices in both State First and State Second. Alpha is admitted to practice only in State First. Beta is admitted to practice only in State Second, and Delta is admitted to practice in both States First and Second. The following letterhead is on stationery used by their offices in both states:

Alpha, Beta, and Delta

Attorneys at Law

100 State Street	200 Bank Building
City, State First	City, State Second
(200) 555-5555	(202) 555-5555

Attorney Alpha

Admitted to practice only

in State First

Attorney Beta

Admitted to practice only

in State Second

Attorney Delta

Admitted to practice

in States First and Second

Are the members of the partnership subject to discipline?

(A) No, because the letterhead states the jurisdictions in which each partner is admitted.

(B) Yes, because there is no jurisdiction in which both Alpha and Beta are admitted to practice.

(C) Yes, because the firm name used by each office contains the name of a lawyer not admitted to practice in that jurisdiction.

(D) Yes, unless Delta actively practices law in both States First and Second.

Question 23.

An attorney was engaged under a general retainer agreement to represent a corporation involved in the uranium industry. Under the agreement, the attorney handled all of the corporation's legal work, which typically involved regulatory issues and litigation.

The corporation told the attorney that a congressional committee was holding hearings concerning the extent of regulation in the copper industry. Because the corporation was considering buying a copper mine during the next fiscal year, the corporation wanted the attorney to testify that the industry was overregulated. The attorney subsequently testified before the relevant congressional committee. The attorney registered his appearance under his own name and did not disclose that he was appearing on behalf of a client. Afterward, the attorney billed the corporation for fees and expenses related to his testimony.

Was the attorney's conduct proper?

(A) Yes, because the duty of confidentiality prevented the attorney from disclosing the identity of his client.

(B) Yes, because the attorney-client evidentiary privilege prevented disclosure of the identity of his client in this context.

(C) No, because the attorney failed to disclose that he was appearing and testifying in a representative capacity.

(D) No, because the attorney accepted compensation in return for his testimony.

Question 24.

An attorney represented a man in a case set for a jury trial. After the list of potential jurors was made available, the attorney hired a private investigator to interview the potential jurors and their family members concerning their relevant past experiences related to the subject matter of the action. The investigator did not inform the jurors or their family members that he was working on behalf of the attorney. The interviews were entirely voluntary and were not harassing.

The attorney did not provide the report of the interviews to opposing counsel. He used the report to make decisions regarding jury selection.

Is the attorney subject to discipline?

(A) Yes, because the attorney did not provide the report of the interviews to opposing counsel.

(B) Yes, because the investigator, at the attorney's direction, communicated with potential jurors prior to trial.

(C) Yes, because the investigator did not inform the jurors or their family members that he was working on behalf of the attorney.

(D) No, because the interviews were entirely voluntary and not harassing.

Question 25.

For many years, an attorney has served as outside counsel to a corporation. Shortly after a change in management, the attorney discovered what she reasonably believed to be a material misstatement in a document she had drafted that the attorney was about to file on the corporation's behalf with a government agency. The attorney advised the corporation's board of directors that filing the document was probably criminal. However, the board disagreed that there was any material misstatement and directed the attorney to proceed with the filing. When the attorney indicated her intention to resign, the corporation argued that a resignation at this time would send a signal that there was a problem with the filing. The corporation urged the attorney to continue the representation, but offered to use in-house counsel to complete the work on the filing. Although she does not know for certain that filing the document is illegal, the attorney reasonably believes that it is. In any event, the attorney is personally uncomfortable with the representation and wants to withdraw.

May the attorney withdraw from her representation of the corporation?

(A) Yes, because withdrawal is permitted but not required when a client insists on conduct that the lawyer reasonably believes, but does not know, will be criminal.

(B) Yes, because withdrawal is required when a client insists on conduct which the lawyer reasonably believes, but does not know, will be criminal.

(C) No, because the corporation is correct that withdrawal would breach confidentiality by sending a signal that the filing is problematic.

(D) No, because the attorney's withdrawal as outside counsel might affect the corporation's ability to complete the filing in a timely fashion.

Question 26.

A judge and an attorney were formerly law partners. During their partnership, they acquired several parcels of real property as cotenants. After the judge was elected to the trial court in the county, she remained a cotenant with the attorney, but left the management of the properties to the attorney.

The judge's term of office will expire soon and she is opposed for reelection by two members of the bar. The attorney, who has not discussed the matter with the judge, intends to make a substantial contribution to the judge's campaign for reelection.

The judge is one of 15 judges sitting as trial court judges in the county. The attorney frequently represents clients in cases tried in the trial court of the county.

Is the attorney subject to discipline if the attorney contributes $10,000 to the judge's reelection campaign committee?

(A) Yes, because the attorney frequently represents clients in cases tried in the trial court of the county.

(B) Yes, because the judge and the attorney have not discussed the matter of a campaign contribution.

(C) No, because the contribution is made to a campaign committee organized to support the judge's reelection.

(D) No, because the attorney and the judge have a long-standing personal and business relationship.

Question 27.

Attorney Alpha, a partner in the law firm of Alpha & Beta, was retained by the plaintiff in a personal injury action against the defendant. The jury rendered a verdict in favor of the defendant, and Alpha filed an appeal on the plaintiff's behalf. Alpha reviewed the trial transcript and wrote the brief. The brief stated, "It is uncontroverted that the defendant failed to signal before turning left into the intersection." In fact, a witness called by the defendant testified that the defendant did signal before turning. Alpha was aware of this testimony, having read it while reviewing the trial transcript.

Three days before the appeal was scheduled to be argued in the state's intermediate appellate court, Alpha suffered a heart attack. Attorney Beta, one of Alpha's partners, agreed to argue the appeal. Beta knew nothing about the case and had no opportunity to confer with Alpha. In preparing for the argument, Beta read Alpha's brief thoroughly and read as much of the trial transcript as was possible in the limited time available, but did not read the witness's testimony. In oral argument, Beta stated to the court, "Your honors, as stated in our brief, it is uncontroverted that the defendant failed to signal before turning left into the intersection." Beta assumed that Alpha's statement in the brief to that effect was correct.

Is Beta subject to discipline for making this statement during oral argument?

(A) Yes, because the statement was false.

(B) Yes, because Beta did not know whether or not the statement was true.

(C) No, because Beta did not know that the statement was false.

(D) No, because all Beta did was to truthfully recount the statement made by Alpha in the brief.

Question 28.

A judge needed to obtain a loan to be secured by a second mortgage on his house. A bank offered him a loan at a very favorable interest rate. The vice-president at the bank told the judge:

> "Frankly, we normally don't give such a large loan when the security is a second mortgage, and your interest rate will be 2 percent less than we charge our other customers. But we know that your salary is inadequate, and we are giving you special consideration."

The judge did not act in any case involving the bank, and was unlikely to do so. However, the same terms are not available to all judges in the state.

Is it proper for the judge to accept the loan?

(A) Yes, because the judge does not act in any case involving the bank.

(B) Yes, because the bank is not likely to be involved in litigation in the court on which the judge sits.

(C) No, because the same terms are not available to all judges in the state.

(D) No, because the amount of the loan and interest rate were not available to persons who were not judges.

Question 29.

A law firm has 300 lawyers in 10 states. It has placed the supervision of all routine administrative and financial matters in the hands of a nonlawyer. The nonlawyer is paid a regular monthly salary and a year-end bonus of 1 percent of the law firm's net income from fees. Organizationally, the nonlawyer reports to an attorney who acts as the managing partner of the law firm. The attorney deals with all issues related to the law firm's supervision of the practice of law. The nonlawyer does not have access to client files and does not control the professional judgment of lawyers in the firm.

Is it proper for the attorney to participate in the law firm's use of the nonlawyer's services in this fashion?

(A) Yes, because the nonlawyer does not have access to client files.

(B) Yes, because the nonlawyer does not control the professional judgment of the lawyers in the firm.

(C) No, because the law firm is sharing legal fees with a nonlawyer.

(D) No, because the law firm is assisting a nonlawyer in the unauthorized practice of law.

Question 30.

An attorney experienced several instances when clients failed to pay their fees in a timely manner, but it was too late in the representation to withdraw without prejudicing the clients. To avoid a recurrence of this situation, the attorney has drafted a stipulation of consent to withdraw if fees are not paid according to the fee agreement. She proposes to have all clients sign the stipulation at the outset of the representation.

Is it proper for the attorney to use the stipulation to withdraw from representation whenever a client fails to pay fees?

(A) Yes, because a lawyer may withdraw when the financial burden of continuing the representation would be substantially greater than the parties anticipated at the time of the fee agreement.

(B) Yes, because the clients consented to the withdrawal in the stipulation.

(C) No, because a client's failure to pay fees when due may be insufficient in itself to justify withdrawal.

(D) No, because clients are not provided an opportunity to seek independent legal advice before signing the stipulation.

Question 31.

An attorney was retained by a client to represent him in a paternity suit. The client's aunt believed the suit was unfounded and motivated by malice. The client's aunt sent the attorney a check for $1,000 and asked the attorney to apply it to the payment of the client's fee. The client's aunt told the attorney not to tell the client of the payment because the client "is too proud to accept gifts, but I know he really needs the money."

Is it proper for the attorney to accept the aunt's check?

(A) Yes, because the client's aunt is not attempting to influence the attorney's conduct of the case.

(B) Yes, because the attorney's charges to the client are reduced accordingly.

(C) No, because the client's aunt is attempting to finance litigation to which she is not a party.

(D) No, because the attorney is not informing the client and obtaining the client's consent to retain the payment.

Question 32.

An attorney has a highly efficient staff of paraprofessional legal assistants, all of whom are graduates of recognized legal assistant educational programs. Recently, the statute of limitations ran against a claim of a client of the attorney's when a legal assistant negligently misplaced a client's file and suit was not filed within the time permitted by law.

Which of the following correctly states the attorney's professional responsibility?

(A) The attorney is subject to civil liability and is also subject to discipline on the theory of respondeat superior.

(B) The attorney is subject to civil liability or is subject to discipline at the client's election.

(C) The attorney is subject to civil liability but is NOT subject to discipline unless the attorney failed to supervise the legal assistant adequately.

(D) The attorney is NOT subject to civil liability and is NOT subject to discipline if the attorney personally was not negligent.

Question 33.

A seller was engaged in negotiations to sell his interest in a large tract of land to a buyer who was unrepresented in the transaction. Before the seller went out of town for a few days, he told the buyer to call his attorney if the buyer had any questions about the property. The buyer called the seller's attorney, asked certain questions about the size of the tract, and expressed hesitations concerning the high asking price for the tract. The attorney responded that, based on his experience handling real estate transactions in the neighborhood, the buyer would be getting a lot of property for the price. At the time the attorney spoke to the buyer, the attorney knew that there was a defect in the title and that the buyer's attempt to purchase the seller's interest in the tract would not result in the buyer's acquisition of any interest in the property.

Relying on the attorney's assurance, the buyer agreed to make the purchase. Shortly after the sale closed, the buyer discovered that his acquisition was worthless.

Is the attorney subject to civil liability to the buyer?

(A) Yes, because the attorney knowingly made false representations of fact to the buyer.

(B) Yes, because the attorney implied that his opinion regarding the value of the property was a disinterested opinion.

(C) No, because the attorney's statement that the buyer would be getting a lot of property for the money was a statement of opinion regarding the value of the property.

(D) No, because the buyer was not a client of the attorney.

Question 34.

A prosecutor was assigned to try a criminal case against a defendant who was charged with robbery of a convenience store. The defendant denied any involvement, contending he was home watching television with his mother on the night in question. At the trial, a customer at the convenience store testified that he had identified the defendant in a police line-up and provided other testimony connecting the defendant to the crime. In addition, the prosecutor entered into evidence a poor-quality videotape of the robbery as recorded by the store surveillance camera. The jury could not make its own identification of the defendant from the videotape. The jury convicted the defendant of the crime charged. Unknown to the defendant's court-appointed lawyer, the customer had first identified another person in the police line-up and selected the defendant only after encouragement by the detective. This information would have been unlikely to lead to the defendant's acquittal, however. The prosecutor was aware of these facts but did not notify the defendant's counsel who made no pretrial discovery request to obtain this information.

Is the prosecutor subject to discipline?

(A) Yes, because the jury could not make its own identification of the defendant from the videotape.

(B) Yes, because this information tended to negate the defendant's guilt.

(C) No, because the defendant's counsel made no pretrial discovery request to obtain this information.

(D) No, because it is unlikely that the jury would have acquitted the defendant had it known that the customer first identified someone else.

Question 35.

An attorney and a client entered into a written retainer and hourly fee agreement that required the client to pay $5,000 in advance of any services rendered by the attorney and which required the attorney to return any portion of the $5,000 that was not earned. The agreement further provided that the attorney would render monthly statements and withdraw her fees as billed. The agreement was silent as to whether the $5,000 advance was to be deposited in the attorney's Clients' Trust Account or in a general account. The attorney deposited the entire fund in her Clients' Trust Account, which also contained the funds of other persons that had been entrusted to the attorney. Thereafter, the attorney rendered monthly progress reports and statements for services to the client after services were rendered, showing the balance of the client's fee advance. However, the attorney did not withdraw any of the $5,000 advance until one year later when the matter was concluded to the client's complete satisfaction. At that time, the attorney had billed the client reasonable legal fees of $4,500. The attorney wrote two checks on her Clients' Trust Account: one to herself for $4,500, which she deposited in her general office account, and one for $500 to the client.

Was the attorney's conduct proper?

(A) Yes, because the attorney deposited the funds in her Clients' Trust Account.

(B) Yes, because the attorney rendered periodic and accurate billings.

(C) No, because the attorney's failure to withdraw her fees as billed resulted in an impermissible commingling of her funds and the clients' funds.

(D) No, because the attorney required an advanced payment against her fee.

Question 36.

Attorneys Alpha and Beta had been political opponents. Alpha was elected to the state legislature after a bitter race in which Beta had managed the campaign of Alpha's opponent. Alpha had publicly blamed Beta at that time for what Alpha reasonably believed were illegal and unethical campaign practices and later had publicly objected to Beta's appointment as a judge.

Alpha represented a client in a widely publicized case tried in Judge Beta's court. At the conclusion of the trial, Beta ruled against Alpha's client. Alpha then held a press conference and said, "All that you reporters have to do is check your files and you will know what I think about Judge Beta's character and fitness."

Is Alpha subject to discipline for making this statement?

(A) Yes, because Alpha's statement might lessen confidence in the legal system.

(B) Yes, because Alpha's past accusations were unrelated to Beta's legal knowledge.

(C) No, because Alpha reasonably believed that the statements about Beta were true.

(D) No, because Beta had equal access to the press.

Question 37.

An attorney who was a member of the state legislature was allowed to engage in private practice under state law. The attorney represented a plaintiff in a personal injury case. The attorney reasonably believed the trial of the case will last at least two weeks. When the case was first scheduled for trial, the attorney requested a continuance, truthfully stating, "As the court knows, I am a member of the legislature, which will be going into special session next week. Because of my legislative duties, I must be in the state capitol for the duration of the session." The defendant objected to the continuance, but the court granted it.

Is the attorney subject to discipline?

(A) Yes, because the defendant objected to the continuance.

(B) Yes, because the attorney used her public position to influence a tribunal.

(C) No, because the attorney's statements to the court were truthful.

(D) No, because the continuance will not give the plaintiff an advantage in the litigation.

Question 38.

Last year, a man's house was severely damaged when a large tree in his neighbor's yard toppled onto the man's roof and porch. The man hired an attorney, who filed a suit against the neighbor on the man's behalf to recover over $40,000 in damages. The neighbor was represented by another attorney, who was uncooperative. When the man's attorney communicated a settlement offer to the neighbor's attorney, the neighbor's attorney said he would consider it. However, the neighbor's attorney did not respond further, and the man's attorney suspected the offer was never communicated to the neighbor. When the man learned of his attorney's suspicions, he asked whether he could go talk to the neighbor himself. The man's attorney said that he should do so and see if they could "put an end to this unpleasantness."

Is the man's attorney subject to discipline?

(A) Yes, because the man's attorney suggested that the man communicate about the subject matter of the representation with a person known to be represented by another lawyer.

(B) Yes, because there was no proof the neighbor's attorney had failed to inform the neighbor of the settlement offer.

(C) No, because the man and the neighbor may communicate with each other.

(D) No, because by entering into settlement negotiations, the neighbor's attorney impliedly consented to direct communications with the neighbor.

Question 39.

An attorney is defending a corporation against a lawsuit brought in federal court by the plaintiff, a consumer injured by one of the corporation's products. The plaintiff is seeking both compensatory and punitive damages. During discovery, the plaintiff's lawyer served a set of interrogatories on the corporation, including requests for the financial data of the corporation.

The president of the corporation directed the attorney to resist providing this information, although the attorney has informed him that, under the rules of discovery, the plaintiff is entitled to the information requested. The president then demanded that the attorney assert that the information is confidential, privileged work product, and a trade secret, but the attorney correctly informed him that it was well settled that such claims would be regarded as frivolous by the courts. The president nonetheless directed the attorney to file objections on the bases stated, so that at least the plaintiff will have to incur the expense of compelling discovery. The attorney filed the objections as directed by the president.

Which of the following statements is true?

(A) The attorney is subject to discipline.

(B) The attorney is subject to litigation sanction.

(C) The attorney is subject to both discipline and litigation sanction.

(D) The attorney is subject to neither discipline nor litigation sanction.

Question 40.

An attorney is a general practitioner with extensive experience in personal injury litigation, including legal and medical malpractice. A man contacted the attorney by telephone and requested that the attorney represent him in a legal malpractice case that the man wanted to file against the attorney who handled the man's divorce. The attorney refused to meet with the man, saying:

> "Look, I just finished renewing my own malpractice insurance policy, and I can't believe how high the premiums have gotten. I'm not taking on any new clients with legal malpractice cases."

The man tried to contact several other lawyers, each of whom indicated that he or she would be happy to accept the representation but was too busy to take on any new matters at this time. Six months later, the statute of limitations expired without the man filing his lawsuit.

If the man can establish that a legal malpractice action against the divorce attorney would have succeeded, is the attorney subject to civil liability for refusing to accept the representation?

(A) Yes, because the attorney did not have good cause to refuse the representation.

(B) Yes, because the attorney did not make reasonable efforts to find a competent lawyer to represent the man.

(C) No, because the attorney did not hold herself out as specially experienced in legal malpractice cases.

(D) No, because the attorney had no legal obligation to accept the man's case.

Question 41.

An attorney, a member of the state bar, placed a printed flyer in the booth of each artist exhibiting works at a county fair. The face of the flyer contained the following information:

"I am an attorney with offices in 800 Bank Building, telephone (555) 555-5555. I have a J.D. from State Law School and an M.A. in fine arts from State University. My practice includes representing artists in negotiating contracts between artists and dealers and protecting artists' interests. You can find me in the van parked at the fair entrance."

All factual information on the face of the flyer was correct. There was a retainer agreement on the back of the flyer. At the entrance to the fair, the attorney parked a van with a sign that read "Attorney at Law."

For which action, if any, is the attorney subject to discipline?

(A) Parking the van with the sign on it at the fair entrance.

(B) Placing copies of the flyer in the booth of each artist and including a retainer agreement on the back of the flyer.

(C) Parking the van with the sign on it at the fair entrance, placing copies of the flyer in the booth of each artist, and including a retainer agreement on the back of the flyer.

(D) None of the above.

Question 42.

Five years ago, an attorney represented a seller in the sale of the seller's home. The attorney has not represented the seller since that time. Recently, the attorney was approached by the seller's partner in a venture capital company formed two years ago. The partner and seller have agreed to dissolve their partnership, but cannot agree on the terms of the dissolution. The partner asked the attorney to sue the seller for an accounting of the partnership assets.

If the attorney accepts the representation, is the attorney subject to disqualification?

(A) Yes, because the representation is directly adverse to the seller.

(B) Yes, because there is no indication that at the time of the sale of the seller's home, the seller agreed that the attorney would not subsequently be precluded from representing other clients in suits against the seller.

(C) No, because the partnership dissolution is unrelated to the sale of the seller's home.

(D) No, because the seller did not sell the home while in the partnership.

Question 43.

An attorney represents a company that produces chemical manufacturing processes that are highly toxic and are reasonably certain to cause substantial bodily harm if disposed of improperly. The president of the company recently informed the attorney that a new employee mistakenly disposed of the waste products in the ground behind the company plant, an area that is part of the source of the city's water supply. The attorney advised the president that, although the conduct was not criminal, the company could be civilly liable for negligence in lawsuits brought by any persons harmed by the waste products. The attorney advised the president to immediately report the problem to city authorities. Fearful of adverse publicity, the president declined to do so. The attorney further advised the president that she believed the president's decision was immoral. The president continued to decline to report the matter. The attorney then informed the president that she was withdrawing from the representation and would inform the authorities herself. Immediately after withdrawing, the attorney reported the company's conduct to the authorities.

Is the attorney subject to discipline?

(A) Yes, because the information was given to the attorney in confidence and may not be revealed without the client's consent.

(B) Yes, because the company's conduct was not criminal.

(C) No, because the attorney reasonably believed that the company's disposal of the waste products was reasonably certain to cause substantial bodily harm.

(D) No, because the attorney reasonably believed that the president was pursuing an imprudent course of conduct.

Question 44.

An attorney's new client asked the attorney to write a letter recommending the client's nephew for admission to the bar. The client told the attorney that he had no direct contact with his nephew, but his sister assured him that his nephew was qualified for the bar because he has never been arrested or accused of any dishonest actions. The attorney knew nothing about the client's nephew.

Which of the following would be proper for the attorney to do?

(A) Write the letter based on the client's assurances.

(B) Write the letter based on the client's assurances, because the attorney has no unfavorable information about the nephew.

(C) Write the letter after making an independent investigation into the client's assurances.

(D) Write the letter after speaking with the nephew himself.

Question 45.

An attorney wants to make it easier for her clients to pay their bills for her fees. Which of the following would be improper for the attorney to do?

(A) Suggest that the client give publication rights concerning the case as payment.

(B) Arrange for clients to obtain bank loans for the purpose of paying the attorney's fees.

(C) Accept property in payment for services.

(D) Accept bank credit cards.

Question 46.

An attorney practices law in a state that has experienced a business recession and where several banks have failed and others are severely pressed to preserve their solvency. The attorney maintains a Clients' Trust Account in a bank and that account is insured by the Federal Deposit Insurance Corporation against losses up to $250,000. The attorney also maintains his regular office account in the same bank and that account is insured up to $250,000. During a particularly busy time, the attorney's bookkeeper told the attorney that the balance in the Clients' Trust Account had increased to $300,000. The bookkeeper noted that the office account had a balance of $30,000.

Which of the following courses of action by the attorney would be proper?

(A) Leave the Clients' Trust Account as is.

(B) Open another Clients' Trust Account in another bank and transfer some funds to the second account to maintain a fully insured balance in both accounts.

(C) Temporarily transfer $50,000 from the Clients' Trust Account to the office account so the balance in both accounts is fully within insured limits.

(D) Leave the Clients' Trust Account as is if the balance is likely to decrease to less than $250,000 within the next 10 days.

Question 47.

A law firm, a professional corporation with five lawyer shareholders, employs 25 additional lawyers.

Which of the following is proper?

(A) Employees who are members of the bar are not made shareholders until they have been with the law firm for 10 years.

(B) The office manager, who is not a member of the bar, is executive vice president of the law firm.

(C) A widow whose husband was a lawyer shareholder in the firm until he died five years ago continues to hold her husband's shares in the firm.

(D) The firm's accountant, who is not a member of the bar, is a shareholder.

Question 48.

An attorney, who was recently admitted to the bar, has been appointed by the court as counsel for an indigent defendant charged with a felony. After consulting with the defendant and attempting for two days to prepare the case for trial, the attorney became convinced that he lacked the knowledge and experience to represent the defendant effectively.

Which of the following would be proper for the attorney?

(A) Request permission of the court to withdraw from representing the defendant.

(B) Request a two-week continuance to allow more time to prepare for trial.

(C) Explain the circumstances to the defendant, and if the defendant consents, proceed to represent the defendant to the best of his ability.

(D) Explain the circumstances to the defendant, and if the defendant consents in writing, proceed to represent the defendant to the best of his ability.

Question 49.

A judge is presently serving on a state intermediate appellate court. This court, in opinions written by her, has decided several controversial cases in which the court has held that the Fourteenth Amendment to the United States Constitution does not guarantee due process protection to state prison inmates who are disciplined by prison authorities for violating the prison's rules of conduct. The judge is now a candidate for election to a vacancy on the state supreme court. She is vigorously opposed by several organizations concerned with the conditions under which prisoners are incarcerated in the state's prison. The judge is scheduled to be interviewed on television and has been informed that questions will be asked of her concerning those decisions and her attitude on the subject of prisoners' rights.

Which of the following is proper for the judge to say during the interview?

(A) "I believe that the issues raised by the organizations opposing me are appropriate matters for legislative consideration."

(B) "In my opinion, incarceration for the commission of a crime carries with it a loss of civil liberties in prison discipline proceedings."

(C) "I am convinced I was right in those cases and will make the same decision in similar cases in the future."

(D) "I would never rule against prison authorities because they have ultimate responsibility for the health and safety of prisoners."

Question 50.

An attorney was formerly employed by an insurance company as a lawyer who solely handled fire insurance claims. While so employed, she investigated a man's fire loss claim against the insurance company. The attorney is now in private practice. The claim remains unsettled and the man consults the attorney and asks the attorney to represent him for a suit on the claim.

Which of the following would be proper for the attorney to do?

(A) Refuse to discuss the matter with the man.

(B) Represent the man.

(C) Refer the man to an associate in her law firm.

(D) Refer the man to an associate in her law firm, provided the attorney does not share in any fee.

Question 51.

An attorney worked at an electric company. While there, he worked on a claim against the company brought by a woman for sexual harassment. That claim was settled and the attorney left the company and went into private practice. Last week, the woman slipped and fell in the company's offices. She now asks the attorney to represent her.

Which of the following would be proper for the attorney to do?

(A) Refuse to discuss the matter with the woman.

(B) Represent the woman.

(C) Give the woman a list of lawyers who the attorney knows are competent and specialize in such claims.

(D) All of the above.

Question 52.

A man has retained an attorney to represent him in a contract suit. The attorney's retainer agreement provided that the attorney's fees would be based on a fixed hourly rate, payable at the end of each calendar month. Two months before trial, the man fell behind in the payment of the attorney's monthly billing for fees. The attorney included the following statement on the attorney's last billing to the man:

> "Your account is more than 30 days past due. If amounts due are not paid promptly in accordance with our agreement, I will terminate the representation. If you cannot pay the amount due, I will accept an assignment of your cause of action as security for your fee to me."

Two weeks after the last billing, the attorney telephoned the man and told him that the attorney would withdraw from representing the man if the bill was not paid within 48 hours or adequate security given for its payment.

If the bill remains unpaid or unsecured after 48 hours, it would be proper for the attorney to:

(A) Upon notice to the man, move the court for permission to withdraw.

(B) Turn the man's file over to another experienced lawyer in town and notify the man that the attorney no longer represents him.

(C) Accept an assignment of the man's cause of action as security for the attorney's fee.

(D) Stop work on the case until the man pays his bill.

Question 53.

An attorney's advertisement in the local newspaper includes the following information, all of which is true:

> "I have a B.A., magna cum laude, Eastern College; J.D., summa cum laude, State Law School; LL.M., Eastern Law School. My offices are open Monday through Friday from 9:00 a.m. to 5:00 p.m., but you may call my answering service 24 hours a day, seven days a week. I speak modern Greek fluently."

For which, if any, of these statements is the attorney subject to discipline?

(A) "I speak modern Greek fluently."

(B) "J.D., summa cum laude, State Law School."

(C) "You may call my answering service 24 hours a day."

(D) None of the statements in the advertisement subjects the attorney to discipline.

Question 54.

An attorney represents a man in bitter and protracted litigation. The attorney at the man's request, has made several offers of settlement to plaintiff's lawyer, all of which have been rejected.

During a week's recess in the trial, the attorney and the plaintiff were both present at a cocktail party. The plaintiff went over to the attorney and said: "Why can't we settle this case for $50,000? This trial is costing both sides more than it's worth."

Which of the following is a proper response by the attorney?

(A) "I can't discuss the matter with you."

(B) "If that's the way you feel, why don't you and my client get together?"

(C) "I agree. We've already made several offers to settle you might not know about."

(D) "Let me get confirmation from my client, but I think this settlement is appropriate."

Question 55.

The law firm of Alpha and Beta has a radio commercial which states:

"Do you have a legal problem? Are you being sued? Consult Alpha and Beta, licensed attorneys at law. Initial conference charge is $25 for one hour. Act now and protect your interests. Call at 1234 Main Street; telephone area code (555) 555-5555."

All the statements in the advertisement are true. The commercial can be heard in several neighboring states.

Are Alpha and Beta subject to discipline for the commercial?

(A) Yes, because the qualifications of the lawyers are not stated.

(B) Yes, because the radio broadcast may encourage litigation.

(C) Yes, because the radio broadcast is heard outside the state in which they are licensed

(D) No, because all of the statements in the radio broadcast are true.

Question 56.

Attorney Alpha was retained by a client to incorporate a client's business, which previously had been operated as a sole proprietorship. Alpha noticed in the client's file copies of some correspondence from the client to Attorney Beta concerning the possibility of Beta's incorporating the client's business. Alpha questioned the client to make certain that any attorney-client relationship between Beta and the client had been terminated. The client told Alpha,

> "It certainly has been terminated. When I discussed the matter with Beta six months ago, he asked for a retainer of $1,000, which I paid him. He did absolutely nothing after he got the money, even though I called him weekly, and finally, last week when I again complained, he returned the retainer, which satisfied me. Don't say anything about it because Beta is an old friend of my family."

Based on what the client told her, Alpha believes that Beta clearly was guilty of professional misconduct, although she didn't think he usually neglected cases entrusted to him.

Is Alpha subject to discipline if she does not report her knowledge of Beta's conduct to the appropriate authority?

(A) Yes, because Alpha believes Beta clearly was guilty of professional misconduct.

(B) Yes, because Alpha believes Beta does not usually neglect matters entrusted to him.

(C) No, because the client was satisfied by Beta's return of the retainer.

(D) No, because the client does not want Alpha to report the information.

Question 57.

A litigation firm and general partnership hires new law school graduates as associates. These new lawyers are largely left to their own resources to practice law. The firm accepts many small litigation matters and assigns them to the associates for training purposes. No senior partners are assigned to supervise this work. It is assumed that if an associate needs help on a case, he or she will seek the guidance of a more senior attorney.

A client retained the firm to pursue a claim for breach of contract against the city. A first-year associate was assigned the case. The associate failed to comply with the applicable 30-day notice requirement for filing a complaint against the city, and the client lost the chance to recover $5,000. When the complaint was dismissed for failure to comply with the notice requirement, the associate told the client that the case was dismissed on the merits.

Which of the following statements is correct?

(A) The law firm is subject to discipline for failure to supervise the associate.

(B) The individual partners are subject to discipline for failure to make reasonable efforts to establish a system providing reasonable assurance that all lawyers in the firm comply with the rules of professional conduct.

(C) The associate, an unsupervised subordinate lawyer, is not subject to discipline.

(D) The law firm is not subject to civil liability for the client's loss.

Question 58.

An attorney received a check from a defendant payable to the attorney's order in the sum of $10,000 in settlement of a plaintiff's claim against the defendant. The plaintiff had previously paid the attorney a fee, so no part of the $10,000 was owed to the attorney.

Which of the following would be proper?

(A) Endorse the check and send it to the plaintiff.

(B) Deposit the check in the attorney's personal bank account and send a personal check for $10,000 to the plaintiff.

(C) Deposit the check in the attorney's personal bank account and await the plaintiff's instructions.

(D) Deposit the check in the attorney's personal bank account and immediately wire $10,000 to the plaintiff.

Question 59.

Alpha and Beta are members of the bar in the same community but have never practiced together. Beta is a candidate in a contested election for judicial office. Beta is opposed by Delta, another lawyer in the community. Alpha believes Beta is better qualified than Delta for the judiciary and is supporting Beta's candidacy. She has also heard rumors regarding Delta's possible drug problems.

Which of the following would be improper for Alpha to do?

(A) Solicit public endorsements for Beta's candidacy by other attorneys in the community.

(B) Solicit contributions to Beta's campaign committee from other attorneys in the community, including those who are likely to appear before Beta if Beta becomes a judge.

(C) Publicly oppose the candidacy of Delta.

(D) Report the rumors she has heard regarding Delta's possible drug use.

Question 60.

An attorney represents a defendant who has been indicted for auto theft. The prosecutor reasonably believes that the defendant committed the offense, but, because of the defendant's youth, it is in the interest of justice to permit the defendant to plead guilty to the lesser offense of "joyriding" in return for an agreement by the prosecutor to recommend probation. The prosecutor has so advised the attorney, but the attorney told the prosecutor she would not plea bargain and would insist on a jury trial. The attorney informed the defendant of the prosecutor's offer and advised the defendant not to accept it. The defendant followed the attorney's advice. The attorney is a candidate for public office, and the prosecutor suspects that the attorney is insisting on a trial of the case to secure publicity for herself.

Which of the following would be improper for the prosecutor to do?

(A) Send a member of his staff who is not a lawyer to consult with the defendant.

(B) Move the trial court to dismiss the indictment and accept a new complaint charging the offense of "joyriding."

(C) Proceed to trial on the indictment and prosecute the case vigorously.

(D) Disclose to the defense all evidence or information that tends to negate the defendant's guilt.

3. Practice MPRE 3

Question 1.

A prosecutor reasonably believed that a defendant committed a burglary, but thought it was in the interest of justice for the defendant to plead guilty to a lesser offense of "criminal mischief" because of the defendant's age. The defendant's attorney advised the defendant about the potential plea bargain, but advised the defendant not to accept it. The defendant followed the attorney's advice. The attorney zealously and competently represented the defendant at trial, but the defendant was ultimately convicted and sentenced to two years in prison. The prosecutor suspected that the attorney, a candidate for public office, insisted on a trial as a way to secure publicity for herself. In fact, because of the trial, the attorney appeared in several newspapers and on several television shows.

Must the prosecutor report to the disciplinary authority his suspicions about the attorney's conduct in this case?

(A) Yes, because the defendant suffered a detriment from the attorney's refusal to plea bargain.

(B) Yes, because the attorney in fact received widespread publicity as a result of the trial.

(C) No, because the prosecutor does not have actual knowledge that the attorney's refusal to plea bargain was due to personal motives.

(D) No, because the attorney zealously and competently represented the defendant at trial.

Question 2.

An attorney represents a plaintiff in a personal injury action. An eyewitness to the accident lives about 500 miles distant from the city where the case will be tried. The attorney interviewed the witness and determined that the witness's testimony would be favorable for the client.

Which of the following would be improper for the attorney to pay to secure the witness's testimony?

(A) Statutory witness fees.

(B) Reimbursement for travel expenses.

(C) Reimbursement for lost wages while present at the trial.

(D) An amount equal to 5 percent of any recovery in the matter.

Question 3.

With her client's approval, an attorney settled a claim against a defendant for $60,000. The settlement agreement provided that one-half would be paid by the defendant's primary insurance carrier, and one-half by a coinsurer. The attorney's agreed fee was 30 percent of the amount of the settlement. The attorney received the primary carrier's check for $30,000 and a letter from the coinsurer advising that its check would be sent in two weeks. The attorney promptly advised her client and deposited the $30,000 in her Clients' Trust Account. Her client demanded that the attorney send him the entire $30,000 and take her fee out of the funds to be received from the coinsurer.

Which of the following would now be proper for the attorney to do?

(A) Send the client $21,000, and retain $9,000 in her Clients' Trust Account.

(B) Send the client $21,000, and transfer $9,000 to her personal account.

(C) Send the client $12,000, and transfer $18,000 to her personal account.

(D) Send the client $12,000, and transfer $18,000 to her Clients' Trust Account.

Question 4.

An attorney is a candidate for a judicial office that has been occupied by the incumbent for six years. The attorney has conducted a thorough investigation of the incumbent's personal and professional life.

Assume all factual statements below are accurate. Which of the following statements is it improper for the attorney to make during the campaign?

(A) "The incumbent has been reversed by the appellate courts more than any other judge in the state during the preceding two years."

(B) "The incumbent was publicly censured by the state Judicial Qualification Commission on one occasion for his overbearing conduct in court."

(C) "The incumbent was given a poor rating for judicial temperament in a county bar association poll."

(D) "During the previous year, the average sentence in armed robbery cases tried in the incumbent's court was three years, and in murder cases, eight years. If I am elected, I won't be soft on crime."

Question 5.

An attorney and former state senator represents a well-known contractor before a state administrative agency. The agency has ordered the client to show cause why the client's license as a contractor should not be revoked for violation of agency regulations.

In a newspaper interview prior to the administrative hearing, the attorney made the following statements. Which of the following statements is improper?

(A) "My client denies the charge made by the agency that he engaged in conduct constituting grounds for revocation of his license as a contractor."

(B) "The next step in the administrative process is the administrative hearing; if the agency is successful, we will appeal, and the agency still cannot revoke my client's license until the court affirms the finding for the agency."

(C) "My client needs witnesses who are aware of the incidents that are the subject of the hearing."

(D) "I would not have agreed to represent my client unless I knew he did not violate the agency regulations; I appointed everyone in the agency and they'll follow my lead."

Question 6.

An attorney represented a plaintiff in litigation that was settled, with the plaintiff's approval, for $25,000. The attorney received a check in that amount from the defendant, payable to the attorney's order. The attorney endorsed and deposited the check in the attorney's Clients' Trust Account.

The attorney promptly notified the plaintiff and billed the plaintiff $5,000 for legal fees. The plaintiff disputed the amount of the fee and wrote the attorney, stating, "I will agree to pay $3,000 as a reasonable fee for the work you did, but I will not pay anything more than that."

Which of the following is proper for the attorney to do?

(A) Retain the entire $25,000 in the attorney's Clients' Trust Account until the fee dispute is settled.

(B) Send the plaintiff $20,000, transfer $3,000 to the attorney's office account, and retain $2,000 in the attorney's Clients' Trust Account until the dispute is settled.

(C) Send the plaintiff $20,000 and transfer $5,000 to the attorney's office account.

(D) Retain $22,000 in the Clients' Trust account, and transfer $3,000 to the attorney's office account.

Question 7.

During the closing argument to the jury in a civil tax fraud case, the attorney representing the government quoted a portion of the defendant's testimony.

Which of the following statements by the attorney regarding the testimony would be improper?

(A) "The testimony of the defendant directly contradicts the testimony of the two witnesses for the government."

(B) "I ask you, who has the reason to lie, the two witnesses for the government or the defendant?"

(C) "I can truthfully say I have never seen a witness less worthy of belief."

(D) "Someone has to be lying here because the different stories don't add up."

Question 8.

An attorney represents a prominent businessman in a civil paternity suit brought by his former employee. Blood tests did not exclude the businessman's paternity, and the case is being tried before a jury. The result turns on questions of fact. The businessman has steadfastly denied that he had sexual relations with the employee, while the employee has testified that they had sexual relations while on business trips and in her home. The trial has generated great public interest and is closely followed by the news media.

When the employee completed her testimony, the attorney was interviewed by a newspaper reporter.

Which of the following statements, if believed by the attorney to be true, would be improper for the attorney to make?

(A) "As stated in our pleadings, we expect to prove that other men could be the father of the plaintiff's child."

(B) "We have scientific medical tests proving that my client is sterile."

(C) "We have been unable to locate several people whose testimony will be helpful to us, and I implore them to contact me immediately."

(D) "The plaintiff's public tax records show that she's had financial problems."

Question 9.

An attorney represented her client on a minor personal injury claim against an uninsured motorist. The attorney represented the client on a 30 percent contingent fee basis. Pursuant to a negotiated settlement in the amount of $2,000, the motorist agreed to send the attorney a $100 check, made payable to the attorney, in each of the ensuing 20 months.

Which of the following dispositions of each monthly check would be improper?

(A) Deposit the check into her office account and immediately write her client a check for $70 from that account.

(B) Deposit the check into a separate account established for the client and immediately request the client pay the attorney $30.

(C) Deposit the check into a trust account in which funds belonging to all of the attorney's clients are deposited and immediately write the client a check for $70 and herself a check for $30 from that account.

(D) Endorse the check over to the client, send it to the client, and request immediate payment of $30.

Question 10.

An attorney represented a plaintiff who sued a defendant for injuries sustained in a car accident. The defendant was the son of a very rich businessman. Prior to trial, the attorney interviewed a witness who stated that she had observed the defendant drinking heavily hours before the accident. Unfortunately, on the eve of trial, the witness informed the attorney that she was ill and could not testify at trial. The attorney tried but could not obtain a continuance. As a result, the plaintiff's direct case rested solely on the plaintiff's testimony that the defendant was speeding and that the defendant's car crossed the middle line and hit the plaintiff's car. The defendant testified that he was driving safely in compliance with all rules and that the accident was entirely the plaintiff's fault. On cross-examination, the attorney asked the defendant, "Isn't it a fact that you were drinking prior to the accident?" The defendant answered that he had not consumed alcoholic beverages on the day of the accident. In summation to the jury, the attorney stated:

> "Ladies and gentlemen of the jury, you and I know that the defendant lied when he stated that he had not consumed alcoholic beverages on the day of the accident. We know that he was impaired. While we don't have the money to buy off the judge like he does, I know you won't let him buy off you!"

Which of the following is least likely to make the attorney subject to discipline?

(A) The attorney's question to the defendant implying that the defendant had consumed alcoholic beverages when the attorney knew that he could not offer evidence of the defendant's drinking.

(B) The attorney's statement to the jury asserting that the attorney knew that the defendant was drunk when no evidence in the record supported this allegation.

(C) The attorney's statement asserting a personal belief that the defendant was drunk and lying.

(D) The attorney's statement asserting that the defendant's money could buy off the judge.

Question 11.

An attorney tells his firm he will not attend any continuing legal education courses because they are expensive and the state doesn't require it.

However, because the attorney does not have malpractice insurance, he assures his colleagues that he will keep up to date on legal topics by studying on his own.

Is the attorney's action proper?

(A) No, because the attorney does not have malpractice insurance.

(B) No, because the attorney cannot maintain competence without attending continuing legal education courses.

(C) Yes, because the attorney will independently undertake continuing study and education in the law.

(D) Yes, because the state does not offer free continuing legal education courses.

Question 12.

An attorney was employed by the state's water department for five years. During the last year of her employment, the attorney spent most of her time in the preparation of a case against a corporation for the corporation's overuse of state water and equipment. The corporation lost the case and was assessed a large fine. All of the information regarding the case was entered into the public record.

The attorney recently went into private practice. Several individual plaintiffs have now brought private claims against the corporation over the same alleged overuse of the state's water and equipment. The corporation's CEO, who was impressed with her work on the earlier case, called and asked if she would represent the corporation in these new claims.

May the attorney represent the corporation in these matters?

(A) Yes, because the attorney is likely the most competent lawyer to do so.

(B) Yes, because all information acquired by the attorney while representing the water department is now a matter of public record.

(C) No, because the judgment in the prior case could be determinative of the corporation's liability.

(D) No, because the attorney had substantial responsibility in the matter while employed by the water department.

Question 13.

A judge is presiding in a case that has, as its main issue, a complicated point of environmental law. After the two parties present their cases, she still feels that she doesn't understand the claim. Consequently, she calls a friend of hers who specializes in environmental law and asks him several questions. Her friend has no interest in the case, but knows a lot about this area, so he emails her a lot of helpful information. She does not tell the two parties about the call or the information she received.

Was it proper for the judge to consult her friend?

(A) Yes, because her friend has no interest in the case.

(B) Yes, because the judge did not feel like she understood the claim.

(C) No, because the parties in the case did not give their consent to the call.

(D) No, because the judge did not inform the parties of the call.

Question 14.

An attorney drafted a stipulation of consent to withdraw if fees are not paid on time. She has her clients sign the stipulation at the outset of the representation.

Is it improper for the attorney to use the stipulation to withdraw from representation whenever a client fails to pay fees on time?

(A) Yes, because a client's failure to pay fees on time may be insufficient in itself to justify withdrawal.

(B) Yes, because clients are not provided an opportunity to seek independent legal advice before signing the stipulation.

(C) No, because a lawyer may withdraw when the financial burden of continuing the representation is unreasonable.

(D) No, because the clients consented to the withdrawal.

Question 15.

An attorney represented a client who was being prosecuted for securities violations. During the course of the representation, the client told the attorney that he had failed to file five years of tax returns, which was a felony and could add to the amount of any sentence that was imposed by the court because it indicated general financial malfeasance. The client asked the attorney not to disclose his failure to file returns during the course of the representation and told the attorney that, if called as a witness, he would lie about the tax returns. When the attorney called the client as a witness, the attorney asked him about the tax returns. The client said that he was up to date in filing his taxes.

Were the attorney's actions proper under the Rule?

(A) Yes, because the tax returns were not the primary issue in the case.

(B) Yes, because the attorney obtained the information during the course of representation.

(C) No, because the client's failure to file tax returns is a felony.

(D) No, because the attorney knowingly used false testimony.

Question 16.

An attorney representing a plaintiff in a car accident reasonably believed that the defendant's lawyer had not informed the defendant about the attorney's recent settlement offer. She suspected the defendant's lawyer hadn't done so in order to run up his fees. The attorney instructed her office assistant, who was not a lawyer, to tell the defendant about the settlement offer.

Are the attorney's actions proper?

(A) Yes, because the lawyer reasonably believed that the defendant's lawyer had not informed him of the settlement offer.

(B) Yes, because the defendant's lawyer was attempting to run up his fees.

(C) No, because the defendant did not consent to the contact.

(D) No, because the defendant's lawyer did not consent to the contact.

Question 17.

An attorney's standard retainer contract in divorce cases provides for the payment of a fee of one-third of the amount of alimony or property settlement secured by the attorney.

Is the attorney subject to discipline?

(A) Yes, because the fee is contingent.

(B) Yes, because a lawyer may not acquire a proprietary interest in a cause of action.

(C) No, because this helps clients who may not otherwise be able to afford an attorney.

(D) No, because clients consent to the fee arrangement by signing the retainer contract.

Question 18.

In order to obtain ample time for settlement negotiations, an attorney immediately requested and obtained from opposing counsel a stipulation extending the client's time to answer the complaint until 10 days after receipt of written demand from the plaintiff's attorney. Several months later, no settlement had been reached, and on March 1, the plaintiff's attorney wrote to the attorney demanding that an answer be filed within 10 days. When no answer was filed by March 15, the plaintiff's attorney had a default judgment entered in favor of the plaintiff.

The attorney was away on a month-long writing retreat when the opposing counsel's letter was received in her office. Because the writing retreat was extremely remote, she had no reasonable way of receiving any messages from her office. When the attorney returned from her writing retreat on April 1, she promptly moved to have the default set aside and her motion was granted.

Are the attorney's actions proper?

(A) Yes, because the default judgment was set aside.

(B) Yes, because she had no reasonable way of knowing that the plaintiff's attorney had demanded an answer be filed within 10 days.

(C) No, because she didn't offer to provide her client with restitution for any losses.

(D) No, because the attorney didn't make provisions for handling her pending cases while she was away.

Question 19.

While representing a client in a personal injury case, the client told the attorney that she had previously killed a man and buried his body in a nearby swamp. The murder is completely unrelated to the personal injury case. The body has not been found, and the client is not a suspect in the crime, which remains unsolved.

Must the attorney voluntarily disclose to the authorities his knowledge of the prior murder and the location of the victim's body?

(A) Yes, because the attorney is an officer of the court.

(B) Yes, because the murder remains unsolved.

(C) No, because the information was obtained by the attorney in the course of representation.

(D) No, because the attorney did not represent or advise his client regarding the prior murder.

Question 20.

An attorney represented a client in an automobile accident. The client's father sent the attorney a check for $20,000 and asked the attorney to apply it to the client's fee and "give it top priority." The client's father told the attorney not to tell the client about the payment. The attorney agreed not to tell his client.

Is it improper for the attorney to accept the father's check?

(A) Yes, because the attorney agreed not to tell his client.

(B) Yes, because the client's father is trying to influence the attorney's actions in the case.

(C) No, because the client's father is a family member of the client.

(D) No, because the client is allowed to pay the attorney's fee in any reasonable manner.

Question 21.

A seller was engaged in negotiations to sell a golf course to a buyer who was unrepresented in the transaction. The seller told the buyer to call his attorney if the buyer had any questions about the property. The buyer called the seller's attorney and expressed hesitations concerning buying the seller's interest in the golf course. The attorney responded that he thought the buyer was getting a wonderful deal. At the time the attorney spoke to the buyer, the attorney knew that there was a defect in the title and that the buyer's attempt to purchase the seller's interest in the golf course would be worthless.

After speaking with the attorney, the buyer agreed to make the purchase. Shortly after the sale closed, the buyer discovered that his acquisition was worthless.

Were the attorney's actions proper?

(A) Yes, because the seller told the buyer to call his attorney if he had any questions.

(B) Yes, because the attorney merely expressed his opinion regarding the sale.

(C) No, because the buyer was not represented by another lawyer, and the attorney should not have implied he had the buyer's best interests in mind.

(D) No, because the attorney made a false statement to the buyer.

Question 22.

An attorney and a doctor entered into a reciprocal referral arrangement. The attorney agreed to prominently display ads for the doctor in her office, and to mention the doctor to all of her clients who requested a doctor recommendation. In return, the doctor agreed to prominently display ads for the attorney's firm in his office and to recommend the attorney to any of his patients who indicated a need for legal services. The agreement was not exclusive, and the clients and patients were informed of the advertising agreement.

Is the attorney subject to discipline?

(A) Yes, because the attorney advertised for the doctor.

(B) Yes, because the doctor gave recommendations regarding legal services.

(C) No, because the patients and clients were informed of the agreement.

(D) No, because the attorney did not pay the doctor for the recommendations.

Question 23.

An attorney was hired by a restaurant owner. The owner asked the attorney whether any restaurants or bars had been prosecuted for violating a local law that stated alcohol could not be served before noon on Sundays. He also asked whether the law's $50 fine could be imposed for every sale on a Sunday before noon.

The attorney accurately told the client that the fine could only be imposed once for each Sunday, not for each transaction, and that no one had been prosecuted under the law. Several weeks later, the attorney learned that the owner's restaurant had begun to have "Sunday booze breakfasts" where alcohol was served starting at 9 a.m. on Sundays.

Is the attorney subject to discipline?

(A) Yes, because the attorney reasonably should have known that the information she gave the client would encourage him to violate the law.

(B) Yes, because the attorney aided the owner in violating the law.

(C) No, because the attorney merely told the owner factual information regarding the law.

(D) No, because the attorney was not acting as an officer of the court.

Question 24.

An attorney and a financial planner decided to form a partnership for the purpose of providing clients with legal and financial services. The announcement of the proposed partnership, the firm stationery, and all public directory listings clearly state that the financial planner is a certified financial planner and that the attorney is a lawyer. The attorney is the only person in the partnership who gives legal advice.

Is the attorney subject to discipline?

(A) Yes, because there is no indication that clients sign anything consenting to the partnership arrangement.

(B) Yes, because the partnership provides legal services.

(C) No, because the attorney is the only person in the partnership who gives advice on legal matters.

(D) No, because all public communications clearly state that the financial planner is a certified financial planner and the attorney is a lawyer.

Question 25.

A bond-trading firm hired an attorney under a general retainer agreement. The firm told the attorney that a congressional committee was holding hearings concerning the extent of regulation in bond-trading industry. The firm wanted the attorney to testify that the industry was overregulated. The attorney agreed with the firm regarding the regulation issue. The attorney subsequently testified before the relevant congressional committee. The attorney registered his appearance under his own name and did not disclose that he was appearing on behalf of a client. Afterwards, he billed the firm for his appearance.

Was the attorney's conduct improper?

(A) Yes, because the firm paid the attorney for his testimony.

(B) Yes, because the attorney failed to disclose that he was testifying in representative capacity.

(C) No, because the attorney is allowed to engage in political activity under his own name.

(D) No, because the attorney agreed with the firm.

Question 26.

The rules of the judicial district in which a judge sits state that parties are allowed two postponements as of right, but any additional postponements should only be approved if the requesting party convinces the judge that a postponement is appropriate. The judge routinely grants postponements because he believes it allows the parties a longer time to reach a settlement and ultimately does little to affect the outcome.

Are the judge's actions improper?

(A) Yes, because the judge should expedite the matters that appear before him.

(B) Yes, because judges should not try to force parties to settle.

(C) No, because the judge has discretion in how to manage his courtroom schedule.

(D) No, because postponements do little to affect the ultimate outcome of the case.

Question 27.

An attorney regularly appears before a trial court judge who is running for reelection in six months. Over the past year, the attorney has noticed that the judge has become increasingly ill tempered and erratic on the bench. Several lawyers she knows are automatically filing requests for judicial substitution whenever a case in which they are to appear is assigned to the judge.

The attorney's law partners suggested that she also file requests for judicial substitution whenever one of her cases is assigned to the judge. Because of the judge's respected standing, they believe reporting the judge might hurt their clients in the eyes of other members of the judiciary. Additionally, they believe the judge is unlikely to win reelection.

Should the attorney report the judge to the authorities?

(A) Yes, because of the judge's courtroom conduct.

(B) Yes, because all the lawyers filing requests for judicial substitution causes unnecessary cost and delay.

(C) No, because reporting the judge may hurt her clients.

(D) No, because the judge is unlikely to be reelected.

Question 28.

An attorney currently represents a plaintiff in a suit to recover for breach of contract. The plaintiff also has pending a personal injury lawsuit against his neighbor. However, the plaintiff is represented by another attorney in the personal injury matter.

The neighbor has asked the attorney to represent him in the plaintiff's personal injury claim. The neighbor knows that the attorney represents the plaintiff in the contract action.

Is it improper for the attorney to represent the neighbor in the personal injury claim?

(A) Yes, because both matters could be appealed to the same court and force the attorney to argue two conflicting causes of action.

(B) Yes, because the attorney is representing the plaintiff in the contract matter.

(C) No, because the neighbor knows that the attorney represents the plaintiff in the contract action.

(D) No, because one claim is in contract and the other is in tort.

Question 29.

An attorney is representing a plaintiff in a wrongful discharge case on a contingent fee basis. The plaintiff cannot afford the expenses of the investigation necessary to prepare for trial. The client asked the attorney to pay for these expenses. The attorney declined to pay, but offered to guarantee the client's promissory note to a local bank in order to secure the necessary funds.

May the attorney guarantee the promissory note?

(A) Yes, because the funds will be used for the investigation.

(B) Yes, because the attorney took the case on a contingent fee basis.

(C) No, because the attorney is lending her credit to the client.

(D) No, because the attorney is financing the plaintiff's claim.

Question 30.

An attorney hired a recent law school graduate as an associate. For the first six months, the attorney carefully reviewed and revised the associate's work. One day, the attorney told the associate that he would be going on vacation and was assigning her the representation of a plaintiff in a personal injury case that was going to trial while he was away. The associate had never conducted or observed a trial before and she was unfamiliar with the relevant law and procedure. She did not believe that she would have enough time to learn everything that she needed to know. Before the trial began, she met with the plaintiff and disclosed that this would be her first trial, but the plaintiff did not object. Although the associate prepared diligently, the plaintiff lost the trial.

Is the attorney subject to discipline?

(A) Yes, because the plaintiff lost the case.

(B) Yes, because the attorney did not ensure that the associate was competent to conduct the trial on her own.

(C) No, because the plaintiff did not object to the associate's representation.

(D) No, because the attorney closely supervised the associate for six months.

Question 31.

An attorney represented a local amusement park in a personal injury claim brought by one of its customers. Although the park had a valid defense to the claim, the attorney advised the park to pay the damages requested by the customer in order to avoid bad publicity. Relying on the attorney's advice, the park paid the claim.

Is the attorney subject to discipline?

(A) Yes, because the attorney did not zealously advocate the interests of his client.

(B) Yes, because the park paid the claim although it had a valid defense.

(C) No, because the park accepted the attorney's advice.

(D) No, because paying the claim avoided bad publicity.

Question 32.

An attorney, who is corporate counsel for a company, is investigating the possibility that an employee has been embezzling from the company. The attorney believes that if the employee were questioned, the employee would not answer truthfully if he knew the real purpose of the questions. The attorney plans to question the employee and falsely tell him that he is not a suspect and that his answers to the questions will be held in confidence.

Are the attorney's actions proper?

(A) Yes, because legal proceedings are not yet pending.

(B) Yes, because the employee should reasonably understand that the attorney does not represent him.

(C) No, because the attorney's conduct involves misrepresentation.

(D) No, because the attorney is corporate counsel for the company, and the employee is an employee of the company.

Question 33.

A client asked an attorney for representation in a suit to establish the client's ownership of certain intellectual property. The client did not have the necessary funds to pay the attorney's usual rate. The client proposed instead to pay the attorney an amount in cash equal to 10 percent of the fees and royalties the client might recover as a result of the suit. The attorney accepted the proposal and took the case. The resulting payment is unlikely to exceed the fee the attorney would have earned from his normal fee agreement.

Are the attorney's actions proper?

(A) Yes, because the client proposed the fee arrangement.

(B) Yes, because the attorney may contract with the client for a reasonable contingent fee.

(C) No, because the resulting payment may exceed the attorney's normal fee.

(D) No, because the attorney is acquiring a proprietary interest in the subject matter of the litigation.

Question 34.

An attorney joined a firm as a salaried associate. The firm engaged solely in the practice of law. The son-in-law of one of the partners, who is not a lawyer, is vice-president of the firm and office manager. He works under the direct supervision of his father-in-law, a named partner in the firm.

Is the attorney subject to discipline?

(A) Yes, because the partner's son-in-law is an officer of the firm.

(B) Yes, because there is no indication client confidences are kept from the son-in-law.

(C) No, because the attorney is only a salaried employee.

(D) No, because the son-in-law is under the direct supervision of a named partner.

Question 35.

A judge is one of three trustees of a trust for her grandchildren's benefit. The trust owns 1,000 shares of stock in a large telecommunications company. The stock has been selling at $1,000 a share. The telecommunications company is suing another company for breach of contract, and the case is assigned to the judge for trial. The judge reasonably believes that she can be fair and impartial. Additionally, she does not personally own stock in either party to the litigation.

May the judge hear the case?

(A) Yes, because she doesn't personally own any stock in either party.

(B) Yes, because the judge reasonably believes that she can remain impartial.

(C) No, because the outcome of the lawsuit is likely to affect the value of the stock.

(D) No, because the trust has a significant financial interest in the telecommunications company.

Question 36.

An attorney represented a local business in a contract dispute against an advertising agency. The attorney received a proposed settlement that required the attorney to agree not to represent the business in any subsequent proceeding involving the agency. The attorney thought the settlement was reasonable and that another attorney could protect the business in any future disputes with the advertising agency. However, the attorney thought he might be able to get more money for his client if he also agreed to not represent any other client against the agency.

Is the attorney subject to discipline if he agrees to the settlement?

(A) Yes, because the proposed settlement restricts the attorney's right to represent the business in the future.

(B) Yes, because the attorney believes it might help the client more to agree to not represent any client against the agency.

(C) No, because the attorney believes the settlement is reasonable.

(D) No, because the attorney believes another attorney could protect the business in future disputes.

Question 37.

A law firm has 1,000 lawyers in six states. It has placed the supervision of all routine administrative and financial matters in the hands of a nonlawyer. The nonlawyer is paid a regular monthly salary and a year-end bonus from the law firm's net income from fees. Organizationally, the nonlawyer reports to an attorney who acts as the managing partner of the law firm. The attorney deals with all issues related to the law firm's supervision of the practice of law. The nonlawyer does not have access to client files and does not control the professional judgment of lawyers in the firm.

Is the attorney subject to discipline?

(A) Yes, because the firm is sharing legal fees with a nonlawyer.

(B) Yes, because the nonlawyer is engaged in the unauthorized practice of law.

(C) No, because the nonlawyer does not control the professional judgment of lawyers in the firm.

(D) No, because the nonlawyer does not have access to confidential information.

Question 38.

A plaintiff filed suit against both an attorney and her client, alleging a violation of state law as the result of a bad business deal. The attorney represented the client in the deal. The attorney and the client are each represented by separate counsel in the plaintiff's suit. In responding to a deposition under subpoena, the attorney revealed, to the extent the attorney reasonably believes necessary to defend herself, confidential information imparted to the attorney by the client that will be favorable to the attorney but damaging to the client.

Is the attorney subject to discipline?

(A) Yes, because disclosure is detrimental to the client.

(B) Yes, because the client revealed confidential information.

(C) No, because the attorney was defending herself.

(D) No, because the attorney and client are each represented by separate counsel.

Question 39.

A stolen painting was found in the possession of an attorney, who was holding it as a favor for one of her clients. The authorities did not believe the attorney was involved in the theft in any way, but they did believe the attorney's client knew important information regarding the theft. The attorney was subpoenaed to testify before a grand jury. The grand jury asked for the name of the client who had left the painting in the attorney's possession, and the attorney provided the name to the grand jury.

Is the attorney subject to discipline?

(A) Yes, because the identity of the client is protected by the attorney-client privilege.

(B) Yes, because the theft does not involve an imminent threat of death or serious bodily harm.

(C) No, because the attorney can provide the information to defend herself.

(D) No, because the client's name is not privileged under the circumstances.

Question 40.

An attorney served as lieutenant governor immediately prior to reopening his law office in the state. The attorney printed and mailed an announcement of his return to private practice to members of the bar, persons who had previously been his clients, and personal friends whom he had never represented. The printed announcement stated that the attorney had reopened his law office, gave his address and telephone number, and added that he had recently served as lieutenant governor.

Are the attorney's actions proper?

(A) Yes, because all of the information is true.

(B) Yes, because all of the information is public.

(C) No, because the attorney is implying an ability to improperly influence the courts.

(D) No, because he mailed the announcement to people who had never been clients.

Question 41.

A sole practitioner recently underwent chemotherapy and was advised that he could not return to work for six months. The attorney delivered all of his clients' files to a friend of his, who is also a sole practitioner. The friend agreed to review each client's file promptly, take any action necessary to protect each client's interests, and treat the information in the files as confidential. The attorney then wrote to his clients, advising each client that the client's file had been delivered to his friend for review and for any action necessary to protect the client's interest, and that the client was free to select another lawyer.

Is the attorney subject to discipline?

(A) Yes, because the attorney did not obtain prior consent from his clients.

(B) Yes, because the attorney did not plan to supervise his friend in providing representation to the clients.

(C) No, because the friend agreed to act diligently in representing the clients.

(D) No, because finding alternative representation was necessary due to the chemotherapy.

Question 42.

An attorney and a client entered into a written retainer and hourly fee agreement that required the client to pay $10,000 in advance of any services rendered by the attorney and which required the attorney to return any portion that was not earned. The agreement further provided that the attorney would render monthly statements and withdraw her fees as billed. The attorney deposited the entire fund in her Clients' Trust Account. Thereafter, the attorney rendered monthly progress reports and statements for services to the client after services were rendered, showing the balance of the client's fee advance. However, the attorney did not withdraw any of the $10,000 advance until one year later when the matter was concluded to the client's complete satisfaction. At that time, the attorney had billed the client reasonable legal fees of $5,000. The attorney wrote two checks on her Clients' Trust Account: one to herself for $5,000, which she deposited in her general office account, and one for $5,000 to the client.

Is the attorney subject to discipline?

(A) Yes, because the attorney required the client to pay in advance.

(B) Yes, because the attorney failed to withdraw her fees as billed.

(C) No, because the client's payment was put in the Clients' Trust Account.

(D) No, because the attorney's fee was reasonable.

Question 43.

An attorney entered into a written retainer agreement with a defendant in a criminal case. Because the defendant couldn't afford the attorney's fee, the defendant asked if they could agree to transfer ownership of certain stocks to the attorney if the attorney successfully prevented him from going to prison. The attorney agreed to the retainer agreement. Later, the charges against the defendant were dismissed.

Is the retainer agreement proper?

(A) Yes, because the charges were dismissed.

(B) Yes, because the defendant couldn't afford the attorney otherwise.

(C) No, because this is a criminal case.

(D) No, because a lawyer may not acquire a proprietary interest in a client's property.

Question 44.

An attorney represents a plaintiff in a civil action that was filed a year ago and is about to be set for trial. In discussing possible trial dates with opposing counsel and the court clerk, three possible trial dates were available. The three dates were all within 60 days of each other. Without first consulting the plaintiff, the attorney requested the latest possible date because she was also representing a defendant in a felony criminal trial and wanted as much time as possible to prepare the criminal case. The later trial date will not prejudice the plaintiff.

Is the attorney subject to discipline?

(A) Yes, because the attorney is not acting diligently in her representation of the plaintiff.

(B) Yes, because the attorney is favoring the criminal defendant over the civil plaintiff.

(C) No, because the later date will not prejudice the plaintiff.

(D) No, because the attorney is the master of her own schedule.

Question 45.

A defendant was on trial for murder. During closing arguments, the prosecutor accurately stated the testimony in the case. He ended his closing argument by saying, "The defendant's whole defense is based on the testimony of his friend. I don't believe the defendant's friend was telling the truth, and I don't think you believe him either." The prosecutor reasonably believed that the defendant's friend didn't tell the truth.

Is the prosecutor subject to discipline?

(A) Yes, because the prosecutor asserted his personal opinion about the friend's credibility.

(B) Yes, because the prosecutor alluded to the beliefs of the jurors.

(C) No, because the prosecutor accurately stated the testimony in the case.

(D) No, because the prosecutor reasonably believed that the defendant's friend had lied.

Question 46.

A recently graduated attorney began a plaintiffs' personal injury practice, but was having a difficult time attracting clients. The attorney filmed an advertisement where the attorney appeared to be arguing a case before the United States Supreme Court. In the commercial, the Court appears to rule unanimously in favor of the attorney's client. The voice-over states that results would vary depending upon particular legal and factual circumstances, but that the attorney would "Fight for what's yours!" The attorney had never appeared in court. As a result of airing the commercial, the attorney received several significant cases.

May the attorney use this commercial to advertise his practice?

(A) Yes, because it is merely a dramatization.

(B) Yes, because the commercial contained an express disclaimer.

(C) No, because the commercial created an unjustified expectation about the results that the attorney could achieve in court.

(D) No, because the commercial implied the attorney had successfully appeared in court.

Question 47.

A prosecutor met with police officers to review the evidence in a case he was working on. During the meeting, the prosecutor discovered that the police had found several social media posts that showed the defendant was out of state at the time the crime was committed.

The defendant's appointed counsel was busy handling a large caseload and neglected to seek access to the prosecution's investigative file. The prosecutor was virtually certain that suspect's counsel was unaware of the social media posts.

Does the prosecutor have to reveal the existence of the posts to the defendant's counsel?

(A) Yes, because the posts show the defendant was out of state at the time the crime was committed.

(B) Yes, because the evidence was obtained by the police.

(C) No, because under the adversary system of criminal justice, it is expected that each party will marshal the evidence best supporting his or her position.

(D) No, because the suspect's counsel did not seek access to the prosecution's investigative file.

Question 48.

Two weeks before the date set for trial, the attorney for the plaintiff discovered that there was an eyewitness to the accident that formed the basis of the plaintiff's claim. The attorney interviewed the witness. The witness's version of the accident was contrary to that of the plaintiff and, if believed by the trier of fact, would establish that the plaintiff was at fault. The witness told the attorney that she had been thinking about taking a vacation to Japan the following week and didn't want to testify because she hated speaking in front of other people. The attorney told the witness that, since no one had subpoenaed her yet, she had no obligation to appear. She told the witness that if she didn't want to testify, the attorney would feel a lot better if the witness took the vacation and avoided the trial.

Are the attorney's actions proper?

(A) Yes, because the witness didn't want to testify.

(B) Yes, because the attorney didn't offer the witness any inducement not to testify.

(C) No, because the attorney asked the witness to leave the jurisdiction.

(D) No, because no one had subpoenaed the witness.

Question 49.

An attorney was employed in the state's environmental protection division during the time that an investigation of a suspected polluter was being conducted by that office. The attorney took no part in the investigation and had no knowledge of the facts other than those disclosed in the press. Two months ago, the attorney left the environmental protection division and entered private practice.

Last week, the suspected polluter was charged with offenses allegedly disclosed by the prior investigation. The suspected polluter asked the attorney to represent him, and the attorney agreed to do so. The environmental protection division was promptly notified and consented to the representation.

May the attorney represent the suspected polluter in this case?

(A) Yes, because the environmental protection division consented to the representation.

(B) Yes, because the attorney had no responsibility for or knowledge of the facts of the investigation of the suspect.

(C) No, because the attorney was employed by the environmental protection division during the time of the investigation.

(D) No, because the charges arose from the prior investigation.

Question 50.

When one of the attorney's regular clients left on a year abroad, the client delivered to the attorney more than enough money to pay the client's taxes when they became due. The attorney placed the money in her Clients' Trust Account. Soon after the client left, the attorney was in need of a temporary loan. Although she was reasonably certain the client would not object, she still tried to call the client before taking any money out of the client's account. However, the attorney could not reach the client. The attorney borrowed the money and replaced it 10 days later, resulting in no fees or other damages to the client. After the client returned, the attorney told the client what she had done, and the client approved the attorney's conduct.

Was it proper for the attorney to take the loan?

(A) Yes, because the client approved the attorney's conduct.

(B) Yes, because the attorney was reasonably certain the client would not object.

(C) No, because the attorney used the client's funds for a personal purpose.

(D) No, because the attorney could not reach her client before taking the funds.

Question 51.

One day, a trial judge was in his office when the telephone rang at his clerk's desk. Since everyone else had already left for the day, the judge answered it. The call was from a lawyer in a case presently pending before the judge. The lawyer was calling to attempt to reschedule a pretrial conference because of a family emergency. The lawyer had tried to call opposing counsel in the case, but she was not answering his calls. The judge agreed to reschedule the pretrial conference for the following week. The next day, the judge instructed the clerk to contact opposing counsel to inform her of the telephone call and the fact that the pretrial conference had been rescheduled.

Did the judge act properly?

(A) Yes, because the communication only dealt with scheduling matters.

(B) Yes, because no one else was in the office to take the call.

(C) No, because the judge engaged in ex parte communication.

(D) No, because the judge waited until the next day to contact opposing counsel.

Question 52.

When an attorney was elected to the state legislature, he closed his law office. Soon thereafter, a tech startup, one of the legislator's former private clients and a constituent in his legislative district, asked him to try to persuade a state agency to rule in its favor in a copyright dispute. The legislator wrote a letter on his legislative letterhead to the agency's chair, urging that the agency rule in the startup's favor. Eventually the agency ruled in the startup's favor, in part because of the legislator's efforts.

Was it proper for the legislator to write the letter to the agency?

(A) Yes, because the legislator acted on behalf of the startup as a constituent and not as a client.

(B) Yes, because the legislator used his legislative letterhead.

(C) No, because the agency ruled in the startup's favor in part due to the legislator's efforts.

(D) No, because the legislator used his public position to influence the agency.

Question 53.

When called by the attorney as witnesses in a personal injury claim, both the client and his wife testified that they had never seen a warning label on the product. The existence of a warning label was the manufacturer's primary defense. After their testimony, but while the trial was still in progress, the attorney learned from the wife's sister that there indeed had been a warning label on the box, but that the wife had removed and destroyed it. When the attorney confronted the wife with her sister's statement, the wife admitted destroying the label but insisted that her husband knew nothing about it. The attorney continued the trial, but made no reference to the absence of a warning label in his summation to the jury.

Is the attorney subject to discipline?

(A) Yes, because the attorney failed to take reasonable remedial action after he realized that the wife had given perjured testimony.

(B) Yes, because the wife committed perjury.

(C) No, because he did not reference the warning label in his summation.

(D) No, because the attorney did not rely on the wife's testimony once he discovered the perjury.

Question 54.

The partners in a firm gave all lawyers in the firm, on a monthly basis, detailed descriptions of the work they were doing for their different clients. One of the partners mentioned this practice to a new client, and the client complained that his confidences had been violated.

Are the partners subject to discipline?

(A) Yes, because sharing the information increased the risk that it might be improperly disclosed to third parties outside the firm.

(B) Yes, because lawyers may not disclose client information, even to other firm lawyers, unless the disclosure is in furtherance of the representation.

(C) No, because, absent client instructions to the contrary, lawyers may discuss client information with other lawyers in the firm.

(D) No, because lawyers may discuss client information with other lawyers in the firm, regardless of client instructions to the contrary, as long as the disclosure does not disadvantage the client.

Question 55.

An attorney accepted the representation of a plaintiff in a products liability case on a contingent fee basis. While preparing the case for trial, the attorney realized that the direct examination and cross-examination of the experts would involve engineering issues with which the attorney was not familiar and, as a consequence, the attorney might not be able to represent the plaintiff competently.

Without informing the plaintiff, the attorney consulted another attorney, who is also an engineer and a recognized specialist in products liability. The two attorneys agreed that the other attorney would participate in the trial to the limited extent of conducting the direct examination and cross-examination of the experts and that the attorneys would divide the fee in proportion to the services performed and the responsibility assumed by each. Upon conclusion of the matter, the attorney provided the plaintiff with a written statement explaining the relevant fees.

Is the attorney subject to discipline?

(A) Yes, because the attorneys' agreement limited the scope of each one's representation.

(B) Yes, because the plaintiff was not advised of the association of the other attorney.

(C) No, because the fee would be divided in proportion to the services performed and the responsibility assumed by each.

(D) No, because the fee to be paid by the plaintiff was not increased by reason of the other attorney's association.

Question 56.

During a legislative committee hearing, an attorney, reasonably believing that it was in the witness's best interest not to answer, advised the witness not to answer certain questions on the grounds that she had a constitutional right not to answer. The committee chairperson directed the witness to answer and cautioned her that refusal to answer was a misdemeanor and that criminal prosecution would be instituted if she did not answer.

Upon the attorney's advice, the witness persisted in her refusal to answer. The witness was subsequently convicted for her refusal to answer.

Were the attorney's actions proper?

(A) Yes, because the attorney reasonably believed the witness had a legal right to refuse to answer the questions.

(B) Yes, because refusing to answer was only a misdemeanor.

(C) No, because the witness committed a crime by refusing to answer.

(D) No, because the witness was successfully convicted for refusing to answer.

Question 57.

While presiding over the trial of a highly publicized case, a judge received a lengthy letter from a local attorney. The letter discussed the law applicable to the case. The judge knew that the attorney did not represent either party or any client whose interests could be affected by the outcome. After reading the trial briefs in the case, the judge concluded that the attorney's letter better explained the law applicable to the case pending before him than either of the trial briefs. The judge followed the attorney's reasoning in formulating his decision. Prior to rendering his decision, the judge did not tell the attorneys arguing the case anything about the letter.

Is the judge subject to discipline?

(A) Yes, because the attorney is not of record as counsel in the case.

(B) Yes, because the judge, prior to rendering his decision, did not communicate its contents to all counsel and give them an opportunity to respond

(C) No, because the judge did not initiate the communication with the attorney.

(D) No, because the attorney did not represent any client whose interests could be affected by the outcome.

Question 58.

An attorney started a new law firm and moved into offices in a building owned by a bank. The attorney borrowed heavily from the bank to finance the firm. At the bank's suggestion, an employee of the bank, who is not a lawyer, serves as a part-time office manager for the law firm without compensation from the firm. The duties of the office manager are to advise the firm generally on fees and time charges, program matters for the computer services, and consult with the attorney on accounting and billing practices to ensure solvency. The attorney and the bank do not discuss client confidences.

Is the attorney subject to discipline?

(A) Yes, because the bank will be involved in the practice of law.

(B) Yes, because a nonlawyer will be advising the law firm on fees and time charges.

(C) No, because the office manager is paid by the bank.

(D) No, because secrets or confidences of clients will not be disclosed to the bank.

Question 59.

An attorney represents a famous actor in an action against a newspaper for libel. The case has attracted much publicity, and a jury trial has been demanded. After one of the pretrial hearings, as the attorney left the courthouse, news reporters interviewed the attorney. In responding to questions, the attorney revealed the identity of the reporter who made the statements that were the subject of the claim.

Were the attorney's actions proper?

(A) Yes, because the trial has not commenced.

(B) Yes, because the statement relates to a matter of public record.

(C) No, because prospective jurors might learn of the attorney's remarks.

(D) No, because the attorney identified a prospective witness in the case.

Question 60.

An attorney is a well-known healthcare expert. During congressional hearings on healthcare, the attorney testified to her personal belief and expert opinion on the pending healthcare package. She failed to disclose in her testimony that she was being compensated by a private client for her appearance. In her testimony, the attorney took the position favored by her client, but the position was also one that the attorney believed was in the public interest.

Is the attorney subject to discipline?

(A) Yes, because a lawyer may not accept a fee for trying to influence legislative action.

(B) Yes, because a lawyer who appears in a legislative hearing should identify the capacity in which the lawyer appears.

(C) No, because Congress is interested in the content of the testimony and not who is paying the witness.

(D) No, because the attorney believed that the position she advocated was in the public interest.

B. Answers

1. Answers to Practice MPRE 1

Question 1.

B is the correct answer. Under Model Rule 7.2(b), an attorney "shall not give anything of value to a person for recommending the lawyer's services." However, there are exceptions for paying the costs of advertisements or communications, legal service plans or not-for-profit or qualified referral plans, or the purchase of a practice. Here, the agreement with the restaurant owner clearly violates this Rule, since the owner is receiving valuable advertising space and recommendations. For this Rule, keep in mind that the Rule says "anything of value," not simply "money."

A is incorrect. The issue here is that the attorney is giving the restaurant owner something of value for recommending the lawyer's services, not that the attorney asked the owner to put up some ads. Keep in mind that the Rules are particularly concerned with advertising practices that could lead to information that is misleading or overreaching, and an arrangement like this could likely lead to the dissemination of problematic information.

C is incorrect. As stated above, the Rule is concerned with "anything of value," not simply "money."

D is incorrect. Keep in mind that many wrong answers on the MPRE will set up a "no-harm, no-foul" situation. This answer choice implies that a lawyer could pay for referrals as long as he or she let everyone in on the action, which clearly makes little sense ethically. An answer choice like this can be eliminated immediately.

Question 2.

B is the correct answer. Model Rule 7.5(d) states that "lawyers may state or imply that they practice in a partnership or other organization only when that is the fact." As Comment [2] explains, "lawyers sharing office facilities, but who are not in fact associated with each other in a law firm, may not denominate themselves as, for example, 'Smith and Jones,' for that title suggests that they are practicing law together in a firm." Model Rule 7.5, Comment [2]. The big issue here is that Alpha and Gamma are holding themselves out to the world as partners, when they clearly are not. Keep in mind the Rules' concern with keeping the public informed.

A is incorrect. A law firm can continue to use "the names of deceased members where there has been a continuing succession in the firm's identity." Model Rule 7.5, Comment [1]. Here, Alpha is still around, so he could use the name. The big issue is that the new "firm" name misleads the public into thinking Alpha and Gamma are somehow connected.

C is incorrect. This answer choice should be discarded immediately, as it contains no mention of Gamma, who is clearly at issue here.

D is incorrect. This answer choice should also be discarded immediately, as paying for rent and office expenses does not make one a partner with another individual, and the new name implies that there is some kind of partnership between Alpha and Gamma.

Question 3.

B is the correct answer. Under Model Rule 1.11(a)(2), "a lawyer who has formerly served as a public officer or employee of the government ... shall not otherwise represent a client in connection with a matter in which the lawyer participated personally and substantially as a public officer or employee" unless authorized to do so by the government agency. Importantly, Comment [3] states that these provisions are "designed not only to protect the former client, but also to prevent a lawyer from exploiting public office for the advantage of another client." Model Rule 1.11, Comment [3].

Here, although the corporation is asking the attorney for help, it does not change the analysis. The attorney still participated personally and substantially in the investigation of the corporation's effluent, and the Rule does not limit itself only to suits against the government. As a side note, don't shy away from an answer choice simply because there have been several in a row (here, the first three correct choices were B).

A is incorrect. As stated above, the issue is that the attorney participated personally and substantially in the investigation of the corporation's effluent and could exploit information used during his government service.

C is incorrect. "Special competence" does not protect a lawyer from actions that have the appearance of impropriety or unfairness.

D is incorrect. Even if the information is in the public domain, the Rule seeks to keep the attorney from exploiting his prior government service.

Question 4.

C is the correct answer. Although an attorney can retain or contract with other lawyers outside the lawyer's own firm to assist in the provision of legal service, "the lawyer should ordinarily obtain informed consent from the client." Model Rule 1.1, Comment [6]. Imagine being a client and suddenly finding out some strange lawyer you had no say in choosing was working on your case. While an attorney has the right to make decisions in many aspects of a representation, in the case of bringing in another attorney, the attorney must ask for client consent.

A is incorrect. This is another example of the "no-harm, no-foul" answer choice, which should be dismissed immediately.

B is incorrect. Similar to answer choice A, this "no-harm, no-foul" answer choice should be dismissed immediately.

D is incorrect. As in the other two choices, this choice implies that the attorney can do something major like retaining another attorney without consulting the client so long as the attorney makes up for it later. Here, simply telling the client how the fees will be split does not fix the problem of an unauthorized and unexpected attorney working on the case.

Question 5.

C is the correct answer. During representation, a lawyer "shall not make an extrajudicial statement that the lawyer knows or reasonably should know will be disseminated by means of public communication and will have a substantial likelihood of materially prejudicing an adjudicative proceeding in the matter." Model Rule 3.6(a). However, there is an exception for "information contained in a public record." Model Rule 3.6(b)(2). Here, since the politician has sued the newspaper for libel, the identity of the reporter is a matter of public record.

A is incorrect. While the reporter may be a prospective witness, the important point is that lawyers may make statements regarding matters of public record.

B is incorrect. While prospective jurors may learn of the attorney's remarks, this does not automatically make any remarks subject to discipline.

D is incorrect. Although the trial has not yet commenced, the Rule is concerned with "prejudicing an adjudicative proceeding." Model Rule 3.6(a). Clearly, prejudice can be created before a trial has actually commenced.

Question 6.

D is the correct answer. Under Model Rule 1.11(a)(2), "a lawyer who has formerly served as a public officer or employee of the government . . . shall not otherwise represent a client in connection with a matter in which the lawyer participated personally and substantially as a public officer or employee" unless authorized to do so by the government agency. Here, the attorney had nothing to do with the investigation. Remember, Model Rule 1.11 is concerned with former government employees exploiting knowledge about a party unfairly. Here, there is no knowledge to exploit.

A is incorrect. As stated above, for Model Rule 1.11 to apply, the lawyer must have "participated personally and substantially" in the matter.

Although the attorney worked in the district attorney's office, he had nothing to do with the earlier investigation.

B is incorrect. Although the district attorney's office consented, the big issue is that the attorney had nothing to do with the earlier investigation. Thus, the district attorney's office's consent was unnecessary.

C is incorrect. Under Model Rule 1.11, if a lawyer is disqualified from representation, no lawyer in that firm may undertake the representation unless the disqualified lawyer is screened, takes no fee, and written notice is given to the appropriate government agency. Here, since the attorney was not "personally and substantially" involved in the earlier investigation, such actions would be unnecessary.

Question 7.

A is the correct answer. A lawyer should act with reasonable diligence and promptness when representing a client. Model Rule 1.3. Here, since the civil action was filed a year ago, the client gave his availability through December, the "delay" is only a little over two months, and the client will not be prejudiced by the delay, it is absolutely reasonable for the attorney to take the December 10 trial date.

B is incorrect. There is no special Rule stating that criminal trials are more important than civil matters.

C is incorrect. As stated above, there is no indication that her actions are causing an unreasonable delay in the civil trial.

D is incorrect. Even if the attorney was court-appointed, that fact would not create special issues concerning scheduling of the two trials in this situation.

Question 8.

A is the correct answer. A lawyer cannot represent two clients if the representation of one client will be directly adverse to another. Model Rule 1.7(a)(1). Here, the one client's plan to turn state's evidence against the other client clearly violates this restriction. Importantly, since the common representation has failed (since one client is turning against another), the attorney must ordinarily withdraw from representing all of the clients. Model Rule 1.7, Comment [29].

B is incorrect. "A lawyer who has formerly represented a client in a matter shall not thereafter represent another person in the same or a substantially related matter in which that person's interests are materially adverse to the interests of the former client unless the former client gives informed consent, confirmed in writing." Model Rule 1.9(a). Importantly, the other man's consent is only to the withdrawal, not to the continued representation. This is an instance showing the importance of careful reading.

C is incorrect. Considering the basic problem, which client the attorney chooses to stay with and that particular client's argument does not change the analysis.

D is incorrect. Choosing not to call one client as a witness does not fix the situation, since one client's interest is directly adverse to the other client's.

Question 9.

C is the correct answer. Each side is entitled to know and to respond to every fact and every argument presented by the other side. If a judge could consult any legal source he or she wished without identifying it and giving each side the right to respond, the adversarial nature of the judicial system would collapse. At the same time, there are instances in which a judge will need to get advice on the law, especially when, as in these facts, the lawyers have not stated the situation clearly. To enable the judge to do this without subverting the adversarial process, Model Code of Judicial Conduct, Rule 2.9(A)(2) permits a judge to "obtain the written advice of a disinterested expert on the law applicable to a proceeding before the judge, if the judge gives advance notice to the parties of the person to be consulted and the subject matter of the advice to be solicited, and affords the parties a reasonable opportunity to object and respond to the notice and to the advice received."

A is incorrect. Always be wary of this type of answer choice. The MPRE frequently uses the idea of an attorney or judge not initiating the initial contact as a wrong answer choice. Considering the concerns addressed by the Rule, who started the communication is clearly irrelevant. This type of answer choice should be discarded immediately.

B is incorrect. It's not enough that the expert consulted by the judge be impartial. The parties are entitled to know what the expert has been asked and what he or she has advised. After all, the expert may be wrong or the judge may not have communicated the issues correctly. The parties may want to respond, and they must be given the opportunity to do so.

D is incorrect. This answer choice seems to imply that an expert's impartiality could make the communication proper. However, as stated above, this is not the case.

Question 10.

D is the correct answer. "A lawyer shall not make a false or misleading communication about the lawyer or the lawyer's services." Model Rule 7.1. Here, the advertisement is misleading because it claims the lawyer will only charge $600 for representation that does not go to trial, when the reality is that the representation may cost more if the attorney spends more time on the matter. Importantly, this is the only answer choice that specifically mentions anything about the advertisement, which is clearly the primary issue.

A is incorrect. Although the fee might have been reasonable, the question specifically deals with a misleading advertisement and the potential ethical problems caused by it.

B is incorrect. Again, this answer choice does not address the issue of the misleading advertisement.

C is incorrect. This is another example of a "no-harm, no-foul" answer choice, which should be immediately tossed out.

Question 11.

A is the correct answer. A lawyer shall not form a partnership with a nonlawyer if any of the activities of the partnership consist of the "practice of law." A lawyer who does so is assisting another in the unauthorized practice of law, and is subject to discipline. Model Rule 5.5(a). Here, the important point is that the *partnership* is delivering the legal services, which choice A states explicitly.

B is incorrect. Although the attorney would be receiving fees for other than legal services, the primary problem is that the partnership with the non-lawyer would be engaged in the practice of law.

C is incorrect. The important fact is that the partnership is providing legal services. However, as a partner, the accountant is receiving a portion of the entity's profits and has control over aspects of the business. Under Model Rule 5.4(a), a lawyer may not share legal fees with a nonlawyer, which would clearly happen here under the partnership agreement. This Rule is the major deterrent to partnerships like this, and even splitting fees with a charity is not allowed. The only exceptions to this Rule involve paying the estates of deceased attorneys or law firm employee compensation or retirement plans, neither of which apply here. Although the intention might be to provide high-quality services, this fact does not change the analysis.

D is incorrect. As stated above, the main issues are the creation of a partnership that provides legal services and the sharing of fees with a nonlawyer. Simply keeping the accountant from interfering with the attorney's legal advice is not enough.

Question 12.

D is the correct answer. As stated in Part One, the MPRE will ask about the propriety of a fee that is in dispute. Remember that the Model Rules specify that a lawyer's fee shall be reasonable (Model Rule 1.5(a)); it's a safe bet, therefore, that a lower fee will be perceived as more reasonable than a higher one. Thus, when a question asks what part of a fee a lawyer may properly keep, you're generally safe if you opt for the choice that best protects the client's interests in the money under dispute. This answer recognizes the three basic principles a lawyer must observe when dealing with client funds: (1) client funds must always be kept separate from the lawyer's funds in a designated clients' escrow account; (2) as soon as the client's interest in the funds is fixed, the client's money must be delivered to the client; and (3) if both the client and the attorney claim any interest in any part of the funds — for example, if a dispute arises as to the lawyer's fees — the funds must remain in the separate client account until there is an accounting and their respective interests can be severed. Model Rule 1.15. Here, the attorney's maximum claim was for fees totaling 6 hours $\times$ $100 = $600. When the bail hearing was completed, the client's interest in the advance was $1,000. The attorney had a duty to return this promptly. Because the client had demanded $1,600, the lawyer's fee of $600 was in dispute. Consequently, the money representing the fee had to be retained in the clients' trust account until the dispute was resolved.

A is incorrect. The funds in dispute totaled only $600. The balance of $1,000 was not in dispute and belonged to the client. The attorney was under a duty to return $1,000 to the client because the money was not used for the purpose intended.

B is incorrect. Because the fee of $600 was in dispute, the attorney had no right to transfer that sum to his fee account. He was required to retain the funds in his clients' trust account until the dispute was resolved. Further, the attorney had no right to retain the balance of $1,000 in either account pending the appeal. The money was deposited with the attorney only in connection with the bail application, not the appeal itself.

C is incorrect. The attorney was right to send the $1,000 to the client, but wrong in transferring $600 to his fee account. So long as his fee was in dispute, the $600 had to be retained in the Clients' Fund Account. Model Rule 1.15(e).

Question 13.

C is the correct answer. "When ordered to do so by a tribunal, a lawyer shall continue representation notwithstanding good cause for terminating the representation." Model Rule 1.16(c). Here, since the court denied the request, the attorney cannot withdraw. This question is a good example of carefully reading the question.

A is incorrect. As stated above, the major issue is that the court denied the request. The attorney and client cannot simply ignore the court's order. This should be an obviously wrong answer choice.

B is incorrect. Even if the client is being unreasonable, the attorney still has to represent the client if the court orders him to do so.

D is incorrect. The issue here is not potential prejudice to the client, but the fact that the court has ordered representation to continue.

Question 14.

C is the correct answer. If the lawyer did not believe there was a basis in law and fact for the defense, it would be improper for him to mount a defense of the company in court. Model Rule 3.1. However, there is no prohibition against arguing a meritorious defense simply because a settlement might be proper as well.

A is incorrect. Although the company has told the attorney that it will not settle, simply telling the attorney this (when there is a good faith defense) does not make representation improper.

B is incorrect. There is no Rule stating a lawyer should avoid litigation in all circumstances, especially when there is a good faith argument at issue. This answer choice should be tossed immediately, because it implies even those with good faith claims should be discouraged from having their day in court.

D is incorrect. While the general counsel may be the attorney's boss, this does not make the representation improper. Again, this is an answer choice that makes no logical sense in that it implies attorneys cannot be the employees of other people or entities. It should be tossed immediately.

Question 15.

D is the correct answer. At trial, an attorney is not allowed to state his or her personal opinion about the credibility of a witness. Model Rule 3.4.

A is incorrect. Even if the statement is accurate, an attorney is not allowed to state his or her personal opinion about the credibility of a witness.

B is incorrect. Even if the prosecutor really believed the witness was lying, he could not make such a statement.

C is incorrect. The issue here is that the prosecutor is stating his beliefs, not that he may be alluding to the beliefs of jurors.

Question 16.

D is the correct answer. "In representing a client, a lawyer shall not communicate about the subject of the representation with a person the lawyer knows to be represented by another lawyer in the matter, unless the lawyer has the consent of the lawyer or is authorized to do so by law or a court order." Model Rule 4.2. The fact the lawyer is using the investigator to communicate with the defendant does not change the analysis.

A is incorrect. The simple fact that a client tells the attorney to do something does not mean the lawyer can go against the requirements of the Rules. This answer choice should have been discarded immediately.

B is incorrect. The Rules bar the lawyer from communicating with a represented person. It would not make sense if an improper action could be made proper because of what was discovered through that improper action.

C is incorrect. There is no Rule stating that attorneys cannot interview people through agents or employees. The issue here is that the person was represented by counsel.

Question 17.

D is the correct answer. Unlike a represented person, a lawyer may communicate with an unrepresented person as long as the lawyer does not imply he or she is disinterested and the lawyer does not give legal advice to a person whose interests are in conflict with the interests of the lawyer's client. Model Rule 4.3. Here, the husband's interests are in conflict with the wife's. Importantly, the letter did not imply disinterest or give legal advice.

A is incorrect. Under the Rule, the attorney does not have to give advice that the unrepresented person seek counsel, unless the attorney chooses to do so. Importantly, this is the only "legal" advice the attorney could properly give.

B is incorrect. As stated above, a lawyer can communicate with an unrepresented person, unless he or she implies disinterest or gives legal advice. Model Rule 4.3.

C is incorrect. A scrivener is someone who simply copies or records the communications of others. The attorney is not doing that here.

Question 18.

D is the correct answer. A judge must disqualify himself or herself in any proceeding in which the judge's impartiality might reasonably be questioned. Model Code of Judicial Conduct, Rule 2.11. Such situations include when the judge "served as a lawyer in the matter in controversy, or was associated with a lawyer who participated substantially as a lawyer in the matter during such association." Model Code of Judicial Conduct, Rule 2.11(A)(6)(a). Consequently, since the judge was associated with the law firm when these matters were pending, she must disqualify herself.

A is incorrect. Whether or not the judge has a financial interest in the case, the primary issue is that she was a partner at the firm when these matters were pending. Model Code of Judicial Conduct, Rule 2.11(A)(6)(a).

B is incorrect. Even if the requests were not contested, the Rules still disqualify a judge if he or she served as a lawyer in the matter in controversy or were associated with a lawyer who did so. Model Code of Judicial Conduct, Rule 2.11(A)(6)(a). This answer choice is the classic "no-harm, no-foul" answer choice that should be avoided.

C is incorrect. The issue is that the judge was associated with the firm when these matters were pending. Model Code of Judicial Conduct, Rule 2.11(A)(6)(a). Simply noting her involvement in record would not solve the problem of the judge's potential lack of impartiality.

Question 19.

D is the correct answer. Generally, "a lawyer shall not represent anyone in connection with a matter in which the lawyer participated personally and substantially" as an arbitrator. Model Rule 1.12(a). However, there is an exception when the lawyer is selected as a partisan arbitrator of a party in a multimember arbitration panel. In that case, the attorney is not prohibited from subsequently representing that party. Model Rule 1.12(d). Here, since the attorney was appointed to the panel as a partisan arbitrator, he can represent the company.

A is incorrect. Under Model Rule 1.12(d), if an attorney is selected as a partisan arbitrator of a party in a multimember arbitration panel, he or she can subsequently represent that party.

B is incorrect. The attorney's firm's prior association with the company would not bar the attorney from serving as a partisan arbitrator.

C is incorrect. This answer choice is a case of giving a Rule that doesn't apply to these facts. Generally, a lawyer who has been an arbitrator on a matter cannot represent a party unless all parties to the proceeding give informed consent, confirmed in writing. Model Rule 1.12(a). However, since the attorney was a partisan arbitrator, he does not need to the parties' consent to subsequently represent the company. Model Rule 1.12(d).

Question 20.

B is the correct answer. "If a lawyer, the lawyer's client, or a witness called by the lawyer, has offered material evidence and the lawyer comes to know of its falsity, the lawyer shall take reasonable remedial measures, including, if necessary, disclosure to the tribunal." Model Rule 3.3. Simply not referring to the absence of the warning label in his summation is not a valid remedial measure.

A is incorrect. While the attorney called the wife as a witness, the issue is that the attorney came to know of the falsity of the testimony and took no reasonable remedial measures to correct it. If the attorney never discovered the lie, he could not reasonably be expected to do something about it.

C is incorrect. This is the classic "no-harm, no foul" answer choice and should be discarded immediately.

D is incorrect. While he may not have relied on the testimony, the attorney still knew of its falsity and did nothing to remediate matters.

Question 21.

C is the correct answer. "A lawyer shall not reveal information relating to the representation of a client unless the client gives informed consent" or the disclosure falls within one of the exceptions related to preventing crime, defending the attorney, or compliance with law or court order. Model Rule 1.6. The IRS is asking the attorney for information regarding his representation in the employment contract case, and the client has not given his consent for the disclosure. Since there is no indication the disclosure falls within any of the exceptions, it would be improper for the attorney to give the information to the IRS.

A is incorrect. "A lawyer shall not reveal information relating to the representation of a client unless the client gives informed consent" or the disclosure falls within certain exceptions. Model Rule 1.6. Importantly, the "confidentiality rule . . . applies not only to matters communicated in confidence by the client, but also to all information relating to the representation." Model Rule 1.6, Comment [3]. Consequently, the Rule covers more than the attorney's work product.

B is incorrect. "The duty of confidentiality continues after the client-lawyer relationship has terminated." Model Rule 1.6, Comment [20].

D is incorrect. The important point in the confidentiality rule is that the client did not consent to disclosure. Consequently, even if the lawyer believed disclosing the information might be beneficial, he still could not do so without his client's consent.

Question 22.

A is the correct answer. Under Model Rule 7.2(b), a lawyer may not give anything of value to a person for recommending the lawyer's services except under certain circumstances. "Anything of value" refers to more than money, so the fact that the attorney is recommending the broker in exchange for the broker's recommendations violates this Rule.

B is incorrect. A close reading of the question shows that the parties have not entered into any association. They are merely recommending each other's services, although the fact that the attorney is giving the broker something of value for the broker's recommendations violates the Rules.

C is incorrect. Even though they are not sharing fees, the arrangement violates Model Rule 7.2(b).

D is incorrect. Although their fees are reasonable, the arrangement violates Model Rule 7.2(b). This is another "no-harm, no-foul" wrong answer.

Question 23.

B is the correct answer. "In dealing on behalf of a client with a person who is not represented by counsel, a lawyer shall not state or imply that the lawyer is disinterested." Model Rule 4.3. Because the attorney simply identified himself as "an officer of the court," he improperly implied he was disinterested in the outcome, when in fact he was working on behalf of the respondent.

A is incorrect. Here, even if the agency had known or given its consent to the attorney's actions, the primary issue is that the attorney contacted the woman and implied that he was disinterested when in fact he was representing the respondent.

C is incorrect. It's debatable whether all of the attorney's statements were true, considering the fact that he implied he was only "an officer of the court." Importantly, in doing so, he violated the Rule regarding implied disinterest.

D is incorrect. As stated above, the primary issue was that the attorney implied he was disinterested. However, if he had given legal advice, it would also be a violation of Model Rule 4.3. Under Model Rule 4.3, "[t]he lawyer shall not give legal advice to an unrepresented person, other than the advice to secure counsel, if the lawyer knows or reasonably should know that the interests of such a person are or have a reasonable possibility of being in conflict with the interests of the client." Here, the woman's interests are likely in conflict with the respondent's interests, since the matter of paternity and support for the child is in question. Even so, in communications questions, an answer choice saying an attorney is not subject to discipline because he or she did not give legal advice is usually incorrect.

Question 24.

B is the correct answer. An attorney who has formerly served as a public officer or government employee may not represent a client in connection "with a matter in which the lawyer participated personally and substantially as a public officer or employee, unless the appropriate government agency gives its informed consent, confirmed in writing, to the representation." Model Rule 1.11(a)(2). Importantly, this Rule is "designed not only to protect the former client, but also to prevent a lawyer from exploiting public office for the advantage of another client." Model Rule 1.11, Comment [3]. Here, since the attorney represented the county in the nonsupport proceeding against the defendant, he cannot now represent the wife in her action for support.

A is incorrect. There is an exception under Model Rule 1.11 when the attorney obtains the informed consent of the government agency. However, the defendant's consent would not change the analysis.

C is incorrect. Model Rule 1.11 applies to attorneys who serve or have "formerly served" as a public officer or government employee. Consequently, whether or not the attorney's responsibility in his public employment has terminated is irrelevant.

D is incorrect. This answer choice shows the important of careful reading. The question specifically states that the attorney "represented the county" in the criminal proceeding. While the ex-wife may have benefited, he was not representing her interest.

Question 25.

A is the correct answer. Under Model Rule 4.2, a lawyer cannot "communicate about the subject of the representation with a person the lawyer knows to be represented by another lawyer in the matter." Since the attorney knew the claimant was represented by counsel, he cannot communicate with him through the use of the investigator.

B is incorrect. Model Rule 4.2 applies even to communications initiated by the represented person. Importantly, the Rule focuses on the communication itself, not on its content.

C is incorrect. Model Rule 4.2 applies to persons represented by counsel. Once the attorney knows the person is being represented by counsel, he or she cannot communicate with the person "unless the lawyer has the consent of the other lawyer or is authorized to do so by law or a court order." Importantly, whether or not a suit has been filed is irrelevant.

D is incorrect. The issue here is that the attorney knows the claimant is represented by counsel. It does not matter that the attorney may not be representing the city in any subsequent litigation on the claimant's claim.

Question 26.

A is the correct answer. "A lawyer shall not practice with or in the form of a professional corporation or association authorized to practice law for a profit, if: . . . a nonlawyer is a corporate director or officer thereof or occupies the position of similar responsibility." Model Rule 5.4(d)(2). Traditionally, the Rules place limitations on allowing a third party to direct or regulate the lawyer's professional judgment. Model Rule 5.4, Comment [2]. Here, since the partner's wife is vice-president of the corporation, her position in the corporation violates the Rule.

B is incorrect. Model Rule 5.4 expressly allows payments to a deceased lawyer's estate. Since the executor is holding the stock while the deceased lawyer's estate is being probated, it does not violate the Rule.

C is incorrect. Model Rule 5.4 prohibits lawyers from practicing with a corporation that is improperly sharing legal fees or decision-making responsibility with a nonlawyer. The Rule does not limit that prohibition to lawyers who only practice as members or shareholders of the corporation.

D is incorrect. Model Rule 5.4 prohibits nonlawyers from being directors or officers of the corporation. It does not make any distinctions regarding the specific responsibilities of that director or officer's job.

Question 27.

B is the correct answer. "Prior to the conclusion of representation of a client, a lawyer shall not make or negotiate an agreement giving the lawyer literary or media rights to a portrayal or account based in substantial part on information relating to the representation." Model Rule 1.8(d). The Rule notes that such agreements can create a conflict between the lawyer and client, because "measures suitable in the representation of the client may detract from the publication value." Model Rule 1.8, Comment [9]. Specifically, the lawyer may be tempted to act in ways that make the story better, even if those actions are to the client's detriment.

A is incorrect. The problem here is not that the attorney is getting a fee contingent on the value of the media rights, the problem is that this agreement may encourage the attorney to conduct his representation in a way that is detrimental to the client.

C is incorrect. This answer choice is a distractor, and it is trying to trick a student who only remembers the Rule that contingency fees are improper in criminal cases. If that's the only relevant Rule the student can remember, he or she might be tempted to pick this choice.

D is incorrect. This is another over-broad statement that should be avoided. The fact a client received independent advice on a matter does not insulate an attorney who may have violated the Rules.

Question 28.

A is the correct answer. Generally, a lawyer may not represent a client if it creates a concurrent conflict of interest with another client. However, "a lawyer may represent a client if: (1) the lawyer reasonably believes that the lawyer will be able to provide competent and diligent representation to each affected client; (2) the representation is not prohibited by law; (3) the representation does not involve the assertion of a claim by one client against another client represented by the lawyer in the same litigation or other proceeding before a tribunal; and (4) each affected client gives informed consent, confirmed in writing." Model Rule 1.7(b). Here, there would be little risk that either the husband's or wife's interests would be hurt by the representation. Importantly, if no settlement is ultimately reached, the husband and wife would be back where they started, since the attorney has stated she will not represent either party if litigation continues.

B is incorrect. While the attorney may have previously represented the husband and wife in their joint affairs, this would not automatically make a joint representation appropriate. Importantly, if the husband and wife were asserting differing claims and were not trying to settle their affairs amicably, the representation would be improper because of conflicts.

C is incorrect. The Rules specifically state that "with regard to the attorney-client privilege, the prevailing rule is that, as between commonly represented clients, the privilege does not attach. Hence, it must be assumed that if litigation eventuates between the clients, the privilege will not protect any such communications, and the clients should be so advised." Model Rule 1.7, Comment [30]. Consequently, "the lawyer should, at the outset of the common representation and as part of the process of obtaining each client's informed consent, advise each client that information will be shared and that the lawyer will have to withdraw if one client decides that some matter material to the representation should be kept from the other." Model Rule 1.7, Comment [31]. Ultimately, the lawyer was correct to condition representation on a waiver of confidentiality.

D is incorrect. The Rules do not require an attorney to recommend independent counsel before clients agree to joint representation.

Question 29.

B is the correct answer. A lawyer may reveal confidential information "to establish a defense to a criminal charge or civil claim against the lawyer based upon conduct in which the client was involved." Model Rule 1.6(b)(5). Here, since the buyer is suing both the client and attorney over the same real estate transaction, the attorney may reveal the information.

A is incorrect. Since the attorney is defending herself against the buyer's civil action, she does not have to obtain the client's permission before revealing the confidential information.

C is incorrect. Model Rule 1.6 covers both civil and criminal actions, so the attorney does not have to wait for criminal charges to be filed before revealing the information.

D is incorrect. Although the disclosure may be detrimental to the client, the Model Rules allow the attorney to defend herself against civil and criminal actions.

Question 30.

A is the correct answer. A lawyer may not "engage in conduct involving dishonesty, fraud, deceit, or misrepresentation." Model Rule 8.4(c). Here, the attorney is planning to falsely tell the employee she is not a suspect and that her answers will be held in confidence. This is a clear violation of the Rules.

B is incorrect. The issue here is not that the attorney failed to advise the employee to obtain counsel. The issue is that the attorney is planning to lie to the employee regarding the theft investigation.

C is incorrect. Although no legal proceedings are pending, the attorney is improperly planning to misrepresent the situation to the employee.

D is incorrect. The limitations on what an attorney can tell another person involve more than simple legal advice. Importantly, the Rules also dis-allow dishonesty. For a communications question like this, an answer choice stating that the attorney is not subject to discipline because the attorney did not give legal advice is usually wrong.

Question 31.

C is the correct answer. A judge is not permitted to engage in ex parte communications or investigate facts independently. Model Code of Judicial Conduct Rule 2.9(A). The Rules recognize the fact that "to the extent reasonably possible, all parties or their lawyers shall be included in communications with a judge." Model Code of Judicial Conduct Rule 2.9, Comment [1]. Here, the judge violated the Code by sending her clerk to investigate the malfunctioning machine and having her clerk speak with the manufacturer's engineer.

A is incorrect. This is the classic "no-harm, no-foul" answer choice, and should be avoided.

B is incorrect. A judge is not allowed to undertake his or her own investigation regarding the facts of a pending trial. Model Code of Judicial Conduct Rule 2.9.

D is incorrect. Even if the engineer was a witness at the trial, the judge still engaged in improper ex parte communications when she used her law clerk to investigate the machine.

Question 32.

B is the correct answer. A lawyer is required to keep a client's funds separate from his or her own. Model Rule 1.15. Importantly, the attorney could not use the funds in her Clients' Trust Account for her personal use, as those funds belonged to her client.

A is incorrect. The important point here is that an attorney may not use a client's funds for his or her own purpose. Whether or not the attorney paid interest on the money does not change the analysis.

C is incorrect. This is an example of the "no-harm, no-foul" wrong answer choice. Whether or not the client is harmed, an attorney may not use a client's funds for his or her personal use.

D is incorrect. This is another example of the "no-harm, no-foul" wrong answer choice. Even though the client may have approved the attorney's conduct, the attorney had already violated the Rules before she told her client and received the client's approval.

Question 33.

A is the correct answer. An attorney cannot charge a contingent fee for representing a defendant in a criminal case. Model Rule 1.5(d)(2). This is an example of a question where careful reading of the facts is very important.

B is incorrect. The issue here is that an attorney cannot charge a contingent fee in a criminal matter. Model Rule 1.5(d)(2). Importantly, "a lawyer may accept property in payment for services, such as an ownership interest in an enterprise, providing this does not involve acquisition of a proprietary interest in the cause of action or subject matter of the litigation." Model Rule 1.5, Comment [4].

C is incorrect. Even though he obtained a good result for his client, the attorney still violated the prohibition against contingency fees in criminal cases.

D is incorrect. The simple fact that a retainer agreement is in writing does not make that retainer agreement proper under the Rules. This answer choice should have been stricken immediately as an overbroad statement.

Question 34.

D is the correct answer. In the case of a represented organization, Model Rule 4.2 prohibits communications with a member of the organization "who supervises, directs or regularly consults with the organization's lawyer concerning the matter or who has authority to obligate the organization with respect to the matter." Model Rule 4.2, Comment [7]. Here, the corporation's president is clearly such a member of the organization, and the attorney cannot communicate with him without the corporation's attorney's knowledge and consent.

A is incorrect. Although the corporation's president may not be personally liable, he still is a person protected by Model Rule 4.2. Considering his position, he likely supervises, directs, or regularly consults with the organization's lawyer, or even if he does not, he has the power to obligate the organization.

B is incorrect. Even without the dictates of Model Rule 4.2, it wouldn't make sense for the attorney to be allowed to talk to the corporation's president alone considering his actions created potential liability for the corporation.

C is incorrect. Even though the corporation's president may be called as an adverse witness, this does not solve the issue of his position and responsibility in the corporation.

Question 35.

C is the correct answer. A lawyer may not "make an agreement prospectively limiting the lawyer's liability to a client for malpractice unless the client is independently represented in making the agreement." Model Rule 1.8(h)(1). Here, the attorney is attempting to do so by having the client sign the retainer agreement.

A is incorrect. This is not a question regarding the creation of a contract. The issue here is the content of that contract, and the content attempting to limit the attorney's malpractice liability is improper under the Rules.

B is incorrect. While his fee may be fair and his work adequate, this does not guarantee that a client may not have a valid malpractice claim. Importantly, the attorney cannot attempt to limit his liability through the use of this retainer agreement.

D is incorrect. There's no particular issue with using preprinted forms. This answer choice seems to be making the assumption that such pre-printed forms will result in unfair agreements or fees, which is not necessarily the case.

Question 36.

C is the correct answer. Under Model Rule 8.3(a), an attorney who knows another attorney has violated the Rules of Professional Conduct must report that information to the appropriate professional authority. However, there is an exception when the attorney learns this information through representing the other attorney and disclosure of the information would violate the protections of confidentiality afforded by Model Rule 1.6. Model Rule 8.3(c). Since the attorney here gained the information while representing his friend, he is not required to report it.

A is incorrect. The accountant merely confirmed the information the attorney had already learned through his representation of his friend. Consequently, he is not required to report it.

B is incorrect. Because the information was protected by attorney-client privilege, the attorney does not need to report the embezzlement to the appropriate disciplinary authority. Additionally, the attorney's failure to inform the disciplinary authority will do nothing to hinder the investigation that is apparently already in progress.

D is incorrect. Although the bank may make the information public, there is no Rule requiring the attorney to "beat them to the punch" and inform the disciplinary authority first.

Question 37.

B is the correct answer. In advertising his or her practice, an attorney may not make false or misleading statements. Model Rule 7.1. As long as none of the information regarding their degrees is false, the attorneys are free to list their degrees in their advertisement.

A is incorrect. Although both law and medicine are licensed professions, this would not make the statement proper if the attorneys were lying about their licenses.

C is incorrect. The Rules do not forbid an attorney from making statements that are self-laudatory, so long as they are not untruthful or misleading.

D is incorrect. The attorney's listing of his medical degree is not done in a way that indicates any specialty or limitation on his practice.

Question 38.

D is the correct answer. In order to provide competent representation as required by Model Rule 1.1, it is appropriate for the attorney to ask her partner for assistance since they are partners in the same firm.

A is incorrect. In order to obtain competence in this matter, it was appropriate for the attorney to consult with her partner even if it did increase the total fee. In fact, there is nothing different in doing this as opposed to charging more because more research in books or online was necessary.

B is incorrect. Under Model Rule 1.1, Comment [6], client consent becomes necessary when the lawyer retains or contracts with other lawyers outside the lawyer's own firm. Here, the attorney is conferring with her own partner, so no client consent is necessary.

C is incorrect. An attorney is allowed to consult with members of his or her own firm, whether or not he or she reveals the identity of the client.

Question 39.

D is the correct answer. Under Model Code of Judicial Conduct Rule 2.11(A), a judge should disqualify himself or herself in any proceeding where the judge's impartiality might reasonably be questioned. However, as long as the judge does not have a personal bias or prejudice concerning a party or a party's lawyer, or personal knowledge of facts that are in dispute in the proceeding, the judge "may disclose on the record the basis of the judge's disqualification and may ask the parties and their lawyers to consider, outside the presence of the judge and court personnel, whether to waive disqualification. If, following the disclosure, the parties and lawyers agree, without participation by the judge or court personnel, that the judge should not be disqualified, the judge may participate in the proceeding." Model Code of Judicial Conduct Rule 2.11(C). If such proceedings are held, the judge may properly hear the case.

A is incorrect. Although the judge may be particularly well qualified, the issue is that his impartiality could reasonably be questioned because of his brother's financial interest in the case.

B is incorrect. The question in this situation is not what the judge himself or herself believes, but whether that impartiality could reasonably be questioned by someone else. Model Code of Judicial Conduct Rule 2.11(A).

C is incorrect. As stated above, if proceedings are held and the parties and lawyers agree to the judge hearing the case, the judge may properly do so.

Question 40.

B is the correct answer. "A lawyer shall not knowingly . . . offer evidence that the lawyer knows to be false." Model Rule 3.3(a)(3). Because the attorney knows the witness is lying, she cannot offer the witness's testimony in court.

A is incorrect. Even if the attorney informed the court of her belief, it would not excuse her actions if she later offered the testimony of a witness who she knows is lying.

C is incorrect. The Rule states that the attorney may not offer false evidence. Importantly, the Rule does not allow the attorney to do so as long the attorney refrains from mentioning the false evidence during her argument before the jury.

D is incorrect. "A lawyer may refuse to offer evidence, other than the testimony of a defendant in a criminal matter, that the lawyer reasonably believes is false." Model Rule 3.3(a)(3). The client cannot force the lawyer to offer such evidence.

Question 41.

B is the correct answer. Under Model Rule 7.1, "[a] lawyer shall not make a false or misleading communication about the lawyer or the lawyer's services. A communication is false or misleading if it contains a material misrepresentation of fact or law, or omits a fact necessary to make the statement considered as a whole not materially misleading." Here, the commercial is misleading in that it implies the young attorney has argued a case in front of a jury, when he has only done so in moot court.

A is incorrect. Model Rule 7.1, Comment [3] states that it is improper for a lawyer to make an advertisement that would lead a reasonable person to form an unjustified expectation that the lawyer will reach the same results in his or her case. Here, however, the larger issue is that the commercial is misleading in that it leads a viewer to believe the lawyer has appeared in court before a jury, when in fact he has not done so.

C is incorrect. A lawyer's commercial speech is regulated by the Rules. This answer choice should be immediately discarded because it implies a lawyer can say anything he or she wants in a commercial due to the protections of the First Amendment.

D is incorrect. While there was a disclaimer regarding the results, the commercial still misled viewers into believing the attorney had argued a case before a jury.

Question 42.

B is the correct answer. " . . . [A] judge may participate in activities sponsored by organizations concerned with the law, the legal system, or the administration of justice." Model Code of Judicial Conduct Rule 3.7(A). Additionally, a judge may accept reasonable compensation for these extrajudicial activities unless such acceptance would appear to undermine the judge's impartiality. Model Code of Judicial Conduct Rule 3.12. Here, since the judge is engaging in an educational activity devoted to the improvement of law, her actions are proper.

A is incorrect. There is no set limit on the amount a judge may receive for proper extrajudicial activities. The only limitation is that the compensation cannot be so large as to appear to undermine the judge's impartiality. Model Code of Judicial Conduct Rule 3.12.

C is incorrect. Although members of the bar association will necessarily appear in the judge's court, nothing in this situation would lead a reasonable person to believe that the association members are trying to buy the judge's impartiality.

D is incorrect. So long as there is no appearance of impropriety, there is no restriction on the bar association also offering free transportation to the judge's spouse.

Question 43.

A is the correct answer. "A lawyer who knows that a judge has committed a violation of applicable rules of judicial conduct that raises a substantial question as to the judge's fitness for office shall inform the appropriate authority." Model Rule 8.3(b). Since the judge is clearly behaving inappropriately, the attorney has a duty to report it.

B is incorrect. The issue here is that the attorney is failing to report the misconduct. The correct answer choice should be fairly clear in that if every attorney simply filed automatic requests for substitution, the judge would continue to remain on the bench indefinitely with no investigation of his conduct. Consequently, only attorneys who are new to the court would end up in front of him, presumably to the disadvantage of their clients.

C is incorrect. Reporting the misconduct has nothing to do with zealous representation. This answer choice implies that zealous representation only occurs so long as the attorney is very careful not to upset a judge.

D is incorrect. This answer choice implies that the attorney can properly bury her head in the sand and just hope the judge goes away.

Question 44.

B is the correct answer. "In an emergency a lawyer may give advice or assistance in a matter in which the lawyer does not have the skill ordinarily required." Model Rule 1.1, Comment [3]. Consequently, although the attorney does not have the general competency to write a will, the emergency situation caused by the accident allows the attorney to try to undertake the work without violating the Rule.

A is incorrect. The fact of the emergency makes the attorney's actions proper. Even if he did a good job on the will, he would still violate the Rules regarding competency if this was not an emergency situation. This is a variation of the "no-harm, no-foul" wrong answer choice.

C is incorrect. A lawyer may not "make an agreement prospectively limiting the lawyer's liability to a client for malpractice unless the client is independently represented in making the agreement." Model Rule 1.8(h)(1). Consequently, if the attorney had in fact gotten the doctor to waive the attorney's malpractice liability, he would be violating the Rules.

D is incorrect. Even though the attorney did not have the required competence, the emergency situation made his actions proper under the Rules.

Question 45.

A is the correct answer. As long as client confidences are not exposed, the arrangement is proper under the Rules. Importantly, no fees are being shared with the bank employee, and the bank employee is not serving as a director or in a similar position in the firm. Model Rule 5.4. Here, the bank employee is merely acting as a part-time office manager, giving advice on how to keep the firm solvent.

B is incorrect. Although there is no sharing of fees, the arrangement could cause a problem if confidences were being shared with the bank.

C is incorrect. It is improper for a nonlawyer third party to direct the lawyer's professional judgment in rendering legal services. Model Rule 5.4, Comment [1]. Here, the bank employee is not giving advice on representation, but merely on office billing and solvency matters.

D is incorrect. There is no indication that this setup will result in the bank improperly practicing law. The bank employee is merely a part-time office manager, giving advice regarding the running of the office.

Question 46.

C is the correct answer. "A lawyer shall not provide financial assistance to a client in connection with pending or contemplated litigation, except that: (1) a lawyer may advance court costs and expenses of litigation, the repayment of which may be contingent on the outcome of the matter." Model Rule 1.8(e)(1). Here, since the funds are being used for trial preparation, they are proper under the Rules.

A is incorrect. So long as an attorney's financial assistance is used for court costs and expenses of litigation, the attorney may lend his or her credit to a client.

B is incorrect. "Lawyers may not subsidize lawsuits or administrative proceedings brought on behalf of their clients, including making or guaranteeing loans to their clients for living expenses, because to do so would encourage clients to pursue lawsuits that might not otherwise be brought and because such assistance gives lawyers too great a financial stake in the litigation. These dangers do not warrant a prohibition on a lawyer lending a client court costs and litigation expenses, including the expenses of medical examination and the costs of obtaining and presenting evidence, because these advances are virtually indistinguishable from contingent fees and help ensure access to the courts." Model Rule 1.8, Comment [10]. Here, the attorney is not financing the litigation, she is merely providing assistance with trial costs.

D is incorrect. The Rules state that a lawyer may advance court costs and litigation expenses, even if repayment is on a contingency fee basis. Model Rule 1.8(e)(1).

Question 47.

A is the correct answer. "In representing a client, a lawyer shall not communicate about the subject of the representation with a person the lawyer knows to be represented by another lawyer in the matter, unless the lawyer has the consent of the other lawyer or is authorized to do so by law or a court order." Model Rule 4.2. Here, the attorney is communicating directly with the plaintiff by serving the plaintiff with a copy of the motion and tender. This is prohibited under the Rules, as the attorney clearly knows the plaintiff is represented by counsel.

B is incorrect. This is an answer choice showing the importance of careful reading. The Rules require the other lawyer's "consent" before an attorney can communicate with a represented person. This answer choice states that the communication would be proper even if the attorney only informed the plaintiff's attorney, which is clearly not enough under the Rules.

C is incorrect. The Rules prohibit communication with a represented person. The subject of that communication does not change the Rule.

D is incorrect. The Rules prohibit communication with a represented person. The simple fact that the plaintiff might learn the information elsewhere does not change the analysis.

Question 48.

C is the correct answer. Under Model Rule 5.6(b), an attorney shall not participate in offering or making "an agreement in which a restriction on the lawyer's right to practice is part of the settlement of a client controversy." Consequently, the proposed settlement violates the Rules.

A is incorrect. As stated above, an attorney cannot be part of a settlement restricting his or her right to represent a client.

B is incorrect. This is clearly a wrong answer choice, as it implies that as long as the attorney believes something is in the client's best interest, it is proper under the Rules.

D is incorrect. This answer choice also centers around the attorney's beliefs, instead of addressing the issue of what the attorney is actually doing; specifically, restricting his right to represent the client in the future.

Question 49.

C is the correct answer. "The scope of the representation and the basis or rate of the fee and expenses for which the client will be responsible shall be communicated to the client, preferably in writing, before or within a reasonable time after commencing the representation." Model Rule 1.5(b). Within a few days of beginning her representation, and apparently at her first meeting with the president, the attorney revealed her fees. This was clearly within a reasonable time and proper under the Rules.

A is incorrect. As long as an attorney reveals his or her fees within a reasonable time, he or she is not in violation of the Rules.

B is incorrect. The Rule only states that the communication be "preferably in writing," it does not absolutely require it. However, the Rule recognizes the fact that a written statement reduces the possibility of a misunderstanding. Model Rule 1.5, Comment [2].

D is incorrect. An attorney is required to explain his or her fee within a reasonable time. Importantly, this requirement is not triggered by the client's request.

Question 50.

C is the correct answer. During trial, a lawyer may not "assert personal knowledge of facts in issue except when testifying as a witness." Model Rule 3.4(e). Here, by stating his belief regarding the street and driveways, he is clearly violating that Rule.

A is incorrect. While the attorney may have been telling the truth, he still violated the Rule against asserting personal knowledge of the facts. This is another variation on the "no-harm, no-foul" wrong answer choice.

B is incorrect. While the Rules of Evidence may be more liberal in certain circumstances, keep in mind that this is a test on the Model Rules of Professional Conduct.

D is incorrect. Even if there were evidence related to the facts asserted by the attorney, he would still be violating the Rule against asserting his personal knowledge.

Question 51.

C is the correct answer. A lawyer may provide legal assistance to *pro se* litigants. ABA Formal Opinion 07-446 (2007). Here, the attorney is not otherwise involved in the case, and his friend is representing himself.

A is incorrect. Here, the attorney is not assisting the plaintiff in the practice of law. Improperly assisting someone in the practice of law does not mean helping a pro se litigant. Improper assistance refers to situations where the lawyer is helping a nonlawyer represent others and collect fees.

B is incorrect. There is no prohibition under the Rules regarding unsolicited legal advice, unless that unsolicited legal advice violates some other Rule, such as communications with represented people or improper advertising.

D is incorrect. Although the attorney was not compensated, the simple fact that no money exchanged hands would not protect the attorney if the attorney was violating some other Rule by giving the advice. Consequently, this is not the best answer choice.

Question 52.

D is the correct answer. A lawyer must keep a client's confidences unless the information needs to be revealed to prevent death or substantial bodily harm, crime or fraud, secure legal advice about the lawyer's compliance with the Rules, establish a lawyer's claim or defense, comply with a law or court order, or detect and resolve conflicts. Model Rule 1.6. The information revealed by the client involves none of these potential problems. Importantly, the client committed perjury before the lawyer's representation. Had the perjury occurred during the lawyer's representation, the lawyer would have been required to take remedial measures under Model Rule 3.3(a)(3). But, since the client acted before representation began, it would be a violation of the Rules to reveal the client's confidential information.

A is incorrect. The attorney is not required to withdraw from representation as the client has simply informed the attorney of a perjury that happened before representation began. This is not a situation where the client is attempting to have the attorney aid in lying to the tribunal.

B is incorrect. As stated above, the attorney should not reveal the client's perjury in this situation.

C is incorrect. As stated above, the client's information was told in confidence, and it meets no exception allowing the attorney to reveal it.

Question 53.

D is the correct answer. "A lawyer shall not reveal information relating to the representation of a client unless the client gives informed consent." Model Rule 1.6(a). Here, it would be improper for the attorney to turn over all the client files and reveal all the confidences therein before receiving consent from the clients.

A is incorrect. While Beta may be competent, this does not mean a client would necessarily want his or her confidences shared with her.

B is incorrect. The simple fact that Beta has agreed to keep the files confidential would not change the fact that Alpha has already shared confidences by sharing the files in the first place.

C is incorrect. While finding alternative representation may have been necessary, Alpha could not share client information without first gaining consent.

Question 54.

C is the correct answer. Under Model Rule 1.12, a lawyer cannot represent anyone in connection with a matter in which the lawyer participated personally and substantially as a judge. However, a lawyer may represent someone in connection with a matter if the lawyer's judicial actions regarding that matter were merely exercising remote or incidental administrative responsibility that did not affect the merits. Model Rule 1.12, Comment [1]. Here, all the lawyer did was enter an administrative order changing a courtroom. Consequently, she did not participate personally and substantially in the matter, and can thus represent the plaintiff.

A is incorrect. While the judge did act officially as a judge with respect to an aspect of the case, she only changed a courtroom, and did not deal personally or substantially with the merits of the action.

B is incorrect. There is no indication here that the court's impartiality is being called into question.

D is incorrect. Although information the judge learned could be a matter of public record, the main concern is the potential bias of the judge if she had already acted personally and substantially in the matter.

Question 55.

D is the correct answer. "A lawyer shall not enter into a business transaction with a client … unless: (1) the transaction and terms on which the lawyer acquires the interest are fair and reasonable to the client and are fully disclosed and transmitted in writing in a manner that can be reasonably understood by the client; (2) the client is advised in writing of the desirability of seeking and is given a reasonable opportunity to seek the advice of independent legal counsel on the transaction; and (3) the client gives informed consent, in a writing signed by the client, to the essential terms of the transaction and the lawyer's role in the transaction, including whether the lawyer is representing the client in the transaction." Model Rule 1.8(a). Here, importantly, the attorney did nothing regarding the desirability of seeking the advice of independent counsel. It's also debatable whether the terms are fair and reasonable.

A is incorrect. Many wrong answer choices highlight the fact that the questionable transaction was initiated by the client (for example, in client communication questions). Remember, simply because the client initiated something does not make it proper under the Rules.

B is incorrect. The fact that the note operated as the attorney intended it to do did not make the note valid under the Rules.

C is incorrect. An attorney can enter into a business transaction with a client, so long as he or she follows the Rules. Consequently, a loan is not completely improper under the Rules.

Question 56.

C is the correct answer. In advertising his or her services, a lawyer may not make a false or misleading statement. Model Rule 7.1. Here, nothing in the mailing is false, and it appears that its main purpose is simply to alert members of the community that the lawyer is returning to private practice.

A is incorrect. Although the mailing was sent to people who were not his clients, this does not violate Model Rule 7.3's prohibitions regarding solicitation of clients. Importantly, written contact is prohibited when the lawyer knows the person does not want to be solicited or the solicitation involves coercion, duress, or harassment. Model Rule 7.3(b). Here, the mailing announcing the new law office appears to do none of these things.

B is incorrect. Although his service as a congressman is unrelated to his ability as a lawyer, there is no prohibition on advertising this fact as long as the statement is truthful. Model Rule 7.1. Additionally, although the lawyer states he was once a congressman, the mailing does not appear to violate Model Rule 8.4(e)'s prohibition against implying an ability to influence improperly government agencies or officials.

D is incorrect. Although all the information was in the public domain, it could still be presented or phrased in a way to create an improper mis-representation under Model Rule 7.1 or an improper implication of influence under Model Rule 8.4(e). Consequently, the simple fact the information was in the public domain does not make the advertisement proper.

Question 57.

D is the correct answer. "A lawyer shall be responsible for another lawyer's violation of the Rules of Professional Conduct if: (1) the lawyer orders or, with knowledge of the specific conduct, ratifies the conduct involved." Model Rule 5.1(c)(1). Here, the supervising attorney is ordering the associate to violate Model Rule 1.1 regarding competence. "Competent representation requires the legal knowledge, skill, thoroughness, and preparation reasonably necessary for representation." Model Rule 1.1. Here, the new associate has no familiarity with title searches, and the attorney is apparently too busy to oversee his work. Consequently, this setup is a violation of the Rules.

A is incorrect. Although the paralegals may know what is going on, this in no way justifies the senior attorney ordering the associate to do title work despite his lack of competence.

B is incorrect. Although the attorney may be ultimately liable, the primary issue is that the attorney is ordering the associate to violate the Model Rules by doing work he lacks competence in.

C is incorrect. This should be an obvious wrong answer choice. Many things could lead to lower fees (for example, having nonlawyers do legal work, or capping all legal work to what can be done in 15 minutes), so a simple price cut cannot justify a lawyer's actions under the Model Rules.

Question 58.

B is the correct answer. Under Model Rule 1.5(b), any changes in the basis or rate of the fee or expenses shall be communicated to the client. Here, there was no indication that the client had any notice of the change in fee. The necessity of informing a client of a fee change and having that client consent to the increase is particularly apparent when an attorney represents an organization, as payments may be automated or done by some other person or department who may have no idea what the agreed-upon rate is.

A is incorrect. Fees may change over time, so the original fee agreement is really irrelevant to the question of a change in fees.

C is incorrect. Although the fee change may be reasonable, the issue is that the client may be paying it without knowledge or consent.

D is incorrect. Careful reading of the question reveals that hourly rates of $180 and $110 were agreed to. Importantly, the agreement did not say the client would pay the firm's "hourly rate" without any further clarification.

Question 59.

A is the correct answer. "A lawyer shall act with reasonable diligence and promptness in representing a client." Model Rule 1.3. Importantly, delay can result in anxiety, statute of limitations issues, and possible destruction of the client's legal position. Model Rule 1.3, Comment [3]. Also, unless the relationship is officially terminated, the lawyer should carry through to conclusion all matters undertaken for a client. Model Rule 1.3, Comment [4]. Although the attorney had gotten another lawyer to do the work, he never officially terminated his relationship with the client, and the lawyer repeatedly sought extensions that resulted in dismissal. Consequently, the attorney is subject to discipline for his lack of diligence in pursuing the matter.

B is incorrect. Fees can be shared between lawyers who are not in the same firm if the division is proportional or each lawyer assumes joint responsibility, the client agrees in writing, and the total fee is reasonable. Model Rule 1.5[e]. However, it should be apparent from the question that the major harm here is the dismissal of the appeal, so the correct answer choice will clearly address that question.

C is incorrect. Although the client agreed in writing to the arrangement, the major problem caused by this arrangement was the dismissal of the appeal. Consequently, the correct answer choice will address the dismissal.

Although the client agreed in writing, this did not excuse the attorneys from diligently pursuing the matter.

D is incorrect. This is another "no-harm, no-foul" wrong answer choice. Although the defendant's appeal might have been without merit, this did not excuse the attorney's lack of diligence in pursuing the matter.

Question 60.

D is the correct answer. "A lawyer shall not enter into an arrangement for, charge, or collect: (1) any fee in a domestic relations matter, the payment or amount of which is contingent upon the securing of a divorce or upon the amount of alimony or support, or property settlement in lieu thereof." Model Rule 1.5(d)(1). Here, the attorney's standard retainer contract violates this Rule.

A is incorrect. While many clients may prefer to pay a contingent fee, this does not mean contingent fees are proper in all situations. This answer choice is another variation of the wrong answer choice that claims an attorney's actions are proper because they are the client's idea.

B is incorrect. Although the fee may be reasonable, the contingent agreement violates the Rules.

C is incorrect. The issue here is not the interest being acquired by the lawyer, but the fact that the lawyer is charging a contingent fee in this domestic matter.

2. Answers to Practice MPRE 2

Question 1.

B is the correct answer. "A lawyer shall act with reasonable diligence and promptness in representing a client." Model Rule 1.3. Importantly, this means that if the attorney is away for a long time or suffers from a disability that causes an attorney to potentially neglect client matters, the lawyer must make some provision for dealing with ongoing matters. Here, the lawyer violated the Rules by failing to do so.

A is incorrect. The issue here is not potential restitution. The bigger issue is that the attorney went away for two months without making provisions for her ongoing cases. This clearly violates the Rules regarding an attorney's diligence.

C is incorrect. This is the classic "no-harm, no-foul" answer choice. While the default judgment was set aside, there was no guarantee that a court would do so.

D is incorrect. The attorney should have known of the plaintiff's attorney's demand. If she had behaved diligently by making provisions for her very long absence, she would have.

Question 2.

A is the correct answer. A lawyer is not allowed to make false or misleading communications about the lawyer or the lawyer's services. Model Rule 7.1. Importantly, "[a]n advertisement that truthfully reports a lawyer's achievements on behalf of clients or former clients may be misleading if presented so as to lead a reasonable person to form an unjustified expectation that the same results could be obtained for other clients in similar matters without reference to the specific factual and legal circumstances of each client's case." Model Rule 7.1, Comment [3]. Here, the attorney's advertisement is clearly trying to give prospective clients the idea that they are also likely to receive a large recovery if they hire the attorney. This is clearly misleading and a violation of the Rules.

B is incorrect. A lawyer may not give anything of value to a person for recommending the lawyer's services. Model Rule 7.2(b). However, as long as the attorney is not giving anything of value for the testimonial, and as long as the client's testimonial is true and not misleading, it is not prohibited under the Rules.

C is incorrect. Although the plaintiff prepared the statement, the advertisement is still misleading in that it implies anyone using the attorney's services will receive a large recovery. Again, answer choices that imply something is proper because the client did it should be avoided.

D is incorrect. While everything was accurate, the advertisement was improper because it would likely lead a reasonable person to conclude the same results could be reached for other clients without any reference to the specifics of that client's case.

Question 3.

A is the correct answer. "Except to the extent that the client's instructions or special circumstances limit that authority, a lawyer is impliedly authorized to make disclosures about a client when appropriate in carrying out the representation . . . . Lawyers in a firm may, in the course of the firm's practice, disclose to each other information relating to a client of the firm, unless the client has instructed that particular information be confined to specified lawyers." Model Rule 1.6, Comment [5]. Consequently, it was proper for the partners to give detailed descriptions of the work being done.

B is incorrect. Lawyers may discuss cases within a firm so long as the client has not given instructions to the contrary. This answer choice should have been crossed out immediately since it implies that lawyers can willfully ignore client instructions regarding confidences.

C is incorrect. Although more people knowing about something could theoretically increase the risk of that information getting out, the Rules allow lawyers to share information within a firm.

D is incorrect. The Rules allow lawyers to disclose information to other lawyers within a firm. This makes sense, considering the desire for competent and efficient representation.

Question 4.

B is the correct answer. A lawyer may withdraw from representing a client if the client insists on taking action with which the lawyer had a fundamental disagreement or if the representation has been rendered unreasonably difficult by the client. Model Rule 1.16(b)(6). Here, the client's insistence on forgoing additional pretrial proceedings has made the representation unreasonably difficult. Importantly, the attorney believes he needs another six months to adequately represent the client's interests, a very significant amount of time, while the client is insisting that they go to trial as soon as possible.

A is incorrect. According to the Rules, an attorney must have cause before withdrawing from representation. Model Rule 1.16(b). Otherwise, a client's rights could be in serious jeopardy if an attorney could withdraw at any time for any reason.

C is incorrect. This answer choice should have been discarded immediately, as it implies that an attorney must absolutely follow a client's instructions, even if those instructions cause the attorney to violate the Rules. Here, the client's insistence on a quick trial would likely lead to incompetent representation, a violation of Model Rule 1.1.

D is incorrect. The Rules regarding withdrawal only require an attorney to act reasonably to protect the client's interests, such as by giving reasonable notice. Model Rule 1.16(d). The Rules do not require the client's consent.

Question 5.

D is the correct answer. A judge is required to perform his or her duties diligently. Model Code of Judicial Conduct Rule 2.5(A). Importantly, issues should be resolved without unnecessary cost or delay. Model Code of Judicial Conduct Rule 2.5, Comment [4]. Here, the judge is granting extensions without any consideration of the individual cases, likely leading to unnecessary cost and delay for the parties involved.

A is incorrect. While a judge has discretion in his or her decision-making, this discretion is not absolute and is regulated by the Model Code of Judicial Conduct.

B is incorrect. The fact that a party could seek appellate review would not have any effect on whether the judge was violating the Rules in the first place. At most, it would give the party recourse for the Rule violation after the Rule violation has already occurred.

C is incorrect. The issue here is the possible harm caused by routine delays. This answer choice fails to address this problem and should be discarded.

Question 6.

C is the correct answer. Generally, a judge is not allowed to engage in ex parte communications. Model Code of Judicial Conduct Rule 2.9. However, "when circumstances require it, ex parte communication for scheduling, administrative, or emergency purposes, which does not address substantive matters, is permitted." Model Code of Judicial Conduct Rule 2.9(A)(1). If a judge does engage in such communication, he or she should make provision to promptly notify all the parties of the substance of the communication. Model Code of Judicial Conduct Rule 2.9(A)(1)(b). Here, the circumstances of the situation made the judge's actions proper, as no one else was there to answer the phone, the lawyer had an emergency and had tried to call opposing counsel, the matter merely involved rescheduling, and the judge promptly informed the opposing party of the rescheduling.

A is incorrect. As stated above, in certain circumstances, it is proper for a judge to engage in ex parte communications.

B is incorrect. While there may have been time to reach opposing counsel, the attorney was not required to do so since the ex parte communication merely involved scheduling issues.

D is incorrect. Although there was no one else to take the call, the communication could have been improper if it had involved some other matter besides scheduling.

Question 7.

A is the correct answer. "A lawyer shall not act as advocate at a trial in which the lawyer is likely to be a necessary witness unless: (1) the testimony relates to an uncontested issue." Model Rule 3.7(a)(1). Here, since there is no contested issue of fact with respect to the formal execution of the will, the attorney is not barred from accepting representation.

B is incorrect. While the executor may have no beneficial interest, the issue is that the attorney is probating and administrating a will he was also a subscribing witness for. The executor's financial position would not address this particular problem.

C is incorrect. Since the attorney's testimony relates to an uncontested issue, there is no need for an evaluation of the possible hardships caused by the attorney's services being unutilized.

D is incorrect. As stated above, if the testimony relates to an uncontested issue, the lawyer can still act as an advocate at trial.

Question 8.

B is the correct answer. "In representing a client, a lawyer shall not use means that have no substantial purpose other than to embarrass, delay, or burden a third person." Model Rule 4.4(a). Here, the lawyer's plan is simply to start malicious gossip that will embarrass the prospective jurors into choosing not to serve.

A is incorrect. Although many of the jurors were selected to serve on the jury, this did not excuse the lawyer's actions in trying to embarrass them.

C is incorrect. Importantly, the lawyer's intent here is not to engage in any real investigation — he just wants to keep all of the parents of minor children off the jury through embarrassment and intimidation.

D is incorrect. Although the lawyer did not directly contact a prospective juror, he did use means that were intended to embarrass them and keep them from serving on the jury.

Question 9.

B is the correct answer. When dealing with client funds: (1) client funds must always be kept separate from the lawyer's funds in a designated clients' escrow account; (2) as soon as the client's interest in the funds is fixed, the client's money must be delivered to the client; and (3) if both the client and the attorney claim any interest in any part of the funds — for example, if a dispute arises as to the lawyer's fees — the funds must remain in the separate client account until there is an accounting and their respective interests can be severed. Model Rule 1.15. Since the fees were unearned, they still belonged to the client, and it was improper for the attorney to transfer those fees to the general office account.

A is incorrect. An attorney can accept legal fees in advance of doing the work, but those fees must be kept separate from the lawyer's funds in a designated clients' escrow account until the fees are earned by the attorney.

C is incorrect. Although the attorney attempted to fix the situation by replacing the money, he had already removed the client funds without justification and violated the Rules.

D is incorrect. The issue is that client funds were taken from the client account and put into the attorney's account. What the attorney believed when he was moving the money is irrelevant.

Question 10.

A is the correct answer. "A lawyer shall act with reasonable diligence and promptness in representing a client." Model Rule 1.3. Importantly, unless the relationship is terminated, the lawyer should carry to conclusion all matters undertaken for a client. Model Rule 1.3, Comment [4]. While the attorney was holding out for payment, he had not terminated representation, and was responsible for diligently continuing the representation.

B is incorrect. While this situation may have been helped if the attorney had withdrawn, the attorney had not terminated representation. Importantly, this answer choice seems to state that the attorney's lack of diligence would be excused merely if the attorney had asked the court to withdraw, not whether in fact the attorney had done so.

C is incorrect. While the plaintiff breached the agreement, the attorney had not terminated representation and was required to continue to carry all matters to conclusion.

D is incorrect. This is the classic "no-harm, no-foul" answer choice. The attorney still violated the Rules, although it ultimately did not hurt the client.

Question 11.

B is the correct answer. "A judge shall disqualify himself or herself in any proceeding in which the judge's impartiality might reasonably be questioned." Model Code of Judicial Conduct Rule 2.11(A). Importantly, if the judge has a personal bias or prejudice concerning one of the parties, the judge should disqualify himself or herself. Model Code of Judicial Conduct Rule 2.11(A)(1). Here, considering her bias against the representatives of the country's government, she should disqualify herself.

A is incorrect. The issue here is her potential bias, not who might be best qualified to hear the action.

C is incorrect. Although only legal questions are being presented, the judge's bias against the country could deeply affect the outcome of those questions. In any event, even if the judge could control her bias (which she seems to feel she cannot), an outside observer would be justified in questioning any decision the judge made in this case because of potential bias.

D is incorrect. Although none of the interested parties have moved to disqualify the judge, her awareness of her potential bias means she needs to disqualify herself.

Question 12.

D is the correct answer. An attorney may withdraw from representation if withdrawal can be accomplished without adverse effect, the client persists in fraudulent action, the client is using the lawyer's services to commit a crime, the attorney fundamentally disagrees with the client's actions, the client has failed to fulfill an obligation, the representation will result in an unreasonable financial burden, or other good cause exists. Model Rule 1.16(b). Here, the attorney is threatening to withdraw unless the client agrees to the fee increase. Importantly, the fee increase meets none of the potentially valid reasons for withdrawal, as the only reason for the fee increase is that the attorney has realized he could be making more money. If something else had occurred (such as the fee increase being necessary to avoid an unreasonable financial burden), the fee increase might have been reasonable. However, as it is now, the attorney is basically extorting the client into paying more to continue the representation.

A is incorrect. While the attorney offered to find another experienced attorney, he had no valid reason for the withdrawal.

B is incorrect. While the contingent fee may have been reasonable, the attorney had already agreed to the 30 percent fee. Consequently, he is threatening to withdraw simply because he thinks he can make more money, not that 35 percent is the only reasonable fee. The Rules do not allow this type of extortion from clients.

C is incorrect. Even if the attorney had suggested independent counsel, the bigger issue is that the attorney is threatening withdrawal without a valid reason to do so.

Question 13.

D is the correct answer. A judicial candidate may not personally solicit or accept campaign contributions other than through a campaign committee. Model Code of Judicial Conduct Rule 4.1(A)(8). Here, the candidate violated this Rule when he personally asked his friends to contribute to his campaign.

A is incorrect. While the funds were ultimately turned over to a committee, the Rule was already violated when the candidate personally solicited the funds.

B is incorrect. A campaign committee may include lawyers likely to practice before the candidate, but the candidate needs to be aware of the dangers of potential disqualification under Model Code of Judicial Conduct Rule 2.11 if the committee includes such lawyers.

C is incorrect. A campaign committee is required to keep records of the employer of each person who makes a campaign contribution. Model Code of Judicial Conduct Rule 4.4(B)(3). However, there is no requirement that at least one of the original contributors be a lawyer.

Question 14.

C is the correct answer. "A lawyer shall not bring or defend a proceeding, or assert or controvert an issue therein, unless there is a basis in law and fact for doing so that is not frivolous, which includes a good faith argument for an extension, modification or reversal of existing law." Model

Rule 3.1. Importantly, the Rule recognizes that the law is "not always clear and never is static" and only requires that the attorney act in good faith when making an argument. Model Rule 3.1, Comments [1] & [2]. Here, the attorney made a good faith argument and withdrew it when it became clear that the argument was no longer valid (importantly, it was a recent decision). Consequently, he acted as required under the Rules.

A is incorrect. The issue here is that the attorney made a claim that was no longer supported by the law. Whether or not he discussed this with the client would not change the analysis of the potential conflict with the Rules.

B is incorrect. While the decision should have been cited, the attorney's failure to do so under these circumstances was not a violation of the Rules.

D is incorrect. This answer choice implies that the attorney could keep arguing the invalid point if he did not know and should not have known of the decision when the complaint was filed. This is clearly a misstatement of the Rule.

Question 15.

B is the correct answer. It is professional misconduct for an attorney to engage in fraud. Model Rule 8.4(c). Importantly, while the attorney was no longer practicing law, he was still on active status as an attorney and was still required to abide by the Rules.

A is incorrect. There is no prohibition on an attorney pursuing a nonlegal occupation while still an active member of the bar.

C is incorrect. While the attorney was not convicted of a crime, he was still found guilty of fraud, which is a violation of the Rules.

D is incorrect. There is no requirement that the standard of proof be the same. The important point is that the attorney committed fraud and thus violated the Rules.

Question 16.

D is the correct answer. A fee may be contingent on the outcome of the matter for which the service is rendered, except in a matter in which a contingent fee involves a domestic matter or a criminal case. Model Rule 1.5(d). "A contingent fee agreement shall be in a writing signed by the client and shall state the method by which the fee is to be determined, including the percentage or percentages that shall accrue to the lawyer in the event of settlement, trial or appeal; litigation and other expenses to be deducted from the recovery; and whether such expenses are to be deducted before or after the contingent fee is calculated. The agreement must clearly notify the client of any expenses for which the client will be liable whether or not the client is the prevailing party. Upon conclusion of a contingent fee matter, the lawyer shall provide the client with a written statement stating the outcome of the matter and, if there is a recovery, showing the remittance to the client and the method of its determination." Model Rule 1.5(c). Here, there is nothing improper in the parties' agreement, and it appears to be reasonable under the circumstances.

A is incorrect. Under Model Rule 1.8(i), "a lawyer shall not acquire a proprietary interest in the cause of action or subject matter of litigation . . . except that the lawyer may . . . contract with a client for a reasonable contingent fee in a civil case." Model Rule 1.8(i)(2). Consequently, there is no general ban against an attorney receiving a proprietary interest in a client's cause of action, so long it is as part of a contract with a client for a reasonable contingent fee in a civil case.

Here, the agreement appears reasonable.

B is incorrect. Although the overall contingent fee may exceed the hourly rate, so long as the agreement is reasonable to the parties, there is nothing making such an agreement automatically improper. Importantly, this answer choice does not say that the fee will be grossly in excess of the hourly rate — it could exceed the hourly cost by only a dollar.

C is incorrect. This is the classic "it was the client's idea" wrong answer choice. Remember, simply because a client thinks something is a good idea does not make it proper under the Rules.

Question 17.

B is the correct answer. A lawyer may reveal information learned in confidence if disclosure of that information is necessary to prevent reasonably certain death or substantial bodily harm. Model Rule 1.6(b)(1). Here, if the attorney does not reveal the information, it will likely result in the death of the client. Consequently, it would be proper for the attorney to disclose the client's intentions to the authorities.

A is incorrect. The starting point of any confidential information provided by a client is that it is protected under Model Rule 1.6. Here, the information is in fact protected. However, it falls under an exception for information relating to certain death or bodily harm, and can be revealed *despite* being protected.

C is incorrect. The issue is that the client has told the attorney he is intending to commit suicide. The analysis does not change in relation to how likely it may be that the client will in fact try to go through with it.

D is incorrect. This Rule is most concerned with a person's safety. Although there is a risk that disclosure could aid in a civil commitment, the primary concern is that a person in danger receive potential help.

Question 18.

B is the correct answer. A lawyer shall not seek to influence a judge by means prohibited by law. Model Rule 3.5(a). Here, the attorney used her public position to attempt to influence the judge. Specifically, she noted that the uncle was the type of solid citizen and influential person who could help garner support for the budget. Clearly, this was an attempt to have the judge rule in the uncle's favor in the pending divorce.

A is incorrect. Although the trial judge ruled in the uncle's favor, if there had been no improper influence brought by the attorney, the simple fact that the judge ruled in the uncle's favor would not lead to a violation of the Rules.

C is incorrect. Whether calling as a legislator or an attorney, the attorney still violated the Rules by improperly trying to influence the judge.

D is incorrect. The ability to engage in law practice does not give an attorney the ability to attempt to improperly influence a judge. A broad answer choice like this should have been thrown out immediately.

Question 19.

B is the correct answer. "A judge shall not accept appointment to serve in a fiduciary position, such as executor, administrator, trustee, guardian, attorney in fact, or other personal representative, except for the estate, trust, or person of a member of the judge's family, and then only if such service will not interfere with the proper performance of judicial duties." Model Code of Judicial Conduct Rule 3.8(A). Here, the judge is serving for her father, and it does not appear to interfere with the judge's performance of her official duties.

A is incorrect. "A judge may accept reasonable compensation for extra-judicial activities permitted by this Code or other law unless such acceptance would appear to a reasonable person to undermine the judge's independence, integrity, or impartiality." Model Code of Judicial Conduct Rule 3.12. Because a judge can accept compensation, there is no Rule stating that if a judge does not receive compensation that judge may take on any particular extrajudicial activity. Importantly, even a noncompensatory position could undermine the judge's impartiality.

C is incorrect. A judge may engage in extrajudicial activities so long as they do not interfere with proper performance of the judge's judicial duties or create the danger of undermining the judge's impartiality. Model Code of Judicial Conduct Rule 3.1. Simply appearing in court would be unlikely to do that.

D is incorrect. A judge may engage in extrajudicial activities so long as they do not interfere with proper performance of the judge's judicial duties or create the danger of undermining the judge's impartiality. Model Code of Judicial Conduct Rule 3.1. Preparing and signing papers will not necessarily interfere with judicial activities.

Question 20.

A is the correct answer. "A lawyer shall not: (a) unlawfully obstruct another party's access to evidence." Model Rule 3.4(a). "Fair competition in the adversary system is secured by prohibitions against destruction or concealment of evidence, improperly influencing witnesses, obstructive tactics in discovery procedure, and the like." Model Rule 3.4, Comment [1]. Here, the attorney's actions in putting the engineer out of the reach of the court are clearly improper.

B is incorrect. Even if the opposing counsel had learned of the engineer's views, the attorney would have still violated the Rules by trying to make access to the evidence impossible.

C is incorrect. This still would not negate the fact that the attorney is clearly trying to get the engineer beyond the reach of the court.

D is incorrect. The main issue is that the attorney is actively trying to hide evidence that he knows might be relevant in the case.

Question 21.

D is the correct answer. A lawyer is required to safeguard a client's property. While in some situations, a third party may have a lawful claim against specific funds or other property in a lawyer's custody, such as a client's creditor who has a lien on funds recovered in a personal injury, unless there is such lawful claim, the lawyer's first priority is to safeguard those funds for the client. Model Rule 1.15, Comment [4]. Here, since the bank has not established any legal right to the funds, the attorney is not required to turn them over.

A is incorrect. While the client does not dispute the debt, there is still no indication that the bank has done anything to gain a legal interest in the funds.

B is incorrect. Although the attorney may know the client is forcing the bank to sue him, this does not create any change regarding legal rights in the money. Additionally, an attorney is under no duty to actively dissuade clients from creating or engaging in litigation so long as that litigation is meritorious.

C is incorrect. The issue here is who has lawful interest in the money. It is not the attorney's responsibility to make sure his client pays his debts.

Question 22.

A is the correct answer. "A law firm with offices in more than one jurisdiction may use the same name or other professional designation in each jurisdiction, but identification of the lawyers in an office of the firm shall indicate the jurisdictional limitations on those not licensed to practice in the jurisdiction where the office is located." Model Rule 7.5(b). Here, since the letterhead states the jurisdictions in which each partner is admitted, it is proper under the Rule.

B is incorrect. There is no Rule stating that a lawyer in a firm has to be licensed in every jurisdiction in which the firm has offices.

C is incorrect. As stated above, as long as the jurisdictional limitations are made clear, the letterhead is not improper.

D is incorrect. This answer implies that the propriety of the situation depends upon Delta splitting his practice between both states (perhaps to the point of limiting the contributions of Alpha and Beta to the firm). As stated above, the law does not require this.

Question 23.

C is the correct answer. "A lawyer representing a client before a legislative body or administrative agency in a nonadjudicative proceeding shall disclose that the appearance is in a representative capacity." Model Rule 3.9. Here, it was improper for the attorney to fail to inform the committee that he was appearing on behalf of the corporation.

A is incorrect. Because of the special Rule concerning legislative bodies or administrative agencies and that Rule's concern for honesty and candor, the attorney could not prevent the disclosure of the identity of his client by claiming it was protected by confidentiality.

B is incorrect. Because of the special Rule concerning legislative bodies or administrative agencies and that Rule's concern for honesty and candor, the attorney could not prevent the disclosure of the identity of his client by claiming attorney-client privilege.

D is incorrect. The issue here is not compensation. The issue is that the attorney is attempting to conceal the fact that he was appearing on behalf of a client and not on behalf of himself. Remember, the correct answer choice will always address the primary problem — here, the problem of the legislative body not knowing the existence of the client behind the scenes.

Question 24.

B is the correct answer. A lawyer shall not communicate ex parte with a judge, juror, prospective juror, or other official during the proceeding unless authorized to do so by law or court order. Model Rule 3.5(b). Here, the attorney violated the Rule by using his investigator to communicate with potential jurors prior to trial.

A is incorrect. The Rule bars communication because an attorney could use such communications to improperly influence a jury. Simply giving a report of the interviews to opposing counsel would not fix this problem.

C is incorrect. The Rule specifically bans communications. If the attorney had informed the jurors or their family members of his affiliation, this would not solve the problem of potential improper influence.

D is incorrect. While voluntary and not harassing, the interviews could still have led to improper influence.

Question 25.

A is the correct answer. A lawyer may withdraw from representing a client if "the client persists in a course of action involving the lawyer's services that the lawyer reasonably believes is criminal or fraudulent." Model

Rule 1.16(b)(2). Here, since the attorney is unsure but reasonably believes there is a material misstatement in the document, she may withdraw.

B is incorrect. When a lawyer reasonably believes an action is criminal or fraudulent, the withdrawal is optional, not mandatory. Withdrawal is mandatory when the attorney knows the representation will result in violation of the Rules of Professional Conduct or other law. Model Rule 1.16(a)(1).

C is incorrect. In this situation, a lawyer may withdraw so long as the withdrawal "can be accomplished without material adverse effect on the interests of the client." Model Rule 1.16(b)(1). Here, the mere possibility that the opposing counsel might realize there is a problem in the filing through the withdrawal would be unlikely to materially affect the client's interests.

D is incorrect. There is no indication that the attorney's withdrawal would affect the corporation's ability to complete the filing in a timely fashion. Even so, this potential issue would not create such a material adverse effect on the client's interests that the attorney would be forced to continue representation.

Question 26.

C is the correct answer. There is no prohibition on the attorney making a contribution to the judge's campaign committee. However, if the attorney does so, the judge has to be aware of potential conflicts that could arise under Model Code of Judicial Conduct Rule 2.11 involving potential bias and disqualification if the attorney appears in the judge's court.

A is incorrect. As long as the judge follows the rules for disqualification in Model Code of Judicial Conduct Rule 2.11, the attorney may still donate to the judge's campaign.

B is incorrect. Whether or not the judge and attorney have discussed the matter is irrelevant, as the donation itself is what is at issue.

D is incorrect. Even if the attorney and judge did not have a long-standing relationship, the attorney would not violate the Rules by giving a donation to the committee.

Question 27.

C is the correct answer. "A lawyer shall not knowingly make a false statement of fact or law to a tribunal." Model Rule 3.3 (a)(1).

Consequently, since the attorney did not know the statement was false, he is not subject to discipline.

A is incorrect. The important point is that the attorney did not actually know the statement was false when he made it.

B is incorrect. "An advocate is responsible for pleadings and other documents prepared for litigation, but is usually not required to have personal knowledge of the matters asserted therein, for litigation documents ordinarily present assertions by the client, or by someone on the client's behalf." Model Rule 3.3, Comment [3]. Consequently, the lawyer was not required to investigate every statement personally in this emergency situation where the litigation materials were prepared by other members of his firm.

D is incorrect. This is a bad choice because if Beta had reason to know the statement was false, he would not be protected simply because he was recounting a statement made by Alpha.

Question 28.

D is the correct answer. "A judge shall act at all times in a manner that promotes public confidence in the independence, integrity, and impartiality of the judiciary, and shall avoid impropriety and the appearance of impropriety." Model Code of Judicial Conduct Rule 1.2. Here, this large, unusual loan clearly creates an appearance of impropriety, and the judge should not accept it.

A is incorrect. Although the judge does not act in any case involving the bank, this loan could clearly create the appearance of impropriety and hurt public confidence in the judiciary.

B is incorrect. As stated above, the problem here is the appearance of impropriety. "A judge should expect to be the subject of public scrutiny that might be viewed as burdensome if applied to other citizens." Model Code of Judicial Conduct Rule 1.2, Comment [2].

C is incorrect. In many ways, it would be worse if the same terms were available to all state judges, as it would create the appearance of widespread impropriety.

Question 29.

B is the correct answer. "A lawyer shall not practice with or in the form of a professional corporation or association authorized to practice law for a profit, if: . . . a nonlawyer has the right to direct or control the professional judgment of a lawyer." Model Rule 5.4(d)(3). Here, the nonlawyer only supervises routine administrative and financial matters and does not control the professional judgment of lawyers in the firm. Importantly, this Rule's limitations "are to protect the lawyer's professional independence of judgment." Model Rule 5.4, Comment [1]. Consequently, this arrangement is proper under the Rules.

A is incorrect. The main issue here would not be the nonlawyer's access to client files. The main issue would be whether the nonlawyer had some ability to control the actions of the attorneys.

C is incorrect. "A lawyer or law firm may include nonlawyer employees in a compensation or retirement plan, even though the plan is based in whole or in part on a profit-sharing arrangement." Model Rule 5.4(a)(3). Consequently, as long as the nonlawyer's position is not violating the Rules in some other way (namely, by controlling the judgment of lawyers), it is proper to share fees with the nonlawyer employee.

D is incorrect. Here, since the nonlawyer is not giving any sort of legal advice, the nonlawyer is not engaged in the unauthorized practice of law.

Question 30.

C is the correct answer. According to the Rules, an attorney may withdraw from representation if the withdrawal can be accomplished without material adverse effect, the client persists in criminal or fraudulent action, the client uses the lawyer's services to perpetrate crime or fraud, the client insists on repugnant action, the client fails to fulfill an obligation and has been given reasonable warning, representation will result in an unreasonable financial burden, or other good cause exists. Model Rule 1.16(b). Consequently, in some cases, the simple fact that a client has failed to pay fees may be insufficient to justify a withdrawal. For example, under the proposed fee agreement, the attorney could withdraw if a client is a day late in paying a fee, which clearly does not meet any of the possible reasons for withdrawal proposed by the Rules.

A is incorrect. The Rules allow withdrawal for "unreasonable" financial burden, not simply a financial burden that was not considered at the onset of representation. Model Rule 1.16(b)(6).

B is incorrect. Although the clients may consent, this does not make the agreement proper under the Rules. Importantly, simply because an attorney gets a client to agree to something does not make it proper.

D is incorrect. The possibility of independent legal advice would still not make the primary agreement proper.

Question 31.

D is the correct answer. "A lawyer shall not accept compensation for representing a client from one other than the client unless: (1) the client gives informed consent." Model Rule 1.8(f)(1). Consequently, the attorney cannot accept the aunt's check without informing the client.

A is incorrect. Although it would clearly be improper for the aunt to attempt to influence the attorney's conduct, the primary issue is that the attorney cannot accept the check without getting the client's consent.

B is incorrect. Even if the charges are reduced, the primary issue is that the aunt is attempting to pay without the client's knowledge.

C is incorrect. Under the Rules, if a client gives informed consent, there is no interference with the attorney's professional judgment or with the client-lawyer relationship, and information relating to the representation is protected, a person other than the client can pay for the representation. Model Rule 1.8(f).

Question 32.

C is the correct answer. "A lawyer having direct supervisory authority over the nonlawyer shall make reasonable efforts to ensure that the person's conduct is compatible with the professional obligations of the lawyer." Model Rule 5.3(b). Importantly, "[a] lawyer must give such assistants appropriate instruction and supervision concerning the ethical aspects of their employment, particularly regarding the obligation not to disclose information relating to representation of the client, and should be responsible for their work product." Model Rule 5.3, Comment [2]. Consequently, unless there is some allegation that the lawyer's supervision was inadequate, he should not be subject to discipline. Obviously, the mistake made by his office would subject him to civil liability.

A is incorrect. As stated above, if the attorney failed to supervise his employees adequately, he would be subject to discipline for his own actions and there would be no need to apply the concept of respondeat superior.

B is incorrect. The decision to sue for civil liability is the client's, but the client has no right to make a decision regarding discipline under the Rules.

D is incorrect. This answer choice should have been discarded immediately, considering it was clear the attorney would be subject to civil liability.

Question 33.

A is the correct answer. "In the course of representing a client a lawyer shall not knowingly: (a) make a false statement of material fact or law to a third person." Rule 4.1(a). Here, the attorney knows of the title defect and is basically committing fraud by encouraging the buyer to purchase it.

B is incorrect. "In dealing on behalf of a client with a person who is not represented by counsel, a lawyer shall not state or imply that the lawyer is disinterested." Model Rule 4.3. This Rule is meant to deal with situations where a person may not know that an attorney is in fact interested in a matter. Here, since the seller told the buyer to contact the seller's attorney, it's clear that the buyer should understand the attorney is interested and working for the seller. Consequently, this answer choice should have been discarded immediately.

C is incorrect. The attorney's statement was not an opinion, considering the title defect made this statement an outright lie.

D is incorrect. In dealing with persons other than the client, the Rules make it very clear that a lawyer is not allowed to make false statements. This answer implies that a lawyer owes a duty to no one but the client, a clearly false statement that should be discarded immediately.

Question 34.

B is the correct answer. "The prosecutor in a criminal case shall: ... (d) make timely disclosure to the defense of all evidence or information known to the prosecutor that tends to negate the guilt of the accused or mitigates the offense." Model Rule 3.8(d). Here, since the prosecutor knew of the prior identification and the detective's encouragement, and since this information tended to negate the guilt of the accused, he was required to disclose these facts to the defendant's counsel.

A is incorrect. The issue here is the fact that the prosecutor has special duties under the Rules not to withhold information from the defense. Whether or not the videotape was clear enough to make an identification is irrelevant.

C is incorrect. Even though the defendant's counsel has not made a discovery request, this does not relieve the prosecutor from his duty to inform the defense counsel of the earlier identification.

D is incorrect. This is the classic "no-harm, no-foul" answer choice that should be avoided.

Question 35.

C is the correct answer. "A lawyer shall hold property of clients or third persons that is in a lawyer's possession in connection with a representation separate from the lawyer's own property." Model Rule 1.15(a). Additionally, "a lawyer shall deposit into a client trust account legal fees and expenses that have been paid in advance, to be withdrawn by the lawyer only as fees are earned or expenses incurred." Model Rule 1.15(c). Importantly, once the funds were identified as belonging to the attorney (i.e., the funds were earned), they should have been removed from the client account.

A is incorrect. Before the fees were earned, it was absolutely proper to place them in the Clients' Trust Account. However, once the fees were earned and became the attorney's property, they had to be removed from the account. The only time a lawyer's own funds should be in the client trust account is when those funds are used for the sole purpose of paying bank service charges on the account, and those funds should only be in the amount necessary for that purpose. Model Rule 1.15(b).

B is incorrect. Although the billings were accurate, the funds remained impermissibly commingled in the account.

D is incorrect. It is proper for a lawyer to accept fees in advance, so long as those fees are kept in the client trust account until they are earned by the lawyer. Model Rule 1.15(c).

Question 36.

C is the correct answer. "A lawyer shall not make a statement that the lawyer knows to be false or with reckless disregard to its truth or falsity concerning the qualifications or integrity of a judge." Model Rule 8.2(a). Here, since the question states that the attorney reasonably believed the accusations to be true, he is not subject to discipline for making the statements.

A is incorrect. As long as a lawyer does not make a statement that is false or with reckless disregard to the truth, a lawyer may properly criticize members of the judiciary. This answer choice should have been discarded immediately, as it implies that judges may never be criticized by attorneys.

B is incorrect. An attorney is allowed to question the character and fitness of judges, not only the extent of their legal knowledge.

D is incorrect. If the attorney was making false statements, the simple fact Beta had equal access to the press would not solve the matter (since Beta's reputation would have already been unfairly damaged).

Question 37.

C is the correct answer. Although Model Rule 3.2 requires a lawyer to make reasonable efforts to expedite litigation, it also notes that "there will be occasions when a lawyer may properly seek a postponement for personal reasons." Model Rule 3.2, Comment [1]. Here, the lawyer requested a continuance to fulfill her legislative duties, which is a valid reason for a postponement.

A is incorrect. Although the defendant objected to the continuance, the defendant's objection did not make the lawyer's request improper.

B is incorrect. The facts in this question do not contain any indication that the lawyer used her public position to influence the tribunal. She only noted that she was a member of the legislature to explain her need for the continuance.

D is incorrect. If the lawyer had asked for a continuance for an improper reason, she would still be subject to discipline whether the request helped her client or not.

Question 38.

C is the correct answer. "Parties to a matter may communicate directly with each other, and a lawyer is not prohibited from advising a client concerning a communication that the client is legally entitled to make." Model Rule 4.2 Comment [4]. Consequently, the lawyer could suggest that his client talk to the other party.

A is incorrect. Model Rule 4.2 only prohibits the lawyer from talking to the opposing party. It does not prohibit any communications between the parties themselves.

B is incorrect. Parties to a matter can communicate directly with each other, whether or not there is any evidence of wrongdoing on an attorney's part.

D is incorrect. Since the parties are allowed to communicate with each other directly, there was no need for the attorney's express or implied consent.

Question 39.

C is the correct answer. By doing what the president asked, the lawyer has violated Model Rule 3.1, which requires meritorious claims and contentions; Model Rule 3.2, which requires the lawyer to expedite litigation; Model Rule 3.3, which requires candor toward the tribunal; and Model Rule 3.4, which requires fairness to the opposing party and counsel. Consequently, the lawyer is subject to discipline under Model Rule 8.4. Additionally, Federal Rules of Civil Procedure Rule 11 provides litigation sanctions for an attorney who files a pleading or other motion for "any improper purpose, such as to harass, cause unnecessary delay, or needlessly increase the cost of litigation."

Consequently, A, B, and D are incorrect. As a side note, although there have been several "C"s in a row, this fact should not have changed your analysis.

Question 40.

D is the correct answer. Model Rule 1.18 Comment [1] notes that "[a] lawyer's consultations with a prospective client usually are limited in time and depth and leave both the prospective client and the lawyer free (and sometimes required) to proceed no further. Hence, prospective clients should receive some but not all of the protection afforded clients." Consequently, the lawyer was not legally obligated to accept the man's case.

A is incorrect. A lawyer's decision not to represent a client is not limited by a need to show good cause to refuse the representation.

B is incorrect. As noted in Model Rule 1.18, while a prospective client receives some protections (such as prohibitions regarding the disclosure of information), a lawyer is not required to help a prospective client find another lawyer to represent him or her if the lawyer decides to decline the representation.

C is incorrect. Even if the lawyer had held herself out as an expert in legal malpractice, the Rules would not have required her to represent this potential client.

Question 41.

D is the correct answer. Under Model Rule 7.2, a lawyer may advertise his or her services through written and public media, subject to Model Rule 7.1's prohibition against false or misleading statements. Here, everything the attorney has stated about his business is true. Importantly, by placing flyers in the artists' booths and parking his van outside the fair, he did not engage in face-to-face or real-time communication as prohibited in Model Rule 7.3. Additionally, there is no prohibition in the Rules stating that the attorney cannot have a retainer agreement on the back of the flyer. Finally, Model Rule 7.4(a) states that "[a] lawyer may communicate the fact that the lawyer does or does not practice in particular fields of law." The attorney is not indicating any sort of certification regarding art law, but is merely stating his degree and general practice area.

Consequently, A, B, and C are incorrect.

Question 42.

C is the correct answer. According to Model Rule 1.9(a), "[a] lawyer who has formerly represented a client in a matter shall not thereafter represent another person in the same or a substantially related matter in which that person's interests are materially adverse to the interests of the former client." Here, the important point is that the partnership dissolution and the sale of the home are completely unrelated, so the attorney may accept the representation.

A is incorrect. Although the representation may be directly adverse to his former client, it does not involve the same or a substantially related matter, so the attorney may accept the representation.

B is incorrect. This answer choice is meant to be a distractor, as it touches on another Rule, but fails to state it correctly. While this choice implies that the attorney could represent other parties adverse to the seller so long as the attorney did not agree not to do so during the earlier representation, a lawyer restricting his or her right to practice in such a way is prohibited by Model Rule 5.6.

D is incorrect. Since the two matters are unrelated, it is immaterial when the sale of the home occurred.

Question 43.

C is the correct answer. "A lawyer may reveal information relating to the representation of a client to the extent the lawyer reasonably believes necessary: (1) to prevent reasonably certain death or substantial bodily harm." Model Rule 1.6(b). Here, since the waste products are "reasonably certain to cause substantial bodily harm," the attorney was not subject to discipline for reporting the company's conduct to the authorities.

A is incorrect. As noted above, a lawyer can reveal confidential information without the client's consent if the lawyer reasonably believes the revelation is necessary to prevent substantial bodily harm.

B is incorrect. The Rules' permission regarding revealing confidential information is not limited to criminal matters.

D is incorrect. The important point is that the waste products could cause substantial bodily harm, not whether or not the president was pursuing an impudent course of conduct.

Question 44.

C is the correct answer. Model Rule 8.1(a) prohibits a lawyer from knowingly making a false statement of material fact in connection with a bar admission application. Here, the attorney shouldn't write the letter until he has made an investigation into the client's statements.

A is incorrect. Since the attorney knows nothing about his new client's nephew, he should not write the letter simply based on the client's assurances.

B is incorrect. This answer choice is the same as A, in that the attorney would be making a statement regarding the nephew's qualifications for the bar without actually knowing anything about the nephew.

D is incorrect. This answer choice simply states that the attorney could write the letter after speaking with the nephew. There is no indication that they would necessarily discuss the client's assurances regarding the nephew's qualifications.

Question 45.

A is the correct answer. Model Rule 1.8(d) states " . . . a lawyer shall not make or negotiate an agreement giving the lawyer literary or media rights to a portrayal or account based in substantial part on information relating to the representation." This Rule guards against a lawyer doing things during representation simply to improve the value of the rights, such as spicing up or complicating the litigation to make it more entertaining.

B is incorrect. There is no prohibition in the Rules that states a lawyer cannot aid a client in obtaining independent bank loans. "However, Lawyers may not subsidize lawsuits or administrative proceedings brought on behalf of their clients, including making or guaranteeing loans to their clients for living expenses, because to do so would encourage clients to pursue lawsuits that might not otherwise be brought and because such assistance gives lawyers too great a financial stake in the litigation." Model Rule 1.8 Comment [10].

C is incorrect. "A lawyer may accept property in payment for services, such as an ownership interest in an enterprise, providing this does not involve acquisition of a proprietary interest in the cause of action or subject matter of the litigation contrary to Rule 1.8 (i). However, a fee paid in property instead of money may be subject to the requirements of Rule 1.8(a) because such fees often have the essential qualities of a business transaction with the client." Model Rule 1.5 Comment [4].

D is incorrect. There is no prohibition in the Rules regarding a client paying a lawyer with bank credit cards.

Question 46.

B is the correct answer. Model Rule 1.15 Comment [1] states that "[a] lawyer should hold property of others with the care required of a professional fiduciary." Consequently, the lawyer should open another Clients' Trust Account in order to make sure the entire $300,000 is protected by insurance.

A is incorrect. If the lawyer fails to take action regarding the funds, a significant portion of them may be lost.

C is incorrect. Under Model Rule 1.15, a lawyer should keep his or her property separate from clients' property. Consequently, it would be improper for the attorney to move clients' funds into his own bank account.

D is incorrect. As in Choice A, this basically means the attorney is crossing his fingers and hoping for the best. A 10-day window does not change the analysis.

Question 47.

A is the correct answer. There is nothing in the Rules that requires lawyers in a firm to be made shareholders within a certain amount of time.

B is incorrect. Model Rule 5.4(d)(2) states that a lawyer cannot be part of a firm where "a nonlawyer is a corporate director or officer thereof or occupies the position of similar responsibility in any form of association other than a corporation." Here, the office manager's position of executive vice president violates the Rule.

C is incorrect. Model Rule 5.4(d)(1) states that a lawyer cannot be part of a firm where "a nonlawyer owns any interest therein, except that a fiduciary representative of the estate of a lawyer may hold the stock or interest of the lawyer for a reasonable time during administration." Here, the widow appears to be a nonlawyer and her husband has been deceased for five years, which would not likely be a reasonable amount of time even if she were a fiduciary representative of the estate.

D is incorrect. Under Model Rule 5.4(b), "[a] lawyer shall not form a partnership with a nonlawyer if any of the activities of the partnership consist of the practice of law." Consequently, the firm's nonlawyer accountant cannot be a shareholder in the firm.

Question 48.

A is the correct answer. Model Rule 1.1 requires a lawyer to give competent representation to a client. Here, since the attorney does not believe he can give competent representation, he should ask the court for permission to withdraw.

B is incorrect. Model Rule 1.1 Comment [2] states that "[a] lawyer can provide adequate representation in a wholly novel field through necessary study." However, this choice simply says that the attorney should ask for a "two-week continuance." It says nothing about whether this would be an adequate amount of time for the lawyer to study this particular area of the law.

C is incorrect. A lawyer cannot represent a client if he or she is not competent to do so, even if the client consents to the representation.

D is incorrect. A lawyer cannot represent a client if he or she is not competent to do so, even if the client consents in writing.

Question 49.

A is the correct answer. Under Model Code of Judicial Conduct Rule 4.1(A)(12), a judge or judicial candidate shall not "make any statement that would reasonably be expected to affect the outcome or impair the fairness of a matter pending or impending in any court." Model Code of Judicial Conduct Rule 4.1 Comment [13] notes that "[t]he making of a pledge, promise, or commitment is not dependent upon, or limited to, the use of any specific words or phrases; instead, the totality of the statement must be examined to determine if a reasonable person would believe that the candidate for judicial office has specifically undertaken to reach a particular result. Pledges, promises, or commitments must be contrasted with statements or announcements of personal views on legal, political, or other issues, which are not prohibited. When making such statements, a judge should acknowledge the overarching judicial obligation to apply and uphold the law, without regard to his or her personal views." Here, choice A is the only statement that does not appear to be promising a specific result.

B is incorrect. This statement implies that the judge will automatically rule in such a way as to limit a prisoner's civil liberties.

C is incorrect. This statement implies that the judge will automatically make the same decision in similar cases without regard to the particular or unique facts of the case.

D is incorrect. This statement explicitly states that the judge will never rule in favor of a prisoner.

Question 50.

A is the correct answer. "A lawyer who has formerly represented a client in a matter shall not thereafter represent another person in the same or a substantially related matter in which that person's interests are materially adverse to the interests of the former client unless the former client gives informed consent, confirmed in writing." Model Rule 1.9(a). Here, since the attorney formerly represented the insurance company in the same matter, she cannot represent the man. Choice A is the only choice that reflects this Rule.

B is incorrect. As stated above, the Rules prohibit the attorney from representing the man.

C is incorrect. Model Rule 1.10(a) states that, except in circumstances not implicated here, lawyers who are associated in a firm shall not knowingly represent a client when any one of them practicing alone would be prohibited from doing so by Rules 1.7 or 1.9. Consequently, an associate in the attorney's firm could not take the case.

D is incorrect. The prohibition in Model Rule 1.10(a) applies whether or not the attorney shares in the fee.

Question 51.

D is the correct answer. "A lawyer who has formerly represented a client in a matter shall not thereafter represent another person in the same or a substantially related matter in which that person's interests are materially adverse to the interests of the former client unless the former client gives informed consent, confirmed in writing." Model Rule 1.9(a). Here, the important point is that the two matters, a sexual harassment claim and a slip-and-fall claim, are not substantially related. Consequently, the attorney can represent the woman if he wants to, refuse to discuss the matter with her, or simply give her a list of competent lawyers.

A, B, and C are therefore incorrect.

Question 52.

A is the correct answer. A lawyer may withdraw from representation if the client fails to abide by the terms of an agreement concerning fees. Model Rule 1.16 Comment [8]. Consequently, the attorney may ask the court for permission to withdraw.

B is incorrect. Model Rule 1.6(a) states that "[a] lawyer shall not reveal information relating to the representation of a client unless the client gives informed consent." Here, the client has not given informed consent, and no exception to the Rule applies, so the attorney should not pass the file onto another lawyer.

C is incorrect. Under Model Rule 1.8(i), a lawyer is prohibited from acquiring a proprietary interest in the cause of action. Thus, the attorney cannot accept an assignment from the client as security.

D is incorrect. If the attorney simply stopped working on the case, he would violate Model Rule 1.3's requirement of reasonable diligence in representing a client.

Question 53.

D is the correct answer. Model Rule 7.2 Comment [2] "permits public dissemination of information concerning a lawyer's name or firm name, address, email address, website, and telephone number; the kinds of services the lawyer will undertake; the basis on which the lawyer's fees are determined, including prices for specific services and payment and credit arrangements; a lawyer's foreign language ability; names of references and, with their consent, names of clients regularly represented; and other information that might invite the attention of those seeking legal assistance." There is no prohibition regarding listing a lawyer's degrees or encouraging potential clients to leave voice messages.

Therefore, A, B, and C are incorrect.

Question 54.

A is the correct answer. Model Rule 4.2 prohibits a lawyer from communicating about the subject of the representation with a person the lawyer knows is represented by another lawyer in the matter. This prohibition applies even if the represented person is the one to initiate the communication. Model Rule 4.2 Comment [3].

B is incorrect. Although the plaintiff could speak directly with the man if he chose to do so, the attorney cannot give him that advice since he knows the plaintiff is represented by another lawyer.

C is incorrect. Even if the attorney has made several settlement offers, this does not allow him to speak with the plaintiff.

D is incorrect. Even if the attorney believes the settlement is appropriate, he still cannot speak to the plaintiff.

Question 55.

D is the correct answer. Model Rules 7.1 and 7.2 allow lawyers to have radio advertisements as long as the statements made in the advertisement are truthful. Model Rule 7.2 Comment [2] notes that "[t]his Rule permits public dissemination of information concerning a lawyer's name or firm name, address, email address, website, and telephone number; the kinds of services the lawyer will undertake; the basis on which the lawyer's fees are determined, including prices for specific services and payment and credit arrangements; a lawyer's foreign language ability; names of references and, with their consent, names of clients regularly represented; and other information that might invite the attention of those seeking legal assistance."

A is incorrect. Although the lawyers could include their qualifications in the radio advertisement, they are not required to do so.

B is incorrect. A close reading of the advertisement shows that it is not actually encouraging litigation. It merely states that if a person is being sued or has another legal problem, that person should contact the attorneys for help. Model Rule 7.2 Comment [1] notes that "[t]o assist the public in learning about and obtaining legal services, lawyers should be allowed to make known their services not only through reputation but also through organized information campaigns in the form of advertising. Advertising involves an active quest for clients, contrary to the tradition that a lawyer should not seek clientele."

C is incorrect. Even though the radio advertisement can be heard outside of the state in which the lawyers are licensed, this does not cause the advertisement to violate the Rules. The question here is clearly focused on the content of the lawyers' message.

Question 56.

D is the correct answer. Model Rule 8.3(a) requires that a lawyer report violations of the Rules that raise "a substantial question as to that lawyer's honesty, trustworthiness, or fitness as a lawyer." However, Model Rule 8.3(c) states that disclosure is not required if the information is protected by Model Rule 1.6's confidentiality rules. Here, the client told the attorney in confidence and does not want her to reveal the information. Consequently, the attorney is not required to report it.

A is incorrect. Even though the attorney believes Beta was guilty of professional misconduct, reporting the information would require revealing the client's confidential information. Importantly, the information does not involve the possibility of substantial harm or any other exception under Model Rule 1.6.

B is incorrect. Beta's normal course of action would not affect the analysis of this question. Importantly, the question is focused on this particular instance of Beta's misconduct.

C is incorrect. Although the client was satisfied with the return of the retainer, the question is really asking about whether the attorney needs to reveal her client's confidential information.

Question 57.

B is the correct answer. Model Rule 5.1(a) states "A partner in a law firm, and a lawyer who individually or together with other lawyers possesses comparable managerial authority in a law firm, shall make reasonable efforts to ensure that the firm has in effect measures giving reasonable assurance that all lawyers in the firm conform to the Rules of Professional Conduct." As the question notes, this law firm doesn't do anything to supervise its new attorneys.

A is incorrect. Model Rule 5.1 specifically states that it applies to the individual partners and managing lawyers, not the firm itself.

C is incorrect. Although the associate is unsupervised, he would still be subject to discipline for his apparent lack of competence and lying to his client.

D is incorrect. Because the client retained the law firm for his claim and the firm had supervisory authority over the associate, the firm would be subject to civil liability for the client's loss.

Question 58.

A is the correct answer. Model Rule 1.15(a) requires that a lawyer keep a client's property separate from his or her own personal property. A is the only choice where the lawyer is not placing the client's funds in his personal bank account.

Because the attorney should not place the plaintiff's funds in his personal bank account, B, C, and D are incorrect, no matter how quickly the attorney gets the funds to the plaintiff.

Question 59.

D is the correct answer. Alpha should not pass along the rumors she has heard regarding Delta. Model Rule 8.2(a) states that a lawyer should not make statements made with reckless disregard as to their truth concerning the qualifications or integrity of a candidate for election or appointment to judicial office. Here, Alpha's passing along of the rumors would likely be in reckless disregard concerning their truth.

A, B, and C are incorrect. Model Rule 8.2 Comment [1] specifically allows lawyers to express their honest and candid opinions regarding judicial candidates. Consequently, Alpha can seek contributions from other lawyers in the community for Beta's campaign committee and publicly oppose Delta, even if the attorneys being contacted are likely to appear before Beta in court.

Question 60.

A is the correct answer. Model Rule 4.2 prohibits communications with persons represented by counsel. Here, the fact the prosecutor would be using a nonlawyer employee to do the communicating does not change the analysis.

B is incorrect. Model Rule 3.8 Comment [1] notes that a prosecutor "has the responsibility of a minister of justice and not simply that of an advocate." If the prosecutor believes "joyriding" is the most appropriate charge, he may file a new complaint reflecting that.

C is incorrect. While Model Rule 3.8(a) states that a prosecutor should not prosecute a claim unsupported by probable cause. That does not seem to be the case here. As the question notes, the prosecutor reasonably believes that the defendant committed the offense. The only issue is that he believes the defendant's youth is a mitigating circumstance.

D is incorrect. Model Rule 3.8(d) specifically states that a prosecutor is required to make such information available to the defense.

3. Answers to Practice MPRE 3

Question 1.

C is the correct answer. Model Rule 8.3(a) states that "A lawyer who knows that another lawyer has committed a violation of the Rules of Professional Conduct that raises a substantial question as to that lawyer's honesty, trustworthiness or fitness as a lawyer in other respects, shall inform the appropriate professional authority." The import word here is "knows." In this question, the prosecutor has his suspicions regarding the attorney's motives, but he doesn't know anything. Importantly, in a question like this, don't read into it facts that are not there, or connect dots that are not connected in the question. As far as the prosecutor actually knows, the attorney has done nothing wrong.

A is incorrect. A lawyer is not subject to discipline simply because a client suffered a detriment by relying on the lawyer's advice.

B is incorrect. The fact the attorney gained publicity as a result of the trial does not necessarily mean she did anything wrong.

D is incorrect. While the attorney did competently represent the defendant, if the prosecutor knew that the refusal to plea bargain was due to the attorney's personal motives and not due to what the attorney thought would be best for the client, the prosecutor would still need to report the attorney.

Question 2.

D is the correct answer. Model Rule 3.4 Comment [3] states that "it is not improper to pay a witness's expenses or to compensate an expert witness on terms permitted by law. The common law rule in most jurisdictions is that it is improper to pay an occurrence witness any fee for testifying and that it is improper to pay an expert witness a contingent fee." Also, Model Rule 3.4(b) prohibits giving a witness an inducement to give false testimony. Here, giving the witness a percentage of the claim is an improper payment that would likely encourage false testimony.

A is incorrect. As noted above, a lawyer is not prohibited from paying witnesses fees permitted by law.

B is incorrect. Clearly, travel expenses would fall under those expenses that an attorney can pay.

C is incorrect. Lost wages would be part of the witness's expenses to testify, so they could be paid for by the attorney.

Question 3.

A is the correct answer. Model Rule 1.15 Comment [3] states that "[l]awyers often receive funds from which the lawyer's fee will be paid. The lawyer is not required to remit to the client funds that the lawyer reasonably believes represent fees owed. However, a lawyer may not hold funds to coerce a client into accepting the lawyer's contention. The disputed portion of the funds must be kept in a trust account and the lawyer should suggest means for prompt resolution of the dispute, such as arbitration. The undisputed portion of the funds shall be promptly distributed." Here, the lawyer has received $30,000, and is entitled to 30 percent of the settlement per her agreed fee. Since she has received $30,000, 30 percent, or $9,000, is currently in dispute. Consequently, she should send the client $21,000 and retain the disputed $9,000 in her Clients' Trust Account until the matter is settled.

B is incorrect. As noted above, the lawyer should keep the disputed portion of the settlement in a trust account.

C is incorrect. While the ultimate settlement may be $60,000, only $30,000 has been received. Thus, only 30 percent of that amount is currently in dispute. Additionally, any disputed funds should not be put in the lawyer's personal account.

D is incorrect. As stated above, only $30,000 of the settlement has been received, so only $9,000 is in dispute at this time.

Question 4.

D is the correct answer. Under Model Code of Judicial Conduct Rule 4.1 Comment [1], a judicial candidate should "be free and appear to be free from political influence and political pressure." Here, the attorney is apparently promising that his sentences will be longer than three years in armed robbery cases and eight years in murder cases, no matter what the particular circumstances are of each case. Also, if you didn't remember the Rule at all, D is clearly different from the other three choices because it includes a statement regarding the attorney's plans should he be elected judge, while the other three choices are simply statements of fact regarding the incumbent.

A, B, and C are incorrect because the attorney is simply making factual statements regarding the incumbent, and the question states that these statements are accurate.

Question 5.

D is the correct answer. Model Rule 8.4(e) prohibits a lawyer from implying an ability to improperly influence a government agency. Here, the attorney's statement seems to imply the agency employees owe him for their appointment. Additionally, it is the only choice that contains more than plain factual statements.

A is incorrect because it simply states the client's position in the matter, which is fairly obvious considering he is fighting the charge.

B is incorrect because it is only outlining how the claim is likely to proceed through the agency and the courts.

C is incorrect because the attorney is only stating that witnesses to the incident are needed to contest the claim.

Question 6.

B is the correct answer. Model Rule 1.15 Comment [3] states that "[l]awyers often receive funds from which the lawyer's fee will be paid. The lawyer is not required to remit to the client funds that the lawyer reasonably believes represent fees owed. However, a lawyer may not hold funds to coerce a client into accepting the lawyer's contention. The disputed portion of the funds must be kept in a trust account and the lawyer should suggest means for prompt resolution of the dispute, such as arbitration. The undisputed portion of the funds shall be promptly distributed." In this case, $2,000 is in dispute. Consequently, that portion should remain in the Clients' Trust Account, and the remainder should be distributed.

A is incorrect. Since the entire amount is not in dispute, it would be incorrect for the lawyer to retain the entire amount in the Clients' Trust Account instead of sending the nondisputed amount to the client.

C is incorrect. Here, $2,000 is in dispute, so the attorney cannot simply place the entire $5,000 he believes he is owed into his office account.

D is incorrect. The amount not in dispute should be sent to the client, as those funds belong to the client and not the attorney.

Question 7.

C is the correct answer. Model Rule 3.4(e) prohibits a lawyer from stating a personal opinion regarding the credibility of a witness during trial. This statement is clearly an example of the attorney's personal opinion.

A is incorrect. This statement is merely a statement of fact regarding the testimony in the case.

B is incorrect. While this statement seems to imply that a witness is lying, the attorney is not stating his personal opinion.

D is incorrect. This statement is similar to the statement in choice B in that it implies a witness is lying, but doesn't actually state the lawyer's personal opinion regarding the credibility of the witnesses.

Question 8.

B is the correct answer. Model Rule 3.6(a) regarding trial publicity prohibits a lawyer from making "an extrajudicial statement that the lawyer knows or reasonably should know will be disseminated by means of public communication and will have a substantial likelihood of materially prejudicing an adjudicative proceeding in the matter." Here, telling the reporter that the defense has medical proof that the client is infertile would clearly prejudice the proceedings by making it impossible for the businessman to have fathered the child, despite witness statements and other evidence to the contrary. Additionally, out of the available choices, choice B is the only statement not specifically allowed by the Rules.

A is incorrect. Model Rule 3.6(b)(1) allows the attorney to tell the reporter the defense involved in the claim.

C is incorrect. Model Rule 3.6(b)(5) allows lawyers to request assistance in obtaining evidence and information regarding the case.

D is incorrect. Model Rule 3.6(b)(2) allows lawyers to state information contained in a public record. Here, the statement notes that the tax records he is referring to are public.

Question 9.

A is the correct answer. Model Rule 1.15(a) states that a lawyer should hold a client's property separate from the lawyer's own property. Consequently, the lawyer should not put the money into her own account, whether or not she immediately writes a check to the client.

B is incorrect. Although the attorney is not immediately sending the funds to the client, the important point is that she is keeping the client's money and her own separate.

C is incorrect. This is probably the best way to handle the checks, as it keeps the funds separate and immediately gives the client the money he is entitled to.

D is incorrect. There is no prohibition against the attorney sending the client the entire check.

Question 10.

A is the correct answer. The attorney violated no Rule of Professional Conduct or Evidence when he asked the defendant on cross-examination to confess to drinking prior to the accident. Although he could not offer any evidence, he was within legal boundaries when he asked the question.

B is incorrect. Model Rule 3.4(e) prohibits a lawyer during trial from asserting personal knowledge or alluding to any matter that will not be supported by admissible evidence.

C is incorrect. As stated above, Model Rule 3.4(e) prohibits a lawyer during trial from asserting personal knowledge regarding the facts at issue.

D is incorrect. Model Rule 8.2(a) prohibits a lawyer from falsely or recklessly attacking the integrity of a judge. The attorney's statement regarding the defendant's money seems to do just that.

Question 11.

C is the correct answer. To maintain the Rules' required level of knowledge, competence, and skill, a lawyer should keep abreast of changes in the law. Model Rule 1.1. Independent study is just as valid as continuing legal education courses in maintaining the attorney's competence. Importantly, the state does not require the attorney to attend continuing legal education.

A is incorrect. The possession of malpractice insurance does not change a lawyer's duty to remain competent.

B is incorrect. Clearly, continuing legal education courses are not the only way a lawyer can maintain his or her competence.

D is incorrect. A lawyer's duty to remain competent is not affected by the cost of doing so.

Question 12.

D is the correct answer. Under Model Rule 1.11(a)(2), "a lawyer who has formerly served as a public officer or employee of the government . . . shall not otherwise represent a client in connection with a matter in which the lawyer participated personally and substantially as a public officer or employee" unless authorized to do so by the government agency. Importantly, Comment [3] states that these provisions are "designed . . . to prevent a lawyer from exploiting public office for the advantage of another client." Model Rule 1.11, Comment [3]. Here, the attorney participated personally and substantially in the preparation of the water department's case against the corporation. Consequently, she cannot now represent the corporation in individual claims involving the same case.

A is incorrect. While the attorney may be the most competent lawyer to represent the corporation in this case, her special competence does not allow her to violate the Rules' prohibition.

B is incorrect. The Rule is concerned with the attorney using her former job as an unfair advantage in the case. Whether or not the information is in the public record doesn't change the basic analysis.

C is incorrect. As stated above, the Rule is concerned with the attorney's exploitation of her prior work experience, not whether the case's prior judgment could be determinative.

Question 13.

D is the correct answer. Model Code of Judicial Conduct Rule 2.9(A)(2) permits a judge to "obtain the written advice of a disinterested expert on the law applicable to a proceeding before the judge, if the judge gives advance notice to the parties of the person to be consulted and the subject matter of the advice to be solicited, and affords the parties a reasonable opportunity to object and respond to the notice and to the advice received." Here, the judge did not inform the parties, which clearly implies that they had no opportunity to object or respond.

A is incorrect. While the friend may have no interest in the case, the important issue is that the parties were not informed.

B is incorrect. Even if the judge did not understand the claim, this does not relieve her of the duty to inform the parties if she seeks outside advice.

C is incorrect. As noted in the Rule above, the judge does not need to get the parties' consent, but she does need to inform them of the advice and give them an opportunity to respond.

Question 14.

A is the correct answer. An attorney may withdraw from representation if the withdrawal can be accomplished without material adverse effect, the client persists in criminal or fraudulent action, the client has used the lawyer's services to perpetrate crime or fraud, the client insists on repugnant action, the client fails to fulfill an obligation and has been given reasonable warning, representation will result in an unreasonable financial burden, or other good cause exists. Model Rule 1.16(b). Thus, the simple fact that a client has failed to pay fees may be insufficient to justify a withdrawal. For example, the attorney in this question could withdraw if a client is a day late in paying a fee, which clearly does not meet any of the possible reasons for withdrawal included in the Rules.

B is incorrect. Even if a client received independent legal advice before signing the stipulation, it would still be improper under the Rules.

C is incorrect. The Rules allow withdrawal for "unreasonable" financial burden. Model Rule 1.16(b)(6). Here, the stipulation comes into effect simply because the client is late paying a fee, which may not be an unreasonable financial burden on the attorney (for example, if the client is one day late in paying).

D is incorrect. Although a client may have consented to the withdrawal, this does not make the underlying stipulation proper under the Rules.

Question 15.

D is the correct answer. Under Model Rule 1.2(d), a lawyer may not counsel or assist a client in conduct that is criminal or fraudulent. Model Rule 3.3(a)(3) prohibits the use of false evidence. When the attorney asked the client about his tax returns, he knew that the response would be a falsehood that would mislead the court in its judgment of the client's offense.

A is incorrect. The fact that the tax returns were not the primary issue does not change the analysis. Importantly, it could change the sentence.

B is incorrect. While the information would ordinarily be protected because it was disclosed to the attorney as a confidence during the course of representation, it cannot be protected if it results in the presentation of testimony that the attorney knows is false.

C is incorrect. The important point in this question is that the testimony is false. The seriousness of the crime is immaterial.

Question 16.

D is the correct answer. A lawyer is prohibited from communicating about a matter with a person known to be represented in the matter unless the person's lawyer consents to the communication or the communication is authorized by law. Model Rule 4.2. In addition, a lawyer may not violate the Rules directly or through the acts of another. Model Rule 8.4(a). Here, the attorney used a nonlawyer agent, the office assistant, to violate the no-contact rule.

A is incorrect. The fact the defendant's lawyer might not have relayed the settlement offer did not justify the prohibited communication.

B is incorrect. As in the case of her belief regarding the settlement offer, her suspicion regarding the lawyer's attempt to run up fees does not excuse the communication.

C is incorrect. As stated above, the important point is that it is the lawyer's consent that is necessary, not the client's.

Question 17.

A is the correct answer. "A lawyer shall not enter into an arrangement for, charge, or collect: (1) any fee in a domestic relations matter, the payment or amount of which is contingent upon the securing of a divorce or upon the amount of alimony or support, or property settlement in lieu thereof." Model Rule 1.5(d)(1). Here, the attorney's standard retainer contract sets up a prohibited contingent fee arrangement.

B is incorrect. The issue here is not the type of interest being acquired by the lawyer, but the fact that the lawyer is charging a contingent fee in a domestic matter.

C is incorrect. While many clients may find it easier to pay a contingent fee, this does not make contingent fees proper in this situation.

D is incorrect. While the clients may consent, this does not make the arrangement proper under the Rules. Always be wary of answer choices that claim something is right because it was the client's idea.

Question 18.

D is the correct answer. "A lawyer shall act with reasonable diligence and promptness in representing a client." Model Rule 1.3. Importantly, if the attorney is away from his or her office for a long time, the attorney must make some provision for dealing with ongoing matters.

A is incorrect. This is the classic "no-harm, no-foul" answer choice. While the default judgment was set aside, there was no guarantee that a court would do so, and the attorney put her client's claim at unreasonable risk.

B is incorrect. If the attorney was going to be unreachable for a long time, she should have made provisions for the handling of her pending cases.

C is incorrect. The issue here is not potential restitution. The bigger issue is that the attorney was unreachable for a month without making provisions for her ongoing cases.

Question 19.

C is the correct answer. A lawyer shall not reveal any information relating to the representation of a client unless the client gives informed consent. Model Rule 1.6(a). Here, the information was obtained during the course of the attorney's representation, and consequently "relates" to that representation. Consequently, the attorney should not reveal it.

A is incorrect. Although there are several exceptions to Model Rule 1.6's confidentiality requirement, none of the exceptions requires an attorney to disclose a client's past crimes of violence. Often, when testing this particular issue, the MPRE uses the idea of an attorney as "an officer of the court" in an incorrect answer choice.

B is incorrect. Although the murder remains unsolved, this does not relieve the attorney from the Rules' prohibition.

D is incorrect. Here, the attorney discovered that information during his representation of the client, so it is protected as confidential information. If the attorney had advised the client regarding how to commit the prior crime or how to hide the body, he would of course be subject to discipline and criminal prosecution.

Question 20.

A is the correct answer. "A lawyer shall not accept compensation for representing a client from one other than the client unless: (1) the client gives informed consent." Model Rule 1.8(f)(1). Consequently, the attorney cannot accept the father's check without informing the client.

B is incorrect. Although it would clearly be improper for the client's father to attempt to influence the attorney's conduct, the primary issue is that the attorney cannot accept the check without getting the client's consent. Additionally, simply asking the attorney to make the case his "top priority" is not really influencing the attorney's conduct.

C is incorrect. The familial relationship between the client and his father does not excuse the attorney from this Rule.

D is incorrect. A close reading of the question shows that the client is not the one who asked his father to pay his bill.

Question 21.

D is the correct answer. "In the course of representing a client a lawyer shall not knowingly: (a) make a false statement of material fact or law to a third person." Rule 4.1(a). Here, the attorney knows of the title defect and is basically committing fraud by telling the buyer that it is a wonderful deal.

A is incorrect. This is another variation of the "it was the client's idea" wrong answer.

B is incorrect. The attorney's statement was not an opinion, considering the title defect made this statement an outright lie.

C is incorrect. Here, the attorney didn't imply anything — he flat-out lied to the buyer because he knew the attempt to purchase the property would be worthless.

Question 22.

A is the correct answer. Under Model Rule 7.2(b), an attorney "shall not give anything of value to a person for recommending the lawyer's services." Here, the agreement with the doctor clearly violates this Rule, since the doctor is receiving valuable advertising space and recommendations for his recommendations regarding the attorney.

B is incorrect. The issue here is that the attorney is giving the doctor something of value for recommending the attorney's services, not that the attorney asked the doctor to put up some ads.

C is incorrect. Remember that many wrong answers on the MPRE will set up a "no-harm, no-foul" situation. Even if the patients and clients knew of the arrangement, this would not cure the problem of the attorney giving the doctor something of value for recommending the attorney's services.

D is incorrect. As stated above, the Rule is concerned with giving someone "anything of value" for recommending the lawyer's services, not simply whether the lawyer is giving that person "money."

Question 23.

C is the correct answer. Although a lawyer is not allowed to counsel or assist a client in criminal or fraudulent conduct, a lawyer may help a client determine the validity, scope, meaning, or application of the law to a client's particular situation. Model Rule 1.2(d). Here, the attorney is not helping the owner break the law; she is simply stating facts regarding the law's fine and enforcement.

A is incorrect. As long as a lawyer is not helping a client to violate the law, he or she is not required to make a guess as to how that client is going to use the lawyer's advice, nor is the attorney subject to discipline if the client decides to use the lawyer's advice to break the law. Here, the attorney is merely telling the owner facts regarding the law.

B is incorrect. Here, all the attorney did was tell her client about the law and its history. She did nothing to aid him in violating the law.

D is incorrect. The primary issue here is that the attorney was merely stating facts regarding the law. Remember that the MPRE often uses the idea of the attorney as an "officer of the court" in wrong answer choices.

Question 24.

B is the correct answer. A lawyer shall not form a partnership with a nonlawyer if any of the activities of the partnership consist of the "practice of law." A lawyer who does so is assisting another in the unauthorized practice of law, and is subject to discipline. Model Rule 5.5(a). While the attorney may be the only person giving legal advice, the partnership itself is in fact delivering legal services.

A is incorrect. As always, a client's consent does not allow an attorney to violate the Rules.

C is incorrect. The important point is that the partnership is providing legal services. It makes no difference that the attorney is the only one in the partnership giving legal advice.

D is incorrect. The fact that the firm's materials clearly delineate each partner's role does not change the overall analysis.

Question 25.

B is the correct answer. "A lawyer representing a client before a legislative body or administrative agency in a nonadjudicative proceeding shall disclose that the appearance is in a representative capacity." Model Rule 3.9. Consequently, the attorney should have disclosed that he was appearing on behalf of the firm.

A is incorrect. The issue here is the attorney's failure to disclose that he was appearing in a representative capacity. The fact he was paid for the testimony is irrelevant to the primary issue.

C is incorrect. While a lawyer may be allowed to engage in political activity under his or her own name as long as such activity does not violate the Rules, the important point here is that he is acting at the behest of the firm.

D is incorrect. Although the attorney may agree with his client, he is still appearing at the committee on the firm's behalf because they asked him to do so.

Question 26.

A is the correct answer. A judge is required to perform his or her duties diligently. Model Code of Judicial Conduct Rule 2.5(A). Importantly, issues should be resolved without unnecessary cost or delay. Model Code of Judicial Conduct Rule 2.5, Comment [4]. Here, the judge is granting postponements without any consideration of the individual cases, likely leading to unnecessary cost and delay for the parties involved.

B is incorrect. The clear focus of the question is on the routine postponements. This question does not address that issue and should be discarded. Additionally, simply granting a postponement is not forcing a party to do anything, so don't read some kind of unlawful pressure into this answer choice.

C is incorrect. While a judge does have discretion in managing the schedule in his or her courtroom, he or she cannot manage it in such a way as to create unnecessary cost or delay.

D is incorrect. While the postponements may not affect the ultimate outcome, they are still likely to cause unnecessary cost and delay.

Question 27.

A is the correct answer. "A lawyer who knows that a judge has committed a violation of applicable rules of judicial conduct that raises a substantial question as to the judge's fitness for office shall inform the appropriate authority." Model Rule 8.3(b). Since the judge is behaving erratically, the attorney has a duty to report it.

B is incorrect. The issue here is not unnecessary cost and delay, but the fact the judge may not be fit for his office.

C is incorrect. While reporting the judge may hurt her clients in some abstract way, this is not enough of a reason to not report the judge's conduct to the authorities.

D is incorrect. This is another example of the "no-harm, no-foul" wrong answer choice. Additionally, even if he doesn't get reelected, he'll be hearing cases for at least another six months.

Question 28.

B is the correct answer. A lawyer may not represent one client if it will be directly adverse to another client without the client's informed consent. Model Rule 1.7. This is true even if the lawyer would be acting as an advocate against the client in a matter unrelated to the one in which the lawyer represents the client. Model Rule 1.7, Comment [6]. Here, representing the neighbor in the personal injury claim would be directly adverse to the plaintiff.

A is incorrect. The important point is that this situation could cause a conflict between two current clients, not that it might affect the attorney's arguments in the claims.

C is incorrect. While the neighbor might know, there is no indication that the plaintiff knows anything about this.

D is incorrect. The conflict still exists even if one action is in an area of the law that is different from the other.

Question 29.

A is the correct answer. "A lawyer shall not provide financial assistance to a client in connection with pending or contemplated litigation, except that: (1) a lawyer may advance court costs and expenses of litigation, the repayment of which may be contingent on the outcome of the matter." Model Rule 1.8(e)(1). Here, since the funds are being used for the investigation, they are proper under the Rules.

B is incorrect. A lawyer may advance funds, but only if they are used for trial preparation. The contingent fee basis of the case does not make any and all fund advancements lawful, so A is a better answer.

C is incorrect. "Lawyers may not subsidize lawsuits or administrative proceedings brought on behalf of their clients, including making or guaranteeing loans to their clients for living expenses, because to do so would encourage clients to pursue lawsuits that might not otherwise be brought, and because such assistance gives lawyers too great a financial stake in the litigation. These dangers do not warrant a prohibition on a lawyer lending a client court costs and litigation expenses, including the expenses of medical examination and the costs of obtaining and presenting evidence, because these advances are virtually indistinguishable from contingent fees and help ensure access to the courts." Model Rule 1.8, Comment [10]. Here, the attorney is not financing the litigation, she is merely providing assistance with trial costs.

D is incorrect. As long as the attorney's financial assistance is used for court costs and expenses of litigation, the attorney may lend her credit to a client.

Question 30.

B is the correct answer. A newly admitted lawyer in a firm must have his or her work properly supervised by a more experienced lawyer to ensure that all lawyers in the firm conform to the Model Rules of Professional Conduct. Model Rule 5.1. Under Model Rule 1.1, a law firm owes a client a duty of competence, specifically the appropriate "legal knowledge, skill, thoroughness and preparation reasonably necessary for the representation." Consequently, when a firm uses less-experienced lawyers to perform client work, the partners must supervise that work. In this case, the associate, who had never conducted or observed a trial, needed supervision. There was not enough time for the associate to become familiar with the relevant law and procedure, nor did she have the experience to competently handle the case. Importantly, the attorney did not take the proper precautions to make sure that the associate was adequately prepared to carry out the assignment.

A is incorrect. The outcome of the trial is irrelevant to whether the associate was properly supervised. This is another example of the "no-harm, no-foul" wrong answer choice.

C is incorrect. The plaintiff's apparent consent would not mitigate this Rule violation. As always, be wary of choices that imply a client can consent to a violation of the Rules.

D is incorrect. While the attorney may have closely supervised the associate for six months, this did not change the fact she was not prepared to handle the trial.

Question 31.

D is the correct answer. When a lawyer gives a client advice, he or she may rely on considerations other than those involved in giving purely technical legal advice. Model Rule 2.1. Consequently, it is proper for a lawyer to rely on moral, economic, and social factors in doing so, which is what the attorney did here when he took potential bad publicity into consideration.

A is incorrect. This answer choice refers to the issue of a lawyer's responsibility to "act with . . . zeal in advocacy." Model Rule 1.3, Comment [1]. However, the issue is what is the proper scope for the advice a lawyer gives a client. Not only is it proper for a lawyer to refer to considerations other than the law in advising a client, he or she also has a responsibility to exercise independent professional judgment in advising a client and to advise the client in a straightforward, honest manner, in the best interests of the client.

B is incorrect. Although the park may have had a valid defense, this did not mean the attorney violated the Rules by taking other factors into consideration when he gave the park advice.

C is incorrect. While the park did accept the attorney's advice, this would not excuse the attorney if his advice violated the Rules in some other manner. This is another example of a wrong answer choice based around the client's actions.

Question 32.

C is the correct answer. A lawyer may not "engage in conduct involving dishonesty, fraud, deceit, or misrepresentation." Model Rule 8.4(c). Here, the attorney is planning to falsely tell the employee he is not a suspect and that his answers will be held in confidence.

A is incorrect. Even if no legal proceedings are pending, the attorney is still engaging in dishonest behavior.

B is incorrect. The issue here is not which party the attorney represents, but the fact that the attorney is planning to misrepresent the nature of his questioning.

D is incorrect. As stated above, the important issue is that the attorney is planning to lie.

Question 33.

B is the correct answer. A fee may be contingent on the outcome of the matter for which the service is rendered, except in a matter in which a contingent fee involves a domestic matter or a criminal case. Model Rule 1.5(d). Here, there is nothing improper in the parties' agreement, and it appears to be reasonable under the circumstances.

A is incorrect. This is the classic "it was the client's idea" wrong answer choice. Remember, simply because a client thinks something is a good idea does not make it proper under the Rules.

C is incorrect. Although the overall fee may exceed the attorney's normal fee, as long as the agreement is reasonable to the parties, there is nothing making such an agreement automatically improper.

D is incorrect. Under Model Rule 1.8(i), "a lawyer shall not acquire a proprietary interest in the cause of action or subject matter of litigation . . . except that the lawyer may . . . contract with a client for a reasonable contingent fee in a civil case." Model Rule 1.8(i)(2). Consequently, there is no general ban against an attorney receiving a proprietary interest in a client's cause of action, so long as it is part of a reasonable contingent fee in a civil case. Here, the agreement appears reasonable.

Question 34.

A is the correct answer. "A lawyer shall not practice with or in the form of a professional corporation or association authorized to practice law for a profit, if: . . . a nonlawyer is a corporate director or officer thereof or occupies the position of similar responsibility." Model Rule 5.4(d)(2). Here, since the partner's son-in-law is vice-president of the firm, his position in the firm violates the Rule.

B is incorrect. The issue here has to do with the son-in-law's leadership position in the firm, not the fact he may be privy to clients' confidential information.

C is incorrect. Model Rule 5.4 prohibits lawyers from practicing with a corporation that is improperly sharing legal fees or decision-making responsibility with a nonlawyer. The Rule does not limit that prohibition to lawyers who only practice as members, shareholders, or partners.

D is incorrect. Model Rule 5.4 prohibits nonlawyers from being directors or officers. Consequently, it does not matter whether the son-in-law is being supervised by a named partner.

Question 35.

D is the correct answer. If a judge personally or as a fiduciary (trustee of a trust) has more than a *de minimis* economic interest in the subject matter in controversy, disqualification is required. Model Code of Judicial Conduct, Rule 2.11(A)(3). Consequently, the judge should not hear the case.

A is incorrect. Even if the judge does not personally own stock in either party to the litigation, she is a trustee who owns a legal interest in the stock while acting as a fiduciary for others with an equitable interest. Under these circumstances, the judge's impartiality can still be reasonably questioned by others.

B is incorrect. Although the judge believes she can be fair and impartial (and she might, in fact, be correct in this belief), that impartiality could be reasonably questioned by others.

C is incorrect. Even if the value of the stock is unlikely to be affected, disqualification is still necessary to prevent the appearance of judicial impropriety and the judge's impartiality can reasonably be questioned under the circumstances. The overarching goal of the Model Code of Judicial Conduct is to make sure judges act in a manner that promotes public confidence in the integrity, fairness, and impartiality of the judiciary. Consequently, members of the judiciary must avoid creating even an appearance of bias.

Question 36.

A is the correct answer. Under Model Rule 5.6(b), an attorney shall not participate in offering or making "an agreement in which a restriction on the lawyer's right to practice is part of the settlement of a client controversy." Consequently, attorney cannot agree to not represent the business as part of the settlement.

B is incorrect. The issue here is not the potential of a better settlement offer. The issue here is that an attorney cannot be part of a settlement restricting his or her right to represent a client.

C is incorrect. This is clearly a wrong answer choice, as it implies that as long as the attorney believes something is reasonable, it is proper under the Rules.

D is incorrect. This answer choice also centers around the attorney's beliefs, instead of addressing the issue of what the attorney is actually doing; specifically, restricting his right to represent the client in the future.

Question 37.

C is the correct answer. "A lawyer shall not practice with or in the form of a professional corporation or association authorized to practice law for a profit, if: . . . a nonlawyer has the right to direct or control the professional judgment of a lawyer." Model Rule 5.4(d)(3). Here, the nonlawyer only supervises routine administrative and financial matters and does not control the professional judgment of lawyers in the firm.

A is incorrect. "A lawyer or law firm may include nonlawyer employees in a compensation or retirement plan, even though the plan is based in whole or in part on a profit-sharing arrangement." Model Rule 5.4(a)(3). Consequently, as long as the nonlawyer's position is not violating the Rules in some other way (namely, by controlling the judgment of lawyers), it is proper to share fees with the nonlawyer employee.

B is incorrect. Here, since the nonlawyer is not giving legal advice or controlling others in the giving of any sort of legal advice, the nonlawyer is not engaged in the unauthorized practice of law.

D is incorrect. The issue here is whether the nonlawyer can control the actions of lawyers. The issue of confidentiality is irrelevant.

Question 38.

C is the correct answer. A lawyer may reveal confidential information "to establish a defense to a criminal charge or civil claim against the lawyer based upon conduct in which the client was involved." Model Rule 1.6(b)(5). Here, since the plaintiff is suing both the client and the attorney over the same business deal, the attorney may reveal the information.

A is incorrect. Although the disclosure may be detrimental to the client, the Rules allow the attorney to defend herself against civil and criminal actions.

B is incorrect. As stated above, a lawyer may reveal confidential information to defend himself or herself.

D is incorrect. The issue here does not turn on whether the attorney and client are represented by separate counsel. The important point is that the attorney can reveal confidential information to defend herself.

Question 39.

D is the correct answer. Although Model Rule 1.6 protects a client's confidential information under the attorney-client privilege, revealing the name of the client does not appear to invoke the Rule in these circumstances. The question notes that the attorney is simply holding the painting as a favor to a client — it does not appear to have anything to do with the attorney's representation of the client or the client's confidential information.

A is incorrect. As stated above, this situation does not appear to have anything to do with the attorney-client privilege.

B is incorrect. As stated above, the information is not confidential under Model Rule 1.6, so it is irrelevant whether it would fall under the exception that allows the disclosure of confidences to prevent imminent death or substantial bodily harm.

C is incorrect. The question notes that the authorities do not believe the attorney was involved in any way, so revealing the information doesn't have anything to do with the attorney defending herself against a criminal charge.

Question 40.

A is the correct answer. In advertising his or her services, a lawyer may not make a false or misleading statement. Model Rule 7.1. Here, nothing in the mailing is false, and it appears that its main purpose is simply to alert members of the community that the lawyer is returning to private practice.

B is incorrect. Although all the information is public, it could be presented or phrased in a way to create an improper misrepresentation under Model Rule 7.1 or an improper implication of influence under Model Rule 8.4(e). Consequently, the simple fact the information is in the public domain does not make the advertisement proper.

C is incorrect. Although the lawyer states he was once lieutenant governor, the mailing does not appear to violate Model Rule 8.4(e)'s prohibition against implying an improper influence.

D is incorrect. Although the mailing was sent to people who were not his clients, this does not violate Model Rule 7.3's prohibitions regarding solicitation of clients. Importantly, written contact is prohibited when the lawyer knows the person does not want to be solicited or the solicitation involves coercion, duress, or harassment. Model Rule 7.3(b). Here, the mailing announcing the new law office appears to do none of these things.

Question 41.

A is the correct answer. "A lawyer shall not reveal information relating to the representation of a client unless the client gives informed consent." Model Rule 1.6(a). Here, it would be improper for the attorney to turn over all the client files and reveal all the confidences therein before receiving consent from the clients.

B is incorrect. The issue here is not supervision. Additionally, the attorneys do not work in the same firm or partnership, so Model Rule 5.1 doesn't apply.

C is incorrect. While the friend appears to be a diligent attorney, this would not excuse the violation of Model Rule 1.6(a).

D is incorrect. While finding alternative representation may have been necessary, the attorney could not share client information without first gaining consent.

Question 42.

B is the correct answer. "A lawyer shall hold property of clients or third persons that is in a lawyer's possession in connection with a representation separate from the lawyer's own property." Model Rule 1.15(a). Additionally, "a lawyer shall deposit into a client trust account legal fees and expenses that have been paid in advance, to be withdrawn by the lawyer only as fees are earned or expenses incurred." Model Rule 1.15(c). Importantly, once the funds were identified as belonging to the attorney (i.e., the funds were earned), they should have been removed from the Clients' Trust Account.

A is incorrect. It is proper for a lawyer to accept fees in advance, so long as those fees are kept in a client trust account until they are earned by the lawyer. Model Rule 1.15(c).

C is incorrect. Before the fees were earned, it was absolutely proper to place them in the Clients' Trust Account. However, once the fees were earned and became the attorney's property, they had to be removed from the account. The only time a lawyer's own funds should be in the client trust account is when those funds are used for the sole purpose of paying bank service charges on the account, and those funds should only be in the amount necessary for that purpose. Model Rule 1.15(b).

D is incorrect. Although the attorney's fee was reasonable, the issue here is that the attorney's money remained impermissibly commingled in the account.

Question 43.

C is the correct answer. An attorney cannot charge a contingent fee for representing a defendant in a criminal case. Model Rule 1.5(d)(2).

A is incorrect. Even though he obtained a good result for his client, the attorney still violated the prohibition against contingency fees in criminal cases.

B is incorrect. Although the defendant may not have been able to afford the attorney otherwise, this fact does not make the retainer agreement appropriate.

D is incorrect. The issue here is that an attorney cannot charge a contingent fee in a criminal matter. Model Rule 1.5(d)(2). Importantly, "a lawyer may accept property in payment for services, such as an ownership interest in an enterprise, providing this does not involve acquisition of a proprietary interest in the cause of action or subject matter of the litigation." Model Rule 1.5, Comment [4].

Question 44.

C is the correct answer. A lawyer should act with reasonable diligence and promptness when representing a client. Model Rule 1.3. Here, the civil action was filed a year ago, and any "delay" is going to be 60 days at most. Since the question states that the client will not be prejudiced by the delay, it is absolutely reasonable for the attorney to take the latest trial date.

A is incorrect. As stated above, there is no indication the attorney is not acting diligently. Importantly, diligence does not mean that an attorney has to act as quickly as possible.

B is incorrect. Except for the fact the plaintiff could have had an earlier trial date (which might not have actually worked for the plaintiff's schedule), there is no indication the attorney is favoring one client over another.

D is incorrect. While a lawyer can make their own schedule, a lawyer cannot manage his or her schedule in a way that prejudices clients.

Question 45.

A is the correct answer. At trial, an attorney is not allowed to state his or her personal opinion about the credibility of a witness. Model Rule 3.4.

B is incorrect. The issue here is that the prosecutor is stating his beliefs, not that he may be alluding to the beliefs of jurors.

C is incorrect. Even if the prosecutor accurately stated the testimony in the case, an attorney is not allowed to state his or her personal opinion about the credibility of a witness.

D is incorrect. Even if the prosecutor reasonably believed the witness was lying, he could not state his belief to the court.

Question 46.

D is the correct answer. Under Model Rule 7.1, "[a] lawyer shall not make a false or misleading communication about the lawyer or the lawyer's services. A communication is false or misleading if it contains a material misrepresentation of fact or law, or omits a fact necessary to make the statement considered as a whole not materially misleading." Here, the commercial is misleading in that it implies the young attorney has argued a case in court, when he has never actually done so.

A is incorrect. This answer choice should be immediately discarded because it implies an attorney can do whatever he or she wants in a commercial as long as it is "merely a dramatization."

B is incorrect. While the commercial did contain a disclaimer, it still falsely implied that the attorney had appeared in court.

C is incorrect. Model Rule 7.1, Comment [3] states that it is improper for a lawyer to make an advertisement that would lead a reasonable person to form an unjustified expectation that the lawyer will reach the same results in his or her case. Here, however, the larger issue is that the commercial is misleading in that it leads a viewer to believe the lawyer has appeared in court, when in fact he has not done so.

Question 47.

A is the correct answer. With regard to *civil cases,* the adversary system contemplates that the evidence in a case is to be marshaled competitively by the parties. Model Rule 3.4, Comment [1]. Likewise, a lawyer's duty not to conceal evidence in a civil case does not carry with it a duty to report or volunteer all relevant information. Prosecutors, however, have special responsibilities. Model Rule 3.8. "A prosecutor has the responsibility of a minister of justice and not simply that of an advocate" (Model Rule 3.8, Comment [1]) and as such, must "make timely disclosure to the defense of all evidence or information known to the prosecutor that tends to negate the guilt of the accused." Model Rule 3.8(d). The fact that the social media posts show that the defendant was out of state at the time the crime was committed "tends to negate the guilt" of the defendant.

B is incorrect. The fact the information was obtained by the police does not affect the analysis.

C is incorrect. This is a true statement with regard to civil cases. See Model Rule 3.4. However, as discussed above, a prosecutor has special responsibilities in a criminal case. Model Rule 3.8.

D is incorrect. The prosecutor's responsibilities under Model Rule 3.8 exist independently of a request by defense counsel.

Question 48.

C is the correct answer. A lawyer is prohibited from asking a person other than the client to refrain from voluntarily giving relevant information to another party unless that person is a relative, employee, or agent of the client and the lawyer reasonably believes that the person's interests will not be adversely affected by refraining to give that information. Model Rule 3.4(f). In that case, the attorney may instruct the person to refrain from giving information unless subpoenaed. Here, the eyewitness does not appear to fall under any of the exceptions to the Rule.

A is incorrect. While the witness may not want to testify, the attorney should not have asked her to leave the country.

B is incorrect. Even though the attorney did not offer the witness any inducement not to appear at trial, Model Rule 3.4(f) prohibits the attorney from making any "request" to refrain from voluntarily giving relevant information.

D is incorrect. Even if a witness has not yet been subpoenaed, Model Rule 3.4(f) prohibits an attorney from asking that witness to refrain from giving relevant information to another party, unless that witness falls within one of the three exceptions.

Question 49.

B is the correct answer. Under Model Rule 1.11(a)(2), "a lawyer who has formerly served as a public officer or employee of the government . . . shall not otherwise represent a client in connection with a matter in which the lawyer participated personally and substantially as a public officer or employee" unless authorized to do so by the government agency. Here, the attorney had nothing to do with the investigation. Remember, Model Rule 1.11 is concerned with former government employees exploiting knowledge about a party unfairly. Here, there is no knowledge to exploit.

A is incorrect. Although the environmental protection division consented, the big issue here is that the attorney had nothing to do with the earlier investigation. Thus, the consent was unnecessary.

C is incorrect. As stated above, for Model Rule 1.11 to apply, the lawyer must have "participated personally and substantially" in the matter. Although the attorney worked for the environmental protection division, he had nothing to do with the earlier investigation.

D is incorrect. As stated above, for Model Rule 1.11 to apply, the lawyer must have "participated personally and substantially" in the matter. Consequently, the fact this case arose from the earlier investigation doesn't change the analysis.

Question 50.

C is the correct answer. A lawyer is required to keep a client's funds separate from his or her own. Model Rule 1.15. Importantly, the attorney could not use the funds in her Clients' Trust Account to give herself a loan, as those funds belonged to her client.

A is incorrect. This is an example of the "no-harm, no-foul" wrong answer choice. Even though the client may have approved the attorney's conduct, the attorney had already violated the Rules before she told her client and received the client's approval.

B is incorrect. This is another example of the "no-harm, no-foul" wrong answer choice. Whether or not the client is harmed, an attorney may not use a client's funds for his or her personal use.

D is incorrect. While this answer choice implies some sort of issue of consent, the choice simply states that the attorney's actions would have been proper had she reached the client before taking the funds. It doesn't actually say anything regarding consent.

Question 51.

A is the correct answer. Generally, a judge is not allowed to engage in ex parte communications. Model Code of Judicial Conduct Rule 2.9. However, "when circumstances require it, ex parte communication for scheduling, administrative, or emergency purposes, which does not address substantive matters, is permitted." Model Code of Judicial Conduct Rule 2.9(A)(1). If a judge does engage in such communication, he or she should make provision to promptly notify all the parties of the substance of the communication. Model Code of Judicial Conduct Rule 2.9(A)(1)(b). Here, the circumstances of the situation made the judge's actions proper, as no one else was there to answer the phone, the lawyer had an emergency and had tried to call opposing counsel, the matter merely involved rescheduling, and the judge promptly informed the opposing party of the rescheduling.

B is incorrect. Although there was no one else to take the call, the communication could have been improper if it had involved some other matter besides scheduling.

C is incorrect. As stated above, in certain circumstances, it is proper for a judge to engage in ex parte communications.

D is incorrect. There is no time limit for informing the parties, so long as the judge promptly notifies all the parties of the substance of the communication. Model Code of Judicial Conduct Rule 2.9(A)(1)(b).

Question 52.

A is the correct answer. A practicing lawyer who is also a legislator may not use his or her official authority for the benefit of a private client. However, a legislator who is a lawyer but who is no longer practicing law may assist a constituent in his or her dealings with a state agency. Here, the facts show that the legislator is helping the startup as a constituent, not a client. Consequently, the legislator's action would not subject him to discipline.

B is incorrect. The paper the letter was written on does not change the analysis.

C is incorrect. The legislator's efforts on behalf of a constituent were proper because he was no longer practicing law and was not seeking to assist the startup as a private client. Therefore, it does not matter that the legislator in fact influenced the agency in his former client's favor.

D is incorrect. Because the legislator is acting on the startup's behalf as a constituent, his actions are proper.

Question 53.

A is the correct answer. "If a lawyer, the lawyer's client, or a witness called by the lawyer, has offered material evidence and the lawyer comes to know of its falsity, the lawyer shall take reasonable remedial measures, including, if necessary, disclosure to the tribunal." Model Rule 3.3. Simply not referring to the absence of the warning label in his summation is not a valid remedial measure.

B is incorrect. While the attorney called the wife as a witness, the issue is that the attorney came to know of the falsity of the testimony and took no reasonable remedial measures to correct it. If the attorney never discovered the lie, he could not reasonably be expected to do something about it.

C is incorrect. As stated above, simply not referring to the absence of the warning label in his summation is not a valid remedial measure.

D is incorrect. While he may not have relied on the testimony, the attorney still knew of its falsity and did nothing to remediate matters.

Question 54.

C is the correct answer. "Except to the extent that the client's instructions or special circumstances limit that authority, a lawyer is impliedly authorized to make disclosures about a client when appropriate in carrying out the representation . . . . Lawyers in a firm may, in the course of the firm's practice, disclose to each other information relating to a client of the firm, unless the client has instructed that particular information be confined to specified lawyers." Model Rule 1.6, Comment [5]. Consequently, it was proper for the partners to give detailed descriptions of the work being done.

A is incorrect. Although more people knowing about something could theoretically increase the risk of that information getting out, the Rules allow lawyers to share information within a firm.

B is incorrect. The Rules allow lawyers to disclose information to other lawyers within a firm. This makes sense, considering the desire for competent and efficient representation.

D is incorrect. Lawyers may discuss cases within a firm so long as the client has not given instructions to the contrary. This answer choice should have been crossed out immediately since it implies that lawyers can willfully ignore client instructions regarding confidences.

Question 55.

B is the correct answer. Although an attorney can retain or contract with other lawyers outside the lawyer's own firm to assist in the provision of legal service, "the lawyer should ordinarily obtain informed consent from the client." Model Rule 1.1, Comment [6]. While an attorney has the right to make decisions in many aspects of a representation, in the case of bringing in another attorney, the attorney must first ask for client consent.

A is incorrect. The agreement between the attorneys is not an example of a prohibited limitation.

C is incorrect. The division of the fee does not change the fact that the attorney brought in another attorney without asking the client first.

D is incorrect. While this implies a "no-harm, no-foul" situation, the client would still be harmed by having his representation undertaken by an attorney he has no knowledge about.

Question 56.

A is the correct answer. In making decisions and exercising options, a lawyer is required to act with competence. Model Rule 1.1. This means that he or she must employ "the legal knowledge, skill, thoroughness and preparation reasonably necessary for the representation." In other words, the lawyer is not a guarantor of a successful outcome or even of a consequence-free result. He or she is required, however, to exercise his or her judgment in a manner that would be considered reasonable by other lawyers under all the circumstances. There are circumstances in which a lawyer may reasonably advise a client not to respond to questions by a legislative fact-finding committee, even when the client is faced by the risk of imprisonment. These facts do not tell us what the underlying facts were, but they do state clearly that the attorney "reasonably believed" that it was in the best interests of the witness not to answer. Ultimately, the attorney is not subject to discipline so long as he acted reasonably.

B is incorrect. The level of potential criminal punishment does not change the analysis.

C is incorrect. The facts do not disclose the constitutional basis for the refusal by the witness to answer the committee's questions. Obviously, however, the consequences to the witness in failing to exercise her constitutional rights were deemed by the attorney to be more serious and severe than the refusal to answer. Although the general rule is that an attorney may not counsel a client to engage, or assist a client, in conduct that the lawyer knows is criminal (Model Rule 1.2), most courts would support the witness' right to refuse to answer if her constitutional rights were in jeopardy.

D is incorrect. For the reasons stated above, the fact that the witness was successfully convicted does not change the analysis.

Question 57.

B is the correct answer. Each side is entitled to know and to respond to every fact and every argument presented by the other side. If a judge could consult any legal source he or she wished without identifying it and giving each side the right to respond, the adversarial nature of the judicial system would collapse. At the same time, there are instances in which a judge will need to get advice on the law, especially when, as in these facts, the lawyers have not stated the situation clearly. To enable the judge to do this without subverting the adversarial process, Model Code of Judicial Conduct, Rule 2.9(A)(2) permits a judge to "obtain the written advice of a disinterested expert on the law applicable to a proceeding before the judge, if the judge gives advance notice to the parties of the person to be consulted and the subject matter of the advice to be solicited, and affords the parties a reasonable opportunity to object and respond to the notice and to the advice received."

A is incorrect. The issue here is that the judge based his decision on the attorney's letter without informing the attorneys arguing the case.

C is incorrect. The fact that the judge didn't initiate the communication does not solve the primary problem.

D is incorrect. It's not enough that the expert consulted by the judge be impartial. The parties are entitled to know what the expert has been asked and what he or she has advised.

Question 58.

D is the correct answer. So long as client confidences are not exposed, the arrangement is proper under the Rules. Importantly, no fees are being shared with the bank employee, and the bank employee is not serving as a director or in a similar position in the firm. Model Rule 5.4. Here, the bank employee is merely acting as a part-time office manager, giving advice on how to keep the firm solvent.

A is incorrect. There is no indication that this setup will result in the bank improperly practicing law. The bank employee is merely a part-time office manager, giving advice regarding the running of the office.

B is incorrect. It is improper for a nonlawyer third party to direct the lawyer's professional judgment in rendering legal services. Model Rule 5.4, Comment [1]. Here, the bank employee is not giving advice on representation, but merely on office billing and solvency matters.

C is incorrect. Although there is no sharing of fees, the arrangement could cause a problem if confidences were being shared with the bank.

Question 59.

B is the correct answer. During representation, a lawyer "shall not make an extrajudicial statement that the lawyer knows or reasonably should know will be disseminated by means of public communication and will have a substantial likelihood of materially prejudicing an adjudicative proceeding in the matter." Model Rule 3.6(a). However, there is an exception for "information contained in a public record." Model Rule 3.6(b)(2). Here, since the actor has sued the newspaper for libel, the identity of the reporter is a matter of public record.

A is incorrect. Although the trial has not yet commenced, the Rule is concerned with "prejudicing an adjudicative proceeding." Model Rule 3.6(a). Clearly, prejudice can be created before a trial has actually commenced.

C is incorrect. While prospective jurors may learn of the attorney's remarks, this does not automatically make any remarks subject to discipline.

D is incorrect. While the reporter may be a prospective witness, the important point is that lawyers may make statements regarding matters of public record.

Question 60.

B is the correct answer. A lawyer appearing before a legislative body must disclose that the appearance is in a representative capacity. Model Rule 3.9. Requiring a lawyer to disclose the client relationship allows the legislative body to assess any potential bias of the lawyer.

A is incorrect. Lawyers frequently serve as paid lobbyists. This activity is permissible so long as the lawyer-lobbyist complies with applicable rules, such as the requirement to disclose his or her representative capacity when appearing before a legislative body.

C is incorrect. As stated above, the congressional members at the hearing would be very interested in knowing whether a witness is possibly biased in his or her testimony; therefore, Model Rule 3.9 requires a lawyer appearing in a representative capacity to disclose that fact to the legislative body.

D is incorrect. The fact that the attorney believes her client's position is in the public interest does not cure the Rule violation. Always be wary of answer choices that imply a Rule was not violated because the attorney would have said or done the same thing despite the Rule violation.